GERMAN POLITICS, 1945–1995

GERMAN POLITICS 1945–1995

PETER PULZER

Gladstone Professor of Government and Public Administration
Fellow of All Souls College Oxford

OXFORD
UNIVERSITY PRESS

OXFORD

UNIVERSITY PRESS

Great Clarendon Street, Oxford OX2 6DP

Oxford University Press is a department of the University of Oxford.
It furthers the University's objective of excellence in research, scholarship,
and education by publishing worldwide in

Oxford New York

Auckland Bangkok Buenos Aires Cape Town Chennai
Dar es Salaam Delhi Hong Kong Istanbul Karachi Kolkata
Kuala Lumpur Madrid Melbourne Mexico City Mumbai Nairobi
São Paulo Shanghai Taipei Tokyo Toronto

Oxford is a registered trade mark of Oxford University Press
in the UK and in certain other countries

Published in the United States
by Oxford University Press Inc., New York

First published 1995
Reprinted 1996, 1999, 2001, 2002, 2003

British Library Cataloguing in Publication Data

Data available

Library of Congress Cataloging in Publication Data

Pulzer, Peter G. J.
German politics, 1945–1995 / Peter Pulzer.
Includes bibliographical references (p.   ).
1. Germany—Politics and government—1945–1990.   2. Germany—
Politics and government—1990-   .   I. Title.
JN3971.A58P85   1995   320.943'09'045—dc20   95-17200
ISBN 0-19-878110-5
ISBN 0-19-878111-3 (pbk.)

10 9 8 7 6

Printed in Great Britain by
Selwood Printing Ltd
Burgess Hill, West Sussex

To my friends and colleagues
on both sides of the Tunnel

Acknowledgements

M Y conclusions in this book are the outcome of many years of reading, thinking, and lecturing about German politics, as well as the fruitful exchange of ideas with colleagues in Britain, Germany, and North America. In writing this book I have particularly benefited from the help and advice of two of my Oxford colleagues, Dr Nigel Bowles and Dr Jonathan Wright, and of Professor Dieter Grosser of Munich University. They bear no responsibility for any remaining errors or misjudgements. I owe a special debt to my wife, Gillian, not only for her moral support but as proof-reader and as a judge of style; to my son Matthew, for designing the Figure on Economic Performance; and to Michèle Jacottet, who prepared the text for publication in her usual exemplary way.

Contents

Abbreviations

ABC	atomic, bacteriological, and chemical [weapons]
APO	Ausserparlamentarische Opposition (extra-parliamentary opposition)
BDI	Bundesverband der Deutschen Industrie (West German Employers' Federation)
BFD	Bund Freier Demokraten (League of Free Democrats)
BHE	Bund der Heimatvertriebenen und Entrechteten (League of Expellees and those Deprived of their Rights)
BVP	Bayerische Volkspartei (Bavarian People's Party)
BP	Bayernpartei (Bavarian Party)
CDU	Christlich Demokratische Union (Christian Democratic Union)
CDUD	Christlich Demokratische Union Deutschlands (Christian Democratic Union of Germany)
CMEA	Council for Mutual Economic Assistance (COMECON)
COMECON	Council for Mutual Economic Assistance (CMEA)
CPSU	Communist Party of the Soviet Union
CSCE	Conference on Security and Co-operation in Europe
CSU	Christlich-Soziale Union (Christian-Social Union)
CSVD	Christlichsozialer Volksdienst (Christian Social People's Service)
DBD	Demokratische Bauernpartei Deutschlands (Democratic Farmers' Party)
DDP	Deutsche Demokratische Partei (German Democratic Party)
DFD	Demokratischer Frauenbund Deutschlands (Democratic Women's League)
DGB	Deutscher Gewerkschaftsbund (West German Trade Union Federation)
DNVP	Deutschnationale Volkspartei (German Nationalist People's Party)

DP	Deutsche Partei (German Party)
DRP	Deutsche Reichspartei (German Reich Party)
DSU	Deutsche Soziale Union (German Social Union)
DVP	Deutsche Volkspartei (German People's Party)
DVU	Deutsche Volksunion (German People's Union)
EC	European Community
ECSC	European Coal and Steel Community
EDC	European Defence Community
EEC	European Economic Community
EFTA	European Free Trade Association
EMS	European Monetary System
ERP	European Recovery Programme (Marshall Plan)
EU	European Union
FDGB	Freier Deutscher Gewerkschaftsbund (Federation of Free Trade Unions)
FDGO	*freiheitliche demokratische Grundordnung*
FDJ	Freie Deutsche Jugend (Free German Youth)
FDP	Freie Demokratische Partei (Free Democratic Party)
FRG	Federal Republic of Germany
GATT	General Agreement on Trade and Tariffs
GDR	German Democratic Republic
INF	Intermediate Nuclear Forces
KPD	Kommunistische Partei Deutschlands (German Communist Party)
LDP	Liberaldemokratische Partei (Liberal Democratic Party)
LDPD	Liberaldemokratische Partei Deutschlands (Liberal Democratic Party of Germany)
LPG	Landwirtschaftliche Produktionsgenossenschaft (agricultural collective)
NATO	North Atlantic Treaty Organization
NDPD	Nationaldemokratische Partei Deutschlands (National Democratic Party [East])
NLP	Niedersächsische Landespartei (Regional Party of Lower Saxony)
NPD	Nationaldemokratische Partei Deutschlands (National Democratic Party [West])
NVA	Nationale Volksarmee (National People's Army)

OECD	Organization for Economic Co-operation and Development
OEEC	Organization for European Economic Co-operation
OMGUS	Office of the Military Government, United States
OPEC	Organization of Petroleum Exporting Countries
PDS	Partei des Demokratischen Sozialismus (Party of Democratic Socialism)
RAF	Rote Armee Fraktion (Red Army Faction)
SALT	Strategic Arms Limitation Treaty
SBZ	Sowjetische Besatzungszone (Soviet zone of occupation)
SDI	Strategic Defence Initiative
SDS	Sozialdemokratischer Studentenbund (Social Democratic Student League)
SED	Sozialistische Einheitspartei Deutschlands (Socialist Unity Party)
SED-PDS	Sozialistische Einheitspartei Deutschlands-Partei des Demokratischen Sozialismus
SMAD	Sowjetische Militäradministration in Deutschland (Soviet military administration)
SPD	Sozialdemokratische Partei Deutschlands (Social Democratic Party)
SRP	Sozialistische Reichspartei (Socialist Reich Party)
SS	Schutz-Staffel
Stasi	Staatssicherheitsdienst
WAV	Wirtschaftlicher Aufbau-Verein (Economic Reconstruction Union)
UN	United Nations
USA	United States of America
USSR	Union of Soviet Socialist Republics

Chronology

1945	8 May	Unconditional surrender of German armed forces
	17 July–2 Aug.	Potsdam conference
1947	1 Jan.	Fusion of British and US zones into 'Bi-zone'
	5 June	Launch of European Recovery Programme ('Marshall Plan')
1948	20 June	Currency Reform in three Western zones
	24 June	Beginning of Berlin Blockade
1949	4 Apr.	Formation of North Atlantic Treaty Organization (NATO)
	12 May	End of Berlin Blockade
	23 May	Basic Law of the Federal Republic of Germany (FRG) comes into force
	14 Aug.	First Bundestag election
	15 Sept.	Konrad Adenauer elected Chancellor
	7 Oct.	Constitution of German Democratic Republic (GDR) adopted
1951	8 Apr.	Creation of European Coal and Steel Community (ECSC), with FRG as a member
1952	3 March	'Stalin Note' proposing peace treaty with Germany
1953	17 June	Uprising in GDR
1954	23 Oct.	Paris Treaties, extending NATO membership to FRG
1955	22 Sept.	Promulgation of 'Hallstein Doctrine'
1956	14–15 Feb.	20th Congress of Communist Party of the Soviet Union
	23 Oct.–4 Nov.	Revolution in Hungary, crushed by Soviet forces
1957	25 Mar.	Signature of Treaties of Rome, creating European Economic Community (EEC)
1958	27 Nov.	Khrushchev's Berlin Ultimatum, demanding demilitarization of West Berlin

1959	3 June	Law on final phase of collectivization of agriculture in GDR
	15 Nov.	Social Democratic Party (SPD) adopts new programme at Bad Godesberg
1961	13 Aug.	Construction of Berlin Wall
1962	22 Oct.–9 Nov.	Cuban Missile Crisis
	26 Oct.	Beginning of *Spiegel* affair
1963	22 Jan.	Signature of Elysée Treaty between FRG and France
	15 July	New Economic System proclaimed in GDR
	16 Oct.	Konrad Adenauer resigns as Chancellor. Succeeded by Ludwig Erhard
1966	30 Nov.–1 Dec.	Resignation of Erhard. Succeeded by Kurt-Georg Kiesenger at head of Great Coalition
1967	20 Feb.	New Citizenship Law in GDR
	2 June	Shooting of Berlin student Benno Ohnesorg leads to growth of Extra-Parliamentary Opposition (APO)
1968	30 May	Emergency Legislation passed
	1 July	Signature of Nuclear Non-Proliferation Treaty
	21 Aug.	Prague Spring crushed by Warsaw Pact invasion
1969	3 May	Gustav Heinemann elected President of FRG
	28 Sept.	Bundestag election gives narrow majority to SPD and FDP
	21 Oct.	Willy Brandt elected Chancellor
1970	19 Mar.	Willy Brandt visits Erfurt (GDR)
	12 Aug.	Signature of Moscow Treaty between FRG and USSR
	7 Dec.	Brandt in Warsaw for signature of FRG–Polish treaty
1971	3 May	Erich Honecker succeeds Walter Ulbricht as First Secretary of Socialist Unity Party (SED)
	3 Sept.	Four-Power Agreement on Berlin
1972	28 Jan.	'Decree on Extremists'

	27 Apr.	Failure of 'constructive vote of no confidence' against Brandt
	19 Nov.	Bundestag election. Increased majority for Brandt coalition
	21 Dec.	Signature of Basic Treaty between FRG and GDR
1973	17 Oct.	First 'oil shock'; Arab OPEC members restrict exports
1974	15 May	Helmut Schmidt elected Chancellor after resignation of Brandt
	7 Oct.	New GDR constitution
1975	1 Aug.	Ratification of agreement of Conference on Security and Co-operation in Europe (CSCE) ('Helsinki Final Act')
1977	13–18 Oct.	Hijacking of Lufthansa airliner at Mogadishu
	19 Oct.	Kidnapped employers' president Hanns Martin Schleyer found dead
1978	5 Dec.	Agreement on European Monetary System
1979	12 Dec.	NATO 'twin-track' decision in response to stationing of Soviet SS-20 missiles
1981	11–13 Dec.	Schmidt–Honecker summit in GDR
1982	17 Sept.	Resignation of FDP ministers from Schmidt government
	1 Oct.	Bundestag elects Helmut Kohl as Chancellor
1983	6 Mar.	Bundestag election confirms Helmut Kohl as Chancellor
1984	23 May	Richard von Weizsäcker elected Federal President
1985	12 Mar.	Mikhail Gorbachev becomes First Secretary of CPSU
1987	7–11 Sept.	Visit by Honecker to FRG
	8 Dec.	USA and USSR agree on elimination of medium- and short-range nuclear weapons ('INF Treaty')
1989	7 May	Rigged local elections in GDR lead to protests
	4 June	Tiananmen Square massacre in Pekin
	18 June	Victory for Solidarnósc candidates in Polish elections

	11 Sept.	Hungary opens Austrian frontier for GDR citizens
	5 Oct.	Gorbachev visits East Berlin for GDR 40th anniversary celebrations
	9 Oct.	Mass demonstration in Leipzig passes off peacefully
	18 Oct.	Honecker resigns, succeeded by Egon Krenz
	9 Nov.	Berlin Wall opened
	28 Nov.	Kohl's Ten-Point Programme on German unification
	7 Dec.	First meeting of GDR Round Table
1990	18 Mar.	First free elections to GDR Volkskammer
	1 July	German Economic and Monetary Union comes into force
	12 Sept.	'Two-plus-Four' Treaty signed
	3 Oct.	German Unification Treaty comes into force
	2 Dec.	All-German elections. Victory for Kohl
1991	20 June	Bundestag votes to move seat of government from Bonn to Berlin
1992	22–7 Aug.	Rioting against asylum-seekers in Rostock
1993	13 Mar.	Solidarity Pact launched to increase transfers to Eastern *Länder*
	26 May	Amendment to Basic Law on right to asylum
1994	12 July	Federal Constitutional Court approves 'out-of-area' German military operations
	16 Oct.	Bundestag election. Kohl government narrowly re-elected
1995	1 Jan.	*Treuhandanstalt* wound up
	8 May	50th anniversary of VE Day commemorated as liberation

Introduction

IN the fifty years since the end of the Second World War Germany has been occupied, divided among the victor powers, rehabilitated in the community of nations, and unified. The new Germany that emerged from the collapse of Communism has the world's third-largest economy and the largest in Europe. It is, as was the Federal Republic of Germany (FRG) before it, the principal motor of economic and political integration in Europe. This Germany is regarded by the rest of the world with respect and even admiration, but also with suspicion: how will it use its undoubted power? how stable are its institutions? and how cohesive is its society?

My book is aimed at all those who want to understand how Germans got from there to here. In it I try to explain, as simply as possible, how German politics works. The book cannot, in the space of some 180 pages, be either a detailed history of post-war Germany or a comprehensive text on German political institutions. As the Suggestions for Further Reading show, both needs are amply catered for. What I offer instead is a stock-taking of the state of German political life fifty years after unconditional surrender and five years after unification. I do so by paying particular attention to those components that distinguish German politics from those of other European states.

The first of these is constitutional politics. The FRG of 1949 was a new creation, based on a new set of rules: in the course of time this Basic Law, with its emphasis on civil rights and decentralized government, has helped to form a national political identity. The adaptability of the structures adopted in 1949, and widely assumed to be provisional, has been one of the major concerns of the pre- and post-unification public debate. The second special component is foreign policy. Both German states, East and West, owed their very formation to foreign-policy considerations. Both their day-to-day politics and the major decisions that have transformed them have involved dense interactions between German politicians and the victor states of 1945. The 'Two-plus-Four' Treaty that ended the division of Germany is one example of this; the FRG's constitutional commitment to supra-nationalism is another. The third special component is the economy. The two German states had economic as well as diplomatic godparents: in the case of the FRG, the currency reform of 1948; in the case of the GDR, the Soviet-inspired collectivization. Before long a strong internationally oriented economy became the *raison d'état* of the FRG and the integration into COMECON that of the GDR. Lastly there is the fact that until 1990 there were two German states: the existence of the other Germany was a major factor in the politics of each of them. Although post-1990 Germany is the heir of both these states, it is, in its political structures, overwhelmingly a continuation of the FRG and a disavowal of the GDR. For that reason the political development of the Western German state gets the lion's share of attention in this book.

A word should be said about the names of the two states that followed the division of Germany. The British, US, and French zones of occupation formed the Federal Republic of Germany (*Bundesrepublik Deutschland*), which I refer to as the FRG in the text. The Soviet zone of occupation became the German Democratic Republic (*Deutsche Demokratische Republik*), which I refer to as the GDR in the text. Post-unification Germany is also called *Bundesrepublik Deutschland*, but I refer to it simply as Germany.

1 Unified, but not United

What belongs together is growing together.
(Willy Brandt, 10 November 1989)

THREE hundred and twenty-nine days after the opening of the Berlin Wall, on 3 October 1990, the two German states of the post-war world merged. For most Germans this event was a re-unification (*Wiedervereinigung*), the restoration of a normal and natural state of affairs that had been arbitrarily interrupted for the previous four decades. The instrument that sealed the merger used more cautious language. It was the Unification Treaty (*Einigungsvertrag*). In this way it passed no judgement on the process at work; it made a statement about the present and the future, not about the past.

At one level the process of unification was straightforward. The German Democratic Republic (GDR), founded in 1949 under Soviet aegis, acceded to the Federal Republic of Germany (FRG) in accordance with Article 23 of the FRG's Basic Law. This state, too, had been founded in 1949, under the aegis of the Western Allies. Both states thought of themselves as provisional. Their constitutions proclaimed German national unity as the ultimate aim; their dominant political leaders assumed that unification would take place on their terms. Hence the provision in the Basic Law that 'other parts of Germany' might in future apply for accession; hence the parallel provision in the GDR's constitution that Germany was an 'indivisible democratic republic'. For reasons that will emerge in the course of this book, the prospect of unity receded further and further in the forty years that followed until few believed that it would happen in their lifetimes. Yet when it did happen, it went through as the Founding Fathers of the FRG had prescribed. The first democratically elected government of the GDR, which emerged from the elections of 18 March 1990, formally applied to join the FRG.

Political union had been preceded on 1 July 1990 by economic, monetary, and social union, which made the whole of Germany a single economic unit and a single domestic market. Except for some specific exclusions in the two treaties, the West took over the East. From 1 July there was one currency, the Deutsche Mark. Monetary policy for the whole of Germany was henceforth regulated by the Bundesbank in Frankfurt. From 3 October the Basic Law of the FRG applied to the area of unified Germany, as did all legislation passed by the federal parliament in Bonn. The civil and criminal law, the taxation and social security systems, and the administrative apparatus of the FRG were extended, in some instances after a transitional period, to the whole of the new Germany. So were all international obligations, including membership of the European Community (EC) and of NATO. The process culminated in the all-German elections of 2 December from which Chancellor Kohl emerged triumphant. By the end of 1990 the formal process of unification was, to all intents and purposes, complete.

In other respects, however, this was far from being the case. The longer the process of growing together took, the more painful and difficult it proved to be. This applied to any number of policy areas where unanticipated incompatibilities emerged, but it was true above all at the psychological level. As the events of 1989–90 showed throughout Eastern and Central Europe, it is easier to destroy an illegitimate and hated regime than to find a viable replacement for it. A negative consensus does not necessarily give way to a positive one. When the change-over takes place in an ethnically fairly homogeneous state, as in Poland, Hungary, or Bulgaria, the problems of adjustment are relatively few. The regime changes, the socio-economic order changes. But the wider framework of a nation-state provides stability and continuity. Patriotism and national identity can be harnessed to give legitimacy to the new order. Its establishment is not only an act of democratization and domestic self-government, but an anti-colonial one, expressing national self-determination. The transition can also be eased if there is a respected counter-élite of dissidents or reformers waiting in the wings to take over as the old regime crumbles. Lech Walesa in Poland and Vaclav Havel in Czechoslovakia are only the best-known examples of such persons.

The GDR fell into none of these categories the day after the

Wall was opened. In the course of October 1990 the slogan chanted by the demonstrating crowds was 'We are the people'. It expressed a demand for self-government, compatible with the continued existence of a reformed GDR. In November the slogan changed to 'We are one people', expressing a demand for national self-determination, wholly incompatible with the state's continued existence. Elsewhere in Central and Eastern Europe such demands have led to a fragmentation of states, as in the separation of the Czech Republic and Slovakia, or the break-up of Yugoslavia and the Soviet Union. Only in the case of Germany did the dual process of self-government and self-determination lead to the abolition of one state and its absorption by another. This turned out to be a much more seismic and traumatizing experience than most of the participants had anticipated, for 're-unification' was not, in fact, the restoration of a previous normality. It was, on the contrary, yet another upheaval in a German history that has been rich in upheavals, another discontinuity in an impressive series of discontinuities.

The German republic that emerged from the Unification Treaty was the sixth form of the state that Germans had experienced in a hundred years and the eleventh in two hundred years. Up to 1806 the German states had formed the Holy Roman Empire, a loose conglomeration without a hereditary dynasty or a fixed capital city, but one that nevertheless gave some expression to a distinctive German existence. It was destroyed by Napoleon and replaced by a series of kingdoms and principalities that had no links except their dependence on his will. With his defeat the German Confederation of 1815 was created, covering roughly the same territory as the Holy Roman Empire, but with more structured institutions and a phantom constitution. It lasted until 1866, interrupted only by the unsuccessful attempt to establish a democratic, united nation-state in 1848–9. With the defeat of Austria by Prussia at the battle of Königgrätz in 1866, the Confederation, to which both states had belonged, came to an end and Austria was from then on shut out from German national politics. For five years the German states—without Austria and the southern monarchies of Bavaria, Württemberg, and Baden—formed the North German Federation; in 1871, following the Prussian defeat of France, it was replaced by the German Empire, which included the southern monarchies.

The Empire of 1871 was the nearest that Germany had yet experienced to a nation-state. The population was overwhelmingly German, except for small Polish, Danish, and Alsatian–French minorities at the Empire's borders. On the other hand, the Habsburg Monarchy, with its substantial German-speaking population, remained excluded. The Empire was not based on popular acclaim; its constitution defined it as 'a permanent league of princes' and its politics was dominated by its biggest member-state, Prussia, whose King was *ex officio* the Emperor. But with the passage of time it became more cohesive. Industrialization, urbanization, and expansion of commerce drew the population together. The Empire acquired a common currency and a uniform legal code; its parliament, the Reichstag, though limited in its powers, was elected by universal male suffrage. It lasted forty-seven years, longer than any of its successors, until defeat in 1918 at the end of the First World War destroyed it. Germany's first attempt at democracy, the Weimar Republic, lasted until 1933. It rested uneasily on a polarized population. It was a 'democracy without democrats', punctuated by political violence, undermined by reparations, inflation, and the Great Depression, threatened by political extremism. The fourteen-year Weimar Republic was followed by the twelve-year Third Reich, a single-party dictatorship characterized by persecution, terror, and wars of aggression. All autonomous social and cultural organizations were either abolished or subordinated to the National Socialist Party. All local self-government and the parliaments and governments of the individual states were swept aside. The years 1933 to 1945 were the only ones in which Germany was ruled by a totally centralized administration. Like the German Empire before it, it came to an end through military defeat.

This was the political legacy bequeathed to Germans at the end of the Second World War. Within their lifetime and that of their parents and grandparents there had been a change of regime on average once every twenty years. The first head of government of the FRG, Konrad Adenauer, was born when the Empire was only five years old. He lived through the monarchy, the republic, and the dictatorship, two world wars, and two defeats. His life span symbolized the discontinuities of German public life, the expectations disappointed, the hopes dashed. For Germans, more than for any other people in Europe, the past was a black hole and national history a liability. Their neighbours, the French and the British, and their patrons, the Americans, could construct a history that was a source of pride, a story of steady development and broadening liberty. In these 'Whig interpretations' there was a dash of over-simplification and more than a dash of myth-making, but somehow the known facts could be made to match the myth. No one could sit down in 1945 to write a Whig version of the German past. When the doyen of German historians, Friedrich Meinecke, set down his conclusions on a lifetime's experience, he entitled his essay 'The German Catastrophe'.

All German regimes have been attempts to counter the mistakes of the previous one. The evaluation of any regime was, therefore, also an evaluation of its predecessor; the present was invariably judged by the past and haunted by it, in a way that was not true of any other country in Western Europe. This meant that the search for traditions had to be selective and depoliticized, that clean breaks and fresh starts appeared as virtues as much as defects. Much of the political identity of the FRG consisted of its not being the Third Reich or the Weimar Republic. Given the past failures of German democracy, there was not only a domestic need to train up a new generation that could take civic virtues for granted, there was an even more pressing need to persuade foreign opinion that this was happening. *Bonn ist nicht Weimar* ('Bonn is not Weimar'), the influential book by the Swiss publicist Fritz René Allemann, published in 1956, was addressed as much to an audience outside Germany as inside.

What all these considerations led to was the process known as 'coming to terms with the past' (*Vergangenheitsbewältigung*), the principle of which was widely accepted, but the application of which was disputed. It was easy enough to disavow the past, but it was preferable not to ask too many questions. The majority of Germans had never been fanatical Nazis, but neither had they been committed opponents of the regime. A regime like that of the Third Reich depends on widespread collusion, often based on acceptance of one or other of the many components of its eclectic ideology—in this case it could be anti-Semitism, anti-Bolshevism, contempt for democracy, or belief in the racial superiority of Germans. Side-by-side with the disavowal of the Nazi regime there was, therefore, a desire to let bygones be bygones. Asking awkward questions about who did what between 1933 and 1945 might turn out to be inconsistent with building a consensus round the new post-war order. Trials of concentration-camp guards, research into the complicity of the army or the medical profession in war crimes, investigations into the records of local worthies— all of these risked disturbing the smooth construction of a new German identity. Coming to terms with the past sometimes had the opposite effect from that intended. At first it led to a battle of the generations, with those who had grown up since 1945 wondering what skeletons there were in their parents' cupboards. As time went on, the Third Reich became more and more remote, so that its horrors almost appeared to have happened on another planet. The effect of this was to uncouple present-day Germans from their history, so that they saw less and less connection between it and the frontierless utopia of travel, consumption, and information technology in which they lived. So much so that some conservative historians and publicists in the 1980s expressed the fear that their contemporaries were losing any sense of national identity and that they had come to regard the whole of German history—in the words of the historian Ernst Nolte—as a negative myth. It was this proposition that detonated the 'historians' dispute' which exercised the passions of academics and the heavyweight press in the years immediately before unification. It led to attempts to restore a historical consciousness, especially in the rising generation, through the creation of museums of German History and influencing school syllabuses to give a more positive picture of the past—attempts that largely came to nothing, since unification superseded their agenda.

In the other Germany, the GDR, the problem of the past was solved differently. From the start the regime disavowed any responsibility for it. Since the GDR was by definition anti-Fascist, it could have no links with National Socialism. Since Fascism was a product of capitalism, and since the GDR was committed to abolishing capitalism, any risk of its resurgence had been removed. From the point of view of the regime, which, like the FRG, wanted to build a new future-oriented consensus, this approach had obvious advantages. Since the crimes of National Socialism had been committed, not by real Germans, but by 'Hitler Fascists' who had all fled to the West, there was no need to ask what had been the role of friends, neighbours, and relations during the Third Reich. Because the question of past collusion was never raised, it was easier for the population to accept the official ideology of anti-Fascism. This has had two consequences for post-unification politics. On the one hand, the conviction that Fascism and racism are bad, and the fear that they might revive, are more widespread in the Eastern *Länder* than in the Western. Opinion-poll findings are quite consistent on this matter, and parties of the far Right, like the Republicans, have done poorly in the East. On the other hand, ignorance of the Nazi regime and the Holocaust is widespread, as these did not feature in the GDR's educational programme. Nor is there much experience of living with foreigners. Vietnamese guest-workers or Mozambican students in the GDR led segregated lives and East Germans had little opportunity for informal social contact with them. The experience of suddenly living in a country of mass immigration was therefore an even greater shock for the Germans of the East than for those of the West.

What do these divergent developments mean for the mentality of unified Germany? They mean not only that the new Germany has two histories, one for the former FRG and one for the former GDR, but that it has two versions of the history before 1945, each derived from the orthodoxy of West and East. That is a matter of some importance in a country where, more than anywhere else in Western Europe, history is politics. This dissensus about the past has a number of consequences. The first has to do with the place of national unity in Germany's political development. As we have seen, although both the FRG and the GDR began their lives with avowals of national unity as a goal, division became an accepted fact. In the West more and more people argued that the existence of more than one state was a normal condition for Germany; that a united Germany, as it had existed between 1871 and 1945, was the anomaly in German history and by no means all that happy an experience. In the GDR the retreat from an aspiration to unity took a different form. Given—so the regime argued—that nationality had a socio-economic base, once the 'real existing Socialism' had been established a separate GDR nationality had emerged. Unification on the basis of two incompatible social systems, of which one was more advanced than the other, was therefore out of the question. Only when the FRG had reached the same level of development as the GDR could such a step be contemplated. For different reasons, therefore, the belief had become widespread in the two states that each would continue to go its way. Thus when unification came it was a shock to both parts of Germany.

For the population of the GDR, the fall of a despised regime was a relief. The prosperity and political freedom on the other side of the Wall were an irresistible magnet. Those dissidents who hoped that a reformed, democratic Socialism would emerge in the GDR were a minority that soon lost the ear of the population. It was only later that it emerged that during forty years of separate statehood East Germans had acquired life-styles, assumptions, and expectations that were less individualistic and more community- and state-centred than those in the West. These, it turned out, did not necessarily fit into those structures of the FRG that were extended overnight. For the population of the FRG the shock was also delayed. Most of them had assumed that unification, if it ever came, would take the form that it did—that is, through accession by the East. After all, the FRG had a legitimacy that its neighbour lacked. It rested on the repeatedly expressed allegiance of the population. It had the world's third-largest economy. It was internationally respected. For its inhabitants and for much of the outside world it was the real Germany, both as the heir of previous German states and as the true representative of the German people. It enjoyed a stability that had been denied to all its predecessors. It was a success story. Why, then, should a united Germany that was an enlarged FRG not be an equal success story?

The answer is that the new Germany could not stay an enlarged FRG for very long. At first the symptoms of continuity were overwhelming, personified by the election victory of Chancellor Kohl in December 1990. Not only were the structures of the old FRG extended to the whole of Germany; much of the personnel was recruited from there. That was inevitably true of the new private-sector managers. But it also applied to most of the public-sector administrators, in particular those in the institutions concerned with transforming the economy. Both the main directors of the Treuhandanstalt, the trustee body responsible for the former GDR's state assets, were Westerners— Detlev Rohwedder and, after his assassination, Birgit Breuel. But even party politics became semi-monopolized by Westerners. True, this did not apply to the successor party of the Communist Socialist Unity Party (Sozialistiche Einheitspartei Deutschlands (SED)), the Party of Democratic Socialism (Partei des Demokratischen Sozialismus (PDS)), nor to Alliance '90 (Bündnis '90), the coalition of former dissidents. But it was increasingly true of the three mainstream parties, partly because the Eastern sections simply lacked experienced persons, partly because too many of those who were available were tainted by collaboration with the previous regime. By 1993 three of the five *Land* Prime Ministers in the East came from the West, as did many of their cabinet colleagues.

On the other hand, it is becoming more and more evident that, in its psychological effect, unification was precisely what those who welcomed it did not wish for. It was yet another discontinuity in Germany history, yet another break in steady development, the tenth of its kind since the end of the Holy Roman Empire in 1806 and, like those of 1918 and 1945, externally induced. As with previous changes in the form of the state, the upheaval was not equally great in every respect. It was most conspicuous in the evaluation of the past and in Germany's external relations. Unification did not do away with the problem of Germany's past, it merely made the past look different. We have seen that in the old FRG and GDR history was a function of those states' post-war status. The Third Reich had been their immediate predecessor and it remained a definer of their politics. United Germany is a post-Cold War state and this has persuaded many Germans that the post-war preoccupations could be abandoned. The 'historians' dispute' of the 1980s is now dead. The question on which it centred—whether national consciousness was possible or desirable in a divided country—has been overtaken. Now that there is once more a German nation-state, it is self-evident that there is a German nationality. What remains unsolved is how the consciousness of this will relate to previous German states. That dilemma was illustrated by the embarrassing episode of Steffen Heitmann's candidature for the Federal Presidency.

Heitmann was Chancellor Helmut Kohl's nominee to succeed Richard von Weizsäcker as head of state in 1994. He was plucked from obscurity as Minister of Justice in Saxony in the hope that, as an

East German, he would act as an integrative figure. However, his ultra-conservative opinions had the opposite effect. His views on family values and the woman's place in the home proved divisive; what killed his candidature was his argument that, with unification achieved, Germans should draw a line under the past and stop being obsessed with the Third Reich. Domestically there was support for such a view, just as there had been before unification, though there was also strong opposition to it. Outside Germany it was as unacceptable as ever, especially if coming from a representative figure like the head of state. Heitmann's withdrawal from the contest closed the incident. Nevertheless, its significance lay in the post-unification conflict about German identity. On the one side were those who declared that the post-war era was over and that the new, unified, self-confident Germany need apologize to no one. On the other were those for whom the ending of the Cold War had not expunged Germany's responsibility for its past. Germany might be unified; it was far from united.

Indeed, far from simplifying the question of the past, unification complicated it, for there was now a new past to come to terms with, that of the GDR. Like the Nazi regime, that of the GDR had counted on the complicity of its citizens. Jobs, careers, and housing depended on conformity, and as long as there was no prospect of the regime's coming to an end the premium on conformity was high. At one time or another one East German in three had acted as an informer for the security service (Staatssicherheitsdienst (Stasi)). After 1989, as after 1945, this posed a dilemma: which was more important—to purge the guilty or to wipe the slate clean? After 1989, as after 1945, the population was divided on the matter—should there be a general amnesty, should there be a thorough combing of the Stasi files, or should there be a selective investigation of those who were holders of high office or aspirants for it? To put it another way: should the motivation be punitive or prophylactic? Once more, German history became German politics. Once more, German unification became a source of division.

The second major upheaval created by unification concerns Germany's international position. Not only is German history inseparable from German politics; foreign policy in modern Germany has been inseparable from domestic policy. The Empire was created by wars and destroyed by a war. The Weimar Republic was the product of a war. The Third Reich existed for the purpose of war. The control of foreign policy and, where relevant, imperial policy has been a topic of permanent domestic dispute, as has been accountability for the armed forces. Above all, Germany's central position in Europe has posed particular choices and dilemmas. Does Germany belong to the industrialized, liberal West of Europe? Should it tend towards the Eurasian land mass and associate its interests with Russia, whatever that country's regime? Should Germany be a committed member of a stable alliance system? Or is it in its interest to balance between East and West, securing the greatest freedom of movement, but also risking its neighbours' distrust?

During the years of the Cold War these dilemmas were in abeyance. The FRG and the GDR were the respective creations of the two superpowers. Their function was to guard the advance posts at the strategic and ideological dividing-line that ran through Europe. Western Germany belonged to the West, Eastern Germany to the East. Once the wartime Grand Alliance had broken down, the Western powers were determined not to permit a neutral Germany to see-saw between the blocs and possibly to be sucked into the Soviet orbit. The Soviet Union in turn responded by accepting half a Communist loaf, once a whole neutral one was no longer available. Two generations of Germans therefore grew up in a world in which integration into one of the blocs was a given. The FRG was, from the start, integrated with the West economically. It was a recipient of Marshall Aid, a founder-member of the European Coal and Steel Community (ECSC) in 1950, a charter signatory of the Treaty of Rome that created the European Economic Community (EEC) in 1957. Its economy was geared to the West, its increasingly formidable export performance dependent on the markets of the West. On the eve of unification some 60 per cent of its trade was with its EC partners, some 80 per cent with the advanced capitalist world. Its military integration followed a parallel path. The West had from the first a strategic interest in the defence of the FRG. The NATO umbrella, created in 1950, was automatically extended to it. In 1955 it became a member of NATO and in the course of time provided the greatest contingent of the alliance's conventional forces.

These developments, a novel experience for Germans, had a

profound effect on their psychological orientation. Not everyone in the FRG approved of the military alignment with the West or—as its opponents saw it—the subordination to the USA. As we shall see in later chapters, at various times massive movements were mobilized against the FRG's defence policy. But in other respects these protests were consistent with the main line of the FRG's ideological development—the disavowal of Germany's militaristic past, indeed the demilitarization of German patriotism. What replaced it were two parallel and connected developments. The first was a slow but cumulative acceptance of the institutions of the West—multi-party democracy, parliamentary government, and a competitive market economy, all of them heavily contested concepts before 1945. The second was an emergent cosmopolitanism and a commitment to European integration. As Eastern Europe, including the GDR, became more and more remote and foreign, a generation grew up that was more at home in Paris and London and even New York and Los Angeles than in Dresden or Leipzig. The orientations of the GDR population are more difficult to trace. The anti-militarism was certainly there. Indeed, the greater militarization of the GDR, including the compulsory training in schools, was one of the causes of the regime's unpopularity. Nor was the orientation towards the East and the political domination by the Soviet Union popular. What the positive political preferences of the population were is less certain. For many GDR citizens, the West represented a substitute normality, though their image of it was not necessarily a true reflection of its reality.

These divergent developments meant that when Germany was unified there was no ready-made recipe for its geo-political future. Since the whole of Germany became automatically integrated in the West—NATO, the EC, GATT, to mention only the most important —the signs pointed to continuity, at any rate continuity with the FRG. But since unification also took place in the context of a new strategic constellation, the omens for continuity were not all that favourable. The Cold War had disciplined politics in the West. It had restricted the options and constrained debate. Once its cement was removed, Germany's future policy orientation became much less certain. Unified Germany once more bestrode the centre of Europe. With a population of eighty million—a quarter more than France, Britain, or Italy—it was clearly no longer one of a number of equal leaders. It was the obvious source of aid and investment for the newly independent states of East and Central Europe and for the Soviet Union. The pressures to take bolder initiatives and to pursue policies more independent than before became stronger. The first signs of a new German policy autonomy came with the recognition of the ex-Yugoslav republics of Slovenia and Croatia in 1992 under the influence of the then Foreign Minister, Hans-Dietrich Genscher. Germany has also taken a more prominent role as a conciliator within the European Union (EU), whether at the time of the negotiations at Maastricht in December 1991 or of the accession of the four European Free Trade Association (EFTA) members, Finland, Sweden, Norway, and Austria, in the spring of 1994.

Continuity is greatest in Germany's military role, where it has remained unassertive. In part this restraint is imposed by the victor powers. The 'Two-plus-Four' Treaty of 1990 between the wartime allies and the two Germanies, which was the basis of unification, limited German conventional forces to 370,000 men (less than the FRG's contribution to NATO) and confirmed the ban on ABC (atomic, bacteriological, and chemical) weapons. The second constraint is constitutional. Article 87a of the Basic Law, adopted after the FRG joined NATO, restricts German armed forces to a defensive role, which was generally taken to mean operations within the NATO area. Germany's defence commitment was defined within the context of the Cold War. The ending of the Cold War has reopened the debate, but not yet defined the new parameters. The Left—the Social Democratic Party (Sozialdemokratische Partei Deutschlands (SPD)) and the Greens— insist that 'out-of-area' actions by German contingents must be restricted to UN peace-keeping operations, and not peace-enforcing operations, as in Somalia in 1993. Public opposition to German involvement in the Gulf War of 1991 led the government to interpret Article 87a very restrictively; the German contribution was financial and logistical only. As we shall see in Chapter 8, the Federal Constitutional Court gave a wider meaning to Article 87a in 1994, thus averting a long and potentially divisive debate about amending the Basic Law, but the political obstacles to greater activism remain. Lastly there is the demand that Germany should join the USA, Russia,

Britain, France, and China as one of the permanent members of the UN Security Council in recognition of its new importance. However, the military constraints imposed by the 'Two-plus-Four' Treaty and the Basic Law might create a situation in which German representatives have to vote on an action in which their country would be prevented from participating. Defence policy in the 1990s therefore presents the usual mix of continuity and discontinuity in German perceptions and German prescriptions. The division in public opinion for or against a more active role mirrors the divisions that existed in the old FRG. The greater pressure for activism reflects the changed geography of Europe.

It is this geopolitical change that has brought about the biggest challenge to Germany's foreign-policy makers. We have seen that the two German states of 1949–80 were created by the superpowers and that their existence was defined by the Cold War blocs. What happens when the Cold War ends, the blocs disintegrate, and only one superpower remains? What does Western integration mean under these new conditions and what are its justifications? The justifications are not lacking. The bulk of Germany's trade continues to be with its EU partners and the West. Investment in the East and trade with the East can supplement it, but not replace it. The Soviet nuclear threat may be over, but the threat of disorder from the East is not. The US defence umbrella has not become superfluous and the European attempts to impose a settlement on ex-Yugoslavia show that such an enterprise is very difficult without American participation. German governments are anxious to draw the newly independent states of Central Europe into the existing Western supra-national institutions, whether formally or informally, and they are anxious to maintain the working relationship with post-Soviet Russia that they had with the Soviet Union. The decision to move the capital from Bonn (60 kilometres from the Belgian frontier) to Berlin (70 kilometres from the Polish frontier) not only symbolizes the return to national unity, but signals an intention to pay more attention to Germany's Eastern neighbours. But none of this can amount to a reorientation. The policy of balance between East and West, of being an independent force that chooses its partners now on one side of the continent and now on the other, which had characterized German statecraft from the creation of the Empire until Hitler's attack on Russia in 1941, is not available. It is practicable only when there are two competing poles for Germany's favour. Post-Communist Russia is not in a position to act as such a pole. The very factor that made German unification possible—the collapse of Communism—has averted the possibility for a policy of balance. To that extent the Western orientation has not only survived unification; it has been strengthened by it.

What has changed is the composition of the Western orientation. Before 1990 this had two principal components, a special relationship with the USA and a special relationship with France. The interests of the USA and Germany had been growing slowly apart even before unification—partly because of the USA's growing preoccupation with the Pacific, partly because of Germany's greater self-confidence in Europe, partly because the perceived military threat from a declining Soviet Union was lessening. Yet the role of the USA in smoothing the path to unification in 1990 showed that in essentials American goodwill was still needed. And the hard bargaining between the USA and the EU in 1994 over the General Agreement on Trade and Tariffs (GATT) showed how high the price of a permanent dissensus would have been. Precisely because the new, larger Germany has neither the desire nor the capacity to be a superpower, the USA remains an overshadowing presence in German politics.

Germany's relationship with France is closer and for that reason more problematical. From the 1960s onwards, and certainly since the creation of the European Monetary System (EMS) in 1979, the Franco-German partnership has been the sheet-anchor of West European politics. Until unification, this partnership slightly privileged France. France was a nuclear power and a permanent member of the UN Security Council. French was a world language, and, as an ex-colonial power, France had cultural and economic spheres of influence in Africa and elsewhere. Justly or not, France enjoyed a status on the world stage that Germany did not. All this compensated for Germany's economic superiority and its greater conventional military strength. But even before unification, as French governments began to fear that this balanced partnership might not last, and that resumed economic growth and greater diplomatic self-confidence on the German side would turn France into a junior partner, they embarked on a strategy of accelerating and tightening European integration in order to constrain Germany. Unification irrevocably tipped the equilibrium in Germany's favour. Germany ceased to be a defeated enemy. It outstripped France more than before in population and economic potential. The collapse of Communism diminished the value of France's nuclear capability and opened Eastern Europe as a sphere of German influence. The only counter-action available to France in this situation was to intensify the pressure for European integration. The Treaty on European Union, signed at Maastricht in December 1991, was the outcome of this. Nothing would be easier than to make a list of Franco-German disputes during and since unification. But the Maastricht Treaty showed that Europe cannot run without Franco-German agreement on essentials and that it cannot run against the wishes of Germany and France where these coincide.

Germany's foreign relations, whether in Europe or outside it, and its military obligations are a matter of continuing public debate and public concern, more so than in the great majority of other European countries, where national existence is less dependent on the international alignment. Nevertheless, except at moments of crisis, they are not the overriding political issue for Germans. What unification has prompted is renewed debate about national identity. This has three main aspects. The first has to do with Germany's newly found sovereignty following the end of the forty-year division and the question, discussed above, whether the destiny of a German nation-state lies in further absorption in supra-national organizations or a rediscovered national interest. The second has to do with social reconciliation in a hastily united state; the third with the ethnic character of a nation in a Europe with open frontiers.

Social reconciliation is in many ways the most urgent of the domestic demands the new Germany faces. Only after the creation of the single German state did it become evident that there were indeed separate East and West German identities which were not necessarily dependent on loyalty towards, or nostalgia for, the former states. In part the erection of the Iron Curtain had merely deepened an existing fault-line. The River Elbe has always been a cultural and economic frontier through German-speaking Europe. *Ostelbien*, implying feudal backwardness, had been a common expression in pre-1933 Germany.

The obvious dependence of the former GDR on Western expertise merely reinforced existing resentments; the arrogance or patronizing attitudes of some of the benefactors made things worse still. In 1994, four years after unification, 80 per cent of East Germans thought they were second-class citizens in their own country and that Bonn had done too little to equalize living standards. West Germans in turn think the costs of unification too high and regard East Germans as too demanding and unenterprising. At the bottom of these divergences there are undeniable real problems. East Germans bear the brunt of the unemployment and disorientation caused by restructuring. West Germans bear most of the additional tax burden. The Bundesbank has calculated that in the years 1991–4 DM 360 billion were transferred by the federal government and the Western *Länder* to the East. In the absence of reliable statistics on the economy of the GDR and in the euphoria of unification, most Germans, East and West, underestimated the size and cost of the task of reconstruction and the complexity of sorting out property claims. After the dismantling of the Berlin Wall there was, unsurprisingly, much talk of 'the wall in people's minds'. Not only had the two populations grown up under different and increasingly divergent systems, they had embarked on the unprecedented experiment of unification with radically contrasting expectations not only of the outcome, but of each others' behaviour. By 1989 the relationships between citizens, civil society, and the state were strikingly different in the two Germanies. Like the extreme free-marketeers of the Anglo-Saxon world, but for different reasons, those who ruled the GDR believed that there was no such thing as society. All significant economic, intellectual, or leisure activities were to be controlled by the state, dominated as it was by the monopoly party, or at the least subject to its veto. That had a number of consequences that were likely to outlive the regime. It meant that people became accustomed to looking to the state for jobs, benefits, and favours. It also meant that they became very good at helping each other to circumvent or evade the requirements of the regime, with its shortages, authoritarianism, and inequities. It meant furthermore that there was a premium on withdrawal into a private world of family, friends, and hobbies, creating a society of nooks and cubby-holes (*Nischengesellschaft*).

In the FRG the developments were more complex. Here, too, the state played a role as provider. The West German welfare state was among the most elaborate and generous inside or outside Europe. But the economy itself was a market economy, putting a premium on competition and individualism. Many East Germans viewed with distaste the materialism, the rat-race, and the society of sharp elbows (*Ellbogengesellschaft*) that characterized the West. But what the West also possessed and what the East by definition lacked was an intermediate sector of voluntary autonomous associations, some to protect material interests, others to advance a variety of causes, ranging from well-endowed nation-wide lobbies to local citizens' initiatives. West Germans could, therefore, take for granted, in a way that East Germans could not, that web of reciprocal rights and obligations that constitute a genuine civil society. Both East and West Germans had ideals of social solidarity, but they were not compatible.

Finally, Germans are divided about what constitutes a German. This is not primarily a division between East and West. It is one that is in many ways inherited not only from the FRG, but from nineteenth-century concepts. It rests on the distinction between citizenship and ethnicity. One can be a German by legal definition, as a citizen of the German state, or a German by cultural identity, irrespective of where one was born or where one lives. The notion of a cultural, as opposed to a state-defined nationality arose through the Romantic movement, but also through the absence of a German nation-state and the scattered nature of the German-speaking population of Europe in the nineteenth century. The French Revolution had introduced the notion of the citizen, who derived his rights from his obligations to the state and from where he lived. A French citizen was anyone born in France, irrespective of where his parents came from. French citizenship was based on *ius soli*, the law of the soil, as was British and US citizenship. German citizenship, as enshrined in the Imperial citizenship law of 1913, rested on *ius sanguinis*, the law of descent: the German-born child of an alien remained an alien. Naturalization was possible, but it was difficult. Article 116(1) of the West German Basic Law accepted the principle of descent in extending citizenship to all who could claim 'membership of the German people'. This device brought numerous advantages and one drawback. It was a justification for refusing to recognize a separate GDR citizenship. Any GDR citizen was automatically entitled to citizenship of the FRG. So was any ethnic German expelled from any of the states of Eastern Europe after the Second World War. So was any ethnic German from Russia, Poland, or Romania who opted for resettlement in the FRG when this became possible in the 1970s and 1980s. There has been a vast ingathering of the German diaspora and it has been relatively painlessly integrated. The drawback of the *ius sanguinis* is, however, considerable and growing. While Germany has generous immigration laws, it has restrictive citizenship laws which the new Germany has inherited from the FRG. From the late 1950s onwards the German economy demanded the recruitment of labour, mainly from Mediterranean countries. Those who came were classified as migrant workers (*Gastarbeiter*), even if they settled with their families. By 1993 there were some 6.9 million of them, constituting about 10 per cent of the West German and 1.5 per cent of the East German population. Turks are the largest group, numbering 1.9 million. Though it is possible for *Gastarbeiter* or their dependants to acquire German citizenship, the obstacles are considerable. For instance, many are deterred from applying because German law does not permit dual citizenship. In 1990 a mere 1,423 Turks were naturalized.

One problem that intensified in the 1990s was the influx of asylum-seekers. Article 16 of the Basic Law granted an unconditional right of asylum to the politically persecuted, a provision that was readily understandable in the context of recovery from the Nazi legacy and the consolidation of Communist rule in Eastern Europe. For the first thirty years of the FRG's existence the small number of asylum-seekers was absorbed without undue difficulty. From the 1980s onwards their numbers began to rise and escalated after the fall of Communism. In 1992 the number of applicants peaked at 438,000. There is no evidence that xenophobic feelings in general are more widespread in Germany than among its neighbours, though large-scale immigration is a more recent phenomenon than in former colonial powers with stronger overseas links. What did happen was something close to a collective public panic at the prospect of an ever-rising flood of immigrants, with opinion polls reporting immigration as the most urgently felt problem in the Western *Länder*. More seriously, there were outbreaks of violence against foreigners, whether *Gastarbeiter* or asylum-seekers, which resulted in thirty-nine fatalities between 1991 and 1993. An amendment to the Basic Law in 1993, which imposed stricter conditions on the right of asylum, seems to have had a calming effect.

Competing social claims, disputes about burden-sharing, divergent mentalities, mutual distrust, doubts about national sovereignty, a fractured relationship with the past, fears about the dilution of an inherited culture—these are some of the factors dividing Germans from each other in the 1990s. Some of the differences are straightforwardly between East and West, directly attributable to the postwar division. Others are between Protestant and Catholic or Left and Right, reflecting much older fault-lines in German society. What are the prospects for compensatory trends? Germans share a language, a literature, a territory, and a national past (though a disputed one). They are part of an increasingly frontierless Europe and advanced industrial world. The values and aspirations of the younger age groups in the Eastern and Western *Länder* are not very different from each other. Socially, culturally, and politically, Germany was much less homogeneous than, say, Britain and France even when it was a single state. Not only the Cold War divide but also the federal structure of the FRG have militated against homogenization. It is a safe prediction that in the course of a generation Germans of East and West will grow closer together, just as those of north and south, town and country, and Protestant and Catholic grew closer together between 1949 and 1990. But those who value variety and pluralism in human affairs should not be too despondent if reconciliation is imperfect and convergence is incomplete.

2 Filling the Vacuum

No political activities shall be countenanced, unless authorized
by you.
*(Directive to the Commander in Chief of United States Forces
of Occupation Regarding the Military Government of
Germany, 26 April 1945)*

The German people should be enabled to develop their
political independence on democratic lines in close association
with the free peoples of Western Europe.
*(Policy Directive for the United States High Commissioner for
Germany, 17 November 1949)*

WHAT is now the past was once the future—uncertain and unpre-
dictable, to be shaped step by step. Sometimes these steps were well
planned and logically coherent, at other times reactive or merely *ad
hoc*. On 8 May 1945 the German armies surrendered unconditionally.
A shadowy German government, headed by Grand Admiral Karl
Dönitz as President and Johann Ludwig Schwerin-Krosigk as Chancellor, continued in office until 23 May, when it was deposed by the
Allies. From that date on it was not merely the Third Reich that had
ceased to exist. There was no German state any more, no overall
administration responsible for the territory of the former Third Reich,
no internal or external representative body to speak for the interests of
Germans individually or collectively. There is no precedent in modern times for the disappearance of a major state in this way. The
victorious Allies recognized the existence of this vacuum. They would,
for the time being, have to run Germany themselves. In the Berlin
Declaration of 5 June they proclaimed the 'supreme authority' of the
Allied Control Council and demanded the Germans' 'full and unconditional compliance' with its instructions.

But there was a vacuum not only in German government, but
also in Allied policy. From 1943 onwards the governments of the
Grand Alliance had devoted increasing thought to the post-war shape
of Germany, even though military victory had remained the first

concern. But at no stage before 1945 had any of the prospective victors elaborated a coherent strategy, nor was there agreement among them on any except the vaguest common aspirations. At three summit conferences in Moscow, Tehran, and finally Yalta (in February 1945) they concurred in some objectives and some specific measures. The general objectives were those of de-Nazification, demilitarization, and democratization. The military defeat of Germany would be worthless if there were to be no permanent guarantee against future aggression; two major wars in twenty-five years had been enough. For the interim the territory of Germany was to be divided into zones of military occupation, one each for Britain, the USA, and the Soviet Union, with France added at a later stage. The capital, Berlin, was to be excluded from the zones and administered separately by an Allied *Kommandatura*, with a sector of occupation for each of the victors. Beyond that the various Allies' ideas were neither specific nor compatible.

The first question that arose concerned the frontiers of a post-war Germany. There was agreement that all annexations by Hitler should be nullified, in particular those of Austria and the German-speaking 'Sudeten' areas of Czechoslovakia. There was agreement that a restored Poland should be compensated in the West by Germany for territories lost to the Soviet Union in the East, but no details were fixed. The second question concerned the territorial organization of a post-war Germany. Many politicians and advisers on the Allied side regarded the existence of a single German state, dominated by Prussia, as the main cause of Europe's disorders and therefore advocated a re-fragmentation into its historic units. But by the end of the war the drawbacks of such a scheme were more evident than its advantages: effective control pointed to a single political and economic unit, rather than a multiplicity of possibly uncoordinated ones.

The third question was economic. Here the conflicts of interest were greatest and the various demands and expectations at their most contradictory. For instance, what implications did the undisputed desire to demilitarize Germany have for its future industrial structure? The most radical answer to this was given by the US Treasury Secretary Henry J. Morgenthau in September 1944, when he advocated the complete dismantling of industry in the Ruhr area—in effect the re-agrarianization of Germany. The Morgenthau Plan was never adopted as official US policy and by the spring of 1945 had ceased, for all practical purposes, to be a policy guideline. But one of the main assumptions behind it—that Germany needed to be punished and Germans needed to be re-educated—remained dominant. It was an assumption that the British government shared, though its economic priorities were different. Britain's economic resources were more strained than those of the USA. As a European state, it was much more aware of the prospective costs of occupation, of the prospective costs of reconstruction not only of Germany but of the rest of the devastated continent, and of the interdependence of European economies. It had a clearer memory of how counter-productive punitive reparations had been after the First World War, not only economically but politically. To repeat that experiment would result, in the words of the Prime Minister, Winston Churchill, in a Britain that was chained to a corpse.

The Soviet Union's priorities were different again. More than Britain or any West European state it would need reparations after the ruinous effects of the war. It, too, therefore, had an interest in a single German economy in a single German state. What concerned the Soviet Union, more than either Britain or the USA at this stage, was who would control its political and economic resources. The resulting struggle for the mastery over the defeated enemy was to be one of the causes of the Cold War and of the division of Germany. As the Allied occupation forces moved into Germany and took up their task of government, they faced the following unsolved problems:

- How were the costs of occupation to be paid for?
- How was reconstruction to be paid for?
- What reparations could they take, in cash or in kind?
- How big a German economy should they tolerate, if only to cover the first three items?
- Who was to own German industrial assets?
- Which German administrators—if any—were to be entrusted with carrying out Allied orders?

Any solution involved multiple trade-offs. The satisfaction of short-term reparations needs could entail long-term economic impoverishment. On the other hand, requiring Germans to pay for occupation and reconstruction costs might entail forgoing generous reparations. Grappling with questions of economic and political control risked early and severe disagreement among the Allies. The first and, as it turned out, the last attempt to arrive at a joint policy was made in July and August at Potsdam. Half-way through the Potsdam conference the results of the British general election were announced; with the Labour victory, Clement Attlee now represented Britain as Prime Minister and Ernest Bevin as Foreign Secretary. As Harry Truman had succeeded to the US Presidency in April 1945 on the death of Franklin Roosevelt, that left only Stalin as the representative of the wartime alliance. The change of personnel, however, made little difference to the proceedings. Superficially Potsdam marked the culmination of the victor powers' common purpose.

The Potsdam Agreement, published on 2 August, repeated the previous commitments to demilitarization and de-Nazification. Germany was to be treated as a single economic unit, with a German administrative apparatus under the supervision of the Allied Control Council. To symbolize the Council's role as the *de facto* government of Germany, its headquarters were set up in Berlin and the British, US, and Soviet military administrations made a point of also moving to Berlin. Only the French, who disapproved of the notion of a single Germany and who had not been represented at Potsdam, made a point of not moving to Berlin. As far as Germany's frontiers were concerned, a number of *faits accomplis* were recognized. The area round Königsberg (renamed Kaliningrad) in former East Prussia was annexed by the Soviet Union; the whole of Germany to the east of the Rivers Oder and the Western Neiße were to be placed under Polish administration pending the final settlement of the frontiers by a peace treaty; the German populations of these territories and of the Czechoslovak Sudetenland were to be transferred in an 'orderly and humane' manner.

The subsequent development of Germany was almost the exact opposite of that indicated by the Potsdam Agreement. In part the reason lay in the fundamentally different interpretations that the Soviet and Anglo–American military governments placed on apparently harmless words. It was not too difficult to agree on the principles of de-Nazification, the fostering of democratic forces, and the decentralization of political life: it soon turned out that they could be interpreted and implemented in quite contrary ways. But what sealed the divergence of the Soviet from the Western zones of occupation was the most heavily contested item in the Potsdam negotiations: reparations. The principle that reparations should be in kind, not money, was maintained, but there was no settlement of the amount involved. Instead, each victor power was to take reparations from its zone, with an additional allowance for the Soviets of 10 per cent of the Western total. This provision made nonsense of the declared aim of treating Germany as a single economic—and therefore administrative—unit. Different reparations policies meant incompatible economic policies; incompatible economic policies led to different political structures. Slowly but inexorably each zone of occupation became a separate political unit.

There is a recognizable and relentless logic about the process by which the Western and Soviet zones acquired separate economic and political systems; became increasingly sovereign states, each drawn into the strategic and economic blocs of the rival superpowers; and finally faced each other as competitors for the allegiance of the German people. There were those on both sides who, as early as 1945, feared, hoped, or accepted that this might be the outcome. But such a course of events was not, at this stage, pre-ordained. None of the Allies had a game-plan; options remained open. When Stalin told the Yugoslav Communist leader Milovan Djilas some weeks before the end of the war that each of the victors would impose his own social system within his military sphere, this did not necessarily imply a division of Germany. There were other ways of bringing about a Germany that was friendly or subordinate to the Soviet Union. The expression 'iron curtain', launched by Churchill in the House of Commons on 16 August 1945, was at this stage no more than a metaphor. Even seven months later, when he repeated it at Fulton, Missouri, he still placed it 'from Stettin on the Baltic to Trieste on the Adriatic'— that is, between the Soviet zone of Germany and Poland. It was not to be long before it ran through the middle of Germany.

One reason for the hesitations on the part of the Allies is that they were far from certain whom they feared and distrusted most. On the one hand, the suspicions between the Anglo-Americans and Soviets were growing and had indeed begun before the war ended. Four days after the ending of the Potsdam conference the first atomic bomb was dropped on Hiroshima, radically altering the strategic balance between the superpowers. On the other hand, the defeated Germans were still seen as a threat to peace and security. The early proclamations of the occupation forces—especially those of Britain and the USA—had a distinctly punitive ring to them. France insisted for longer than any of the other victors on a Carthaginian treatment of Germany, with strict international control of its economy. When the US Secretary of State James F. Byrnes announced that his country intended to withdraw its conventional forces from Europe within two years, his Soviet counterpart was appalled. In addition, distrust of Germans increasingly merged in East–West distrust. Both sides were agreed that 're-education' meant a long haul and that it might take twenty or thirty years before Germans were reliably democratic and could be entrusted with self-government. Meanwhile the Soviets were convinced that only the strictest indoctrination could ensure German political compliance, while the British and US authorities feared that, given the Germans' proclivity for totalitarian doctrines, they might, following the discredit of Nazism, embrace Communism instead. Faced with these uncertainties, the occupying powers veered between authoritarianism and appeasement in their treatment of the defeated enemy, adopting the apartheid of 'no fraternization' one day and the co-optation of local notables the next. In the end it was the East–West rivalry that accelerated the development of a new German politics and the involvement of Germans in the plans of their masters. Between 1945 and 1949 the story of German politics is of the stages by which the occupiers first assumed, then exercised, and finally returned the powers of civil government. With surprising speed and thoroughness Germans advanced during those four years from the status of subordinate participants to being almost equal players.

Initially even the internal geography of occupied Germany was uncertain. True, the boundaries of the zones of occupation had been settled, but it was not until July 1945 that the troops of the various victor armies finally withdrew from conquests outside their assigned areas. The establishment of principal political units—the *Länder* that have become the basis of Germany's federal structure—went forward in a much more haphazard way. Where a region corresponded with a historically established entity and fell within one of the four zones, its reconstitution was fairly straightforward, as the examples of Bavaria in the US zone and Saxony in the Soviet zone show. Elsewhere there were three kinds of difficulties. In the East the territories occupied by Poland cut into established administrative units. In the West zonal boundaries, especially those of the French zone which had been carved out of the area originally allocated to the USA, cut across historic state frontiers. In all four zones there were relics of the patchwork of the former German state structure. Though these had been deprived of all powers under the Third Reich, their populations in many cases retained a distinct identity and there were pressures to reconstitute them after 1945.

The reconstruction of political life was fastest in the US and Soviet zones, in each case in accordance with the ideological assumptions of the occupier. In the Soviet zone this operated from the top down, in the US zone from the bottom up. The Soviet military administration (Sowjetische Militäradministration in Deutschland (SMAD)) was the first to license political parties and trade unions (of which more below) and the first to set up administrative departments—in effect, ministries—to cover the whole of their zone, a decision taken even before the Potsdam Agreement. Of the eleven ministerial directors, six were either members or close collaborators of the Communist Party.

The Soviet and US zones were also the first to constitute *Länder*. In the Soviet zone these were:

- *Saxony*: corresponding roughly to the pre-1933 state;
- *Thuringia*: corresponding roughly to the pre-1933 state;
- *Saxony–Anhalt*: consisting of the Prussian province of Saxony and the former state of Anhalt;
- *Brandenburg*: the former Prussian province of Brandenburg, surrounding Berlin, minus the areas lost to Poland;
- *Mecklenburg*: the former two states of Mecklenburg, plus that part of the Prussian province of Pomerania not lost to Poland.

In the US zone they were:

- *Bavaria*: Bavaria in its historic frontiers, minus the Palatinate on the left bank of the Rhine;

- *Württemberg–Baden*: the Northern halves of the former states of Württemberg and Baden;
- *Hesse*: the former state of Hesse, plus parts of the former Prussian province of Hesse-Nassau.

The creation of the US-zone *Länder* illustrated the way Allied political priorities could conflict with historic German boundaries. The Bavarian Palatinate was detached from the rest of Bavaria because it had been allocated to the French zone; Baden and Württemberg were split, because the southern parts of both were in the French zone. The North Sea port and former city-state of Bremen, geographically in the British zone, was transferred to the US zone at the beginning of 1947 to provide an American outlet to the sea. The *Länder* of the French zone, in fact, respected the historical geography of Germany least. They were:

- *Rhineland–Palatinate*: the Bavarian Palatinate, plus parts of two former Prussian provinces;
- *Baden*: the southern half of the state of Baden;
- *Württemberg–Hohenzollern*: the southern half of the state of Württemberg, plus the detached Prussian province of Hohenzollern.

Territorial reorganization was slowest of all in the British zone, which contained the industrial heartland of the Ruhr, the control of which was an object of intense dispute among the occupying powers. The *Land* of *North Rhine–Westphalia*, then as now much the most populous of the German *Länder*, was not created until July 1946. It consisted of the former Prussian provinces of Westphalia and the Rhine Province, minus that part of it allocated to the French zone. The remaining *Länder* were created later still. They were:

- *Lower Saxony*: the Prussian province of Hanover, plus the former states of Braunschweig, Oldenburg, and Lippe;
- *Hamburg*: an enlarged version of the former Free City;
- *Schleswig-Holstein*: the former Prussian province of that name, plus the Free City of Lübeck.

It was an indication of the piecemeal way in which German territories were reorganized that, though the old state of Prussia was partitioned among eight *Länder* in all four zones, it was not formally abolished until February 1947.

The US administration was also first off the mark in recruiting German politicians into its governmental machinery. Fritz Schäffer, who had belonged to the conservative Bavarian People's Party (Bayerische Volkspartei (BVP)) before 1933, was appointed Prime Minister of Bavaria on 28 May 1945, a bare three weeks after VE Day. The limits of German politicians' discretion at this stage were demonstrated when he was arbitrarily dismissed from this post four months later. Nevertheless, by the end of 1945 there were *Land* governments, headed by appointed German politicians, throughout the US zone. As a sign of the growing coherence of the zones as policy-making units, there was also a *Länder* Council (*Länderrat*), headed by the zone's Prime Ministers. The US military administration (OMGUS) had, indeed, gone further still by appointing 'pre-parliaments' to advise the *Land* governments. Municipal elections took place from January to May 1946 and in June elections were held for constituent assemblies in each of the *Länder*, the first free elections in Germany since Hitler's assumption of power. By October of that year *Land* constitutions were ready for approval by OMGUS and were then submitted for acceptance by referendums in the *Länder*. Simultaneously there were elections to the first regular *Land* parliaments (*Landtage*). The powers of the *Land* governments and legislatures were still circumscribed, but the political evolution of the US zone clearly showed the importance that Americans placed on government by constitution and legitimation by popular sovereignty.

Both the British and the French authorities acted in accordance with different priorities. The French military authorities were initially unwilling to tolerate any unit of government above the district level, but in the end followed the US procedure at some remove. Municipal elections, held in September and October 1946, formed the basis of consultative assemblies for each *Land*. The constitutions they produced were approved by referendums, with simultaneous *Landtag* elections, in May 1947; unlike the US zone, the French zone had no co-ordinating body above the *Land* level. The British favoured the opposite approach from that of the French. For them only the whole zone made sense as an administrative unit and a Central Economic

Office was set up in October 1946. In contrast with the situation in the US zone, the British authorities were slow to recruit politicians into their policy-making apparatuses, such as the Zonal Advisory Council, or to proceed with elections. As in the French zone, municipal elections were held in October and November 1946 and *Landtag* elections in May 1947. Nor did the British attach much value to written constitutions: the *Länder* of the British zone did not acquire them until after the creation of the FRG.

In the first two post-war years the construction of political institutions went ahead faster than many would have forecast. By the middle of 1947 organs of admittedly limited self-government were well in place, at least in the three Western zones, and organs of administration in all four zones. Some of these structures, like the *Land* as the basis of political decision-making, were common to all zones. In other respects there was considerable variety. Local government structures, for instance, reflected the predilections of the individual occupiers. In the US zone the direct election of mayors, which had previously applied only to the state of Württemberg, was extended to Baden and Bavaria. In the British zone, on the other hand, the policy was to downgrade the role of mayors, by separating the political and administrative functions through the *Direktoren*, the equivalent of town clerks or chief executives. In the French zone it was the professional administrators who were downgraded by the introduction of the French mayoral system. Except in the former French zone, these innovations have survived and systems resembling that of the US zone have been introduced in the former GDR.

Political life of this intensity would not have been possible without the mediation of political parties. But here, too, it was difficult for the occupying powers to arrive at rational and consistent policies. In no other respect did they have to decide more quickly whom they distrusted more—their conquered enemy or each other. For this reason alone, as well as for others, they agreed that they alone would have the power to license parties. There were, however, two other powerful motives for such a restrictive course of action. The first was that German experience had shown that democratic institutions did not guarantee democratic outcomes: in the last two free elections of the Weimar Republic in 1932 the parties opposed to parliamentary government had gained absolute majorities. The second was that Weimar politics had been characterized by an increasing fragmentation of the party system, which played its part in discrediting parliamentary democracy. Licensing therefore enabled the occupiers to control the number of parties as well as the kind of parties and thus to play a determining role in the emerging party system.

Such an aim could, however, be realized only in conjunction with German initiatives. And since informal contacts between politically active Germans were difficult to police and impossible to prevent, Allied measures were as often reactive as they were pre-emptive. What gave the Allies such discretion as they had was indecision on the German side and above all the different agendas on the Left. The two parties of the Left, the SPD and the Communists (Kommunistiche Partei Deutschlands (KPD)), had had the strongest organizations before 1933, the clearest aims, and, as they saw it, the best claims to political leadership in view of their anti-Nazi record. The SPD began reorganizing itself even before the war was over by opening an office in Hanover under the leadership of Dr Kurt Schumacher, who was to be its dominant figure until his death in 1952. The KPD re-established itself in Berlin under the leadership of a group, headed by Walter Ulbricht and Wilhelm Pieck, who had spent the Nazi period in exile in Moscow. The unsolved question was the relationship between the two parties. In the Weimar period they had been bitter enemies, but defeat and persecution had softened some of the antagonism and there was some support among rank-and-file members for closer collaboration, even if not fusion, in order to rebuild Germany on democratic and Socialist lines.

On the Right the situation was a great deal more complicated. Non-Socialist politics under both Weimar and the Empire had been divided by religion, region, special interest, and constitutional ideology. The most coherent right-of-centre bloc consisted of the Catholic *Zentrum* and its Bavarian analogue, the BVP. But even these parties had been able to mobilize only half the Catholic electorate. Weimar Liberalism was divided into a small Liberal Left, represented by the Democrats (Deutsche Demokratische Partei (DDP)), and a more nationalist and only dubiously democratic German People's Party (Deutsche Volkspartei (DVP)). Further to the Right were the monarchist nationalists of the Deutschnationale Volkspartei (DNVP), and a whole congeries of minor parties. One of these, a small conservative Protestant grouping, the Christian Social People's Service (Christlichsozialer Volksdienst (CSVD)), was to provide a significant number of post-1945 political leaders. The Nazi Party grew between 1928 and 1932 from 2.6 to 37.3 per cent, largely at the expense of the non-Catholic Right. The majority of the voters of this segment went over to the Nazis, as did at least some of their leaders. Those that did not collaborate did not, in the main, resist either. As the remnants of German right-of-centre politics stood discredited and demoralized in 1945, a number of scenarios emerged for reconstructing it.

To begin with there was widespread agreement that there should be fewer parties than before 1933. One proposal—and the one that ultimately found most favour—was that the division between Protestants and Catholics that had paralysed both denominations before the Nazi onslaught should be bridged. Another proposal was that there should be only one non-Socialist party, combining secular and religious forces as well as both denominations, in face of the presumed strength of the Left after the fall of Hitler. There were, however, dissenters from these two programmes. There were those, especially among Catholics of the Left, who felt that it was more important to overcome the divide between working-class and middle-class politics that had also weakened Weimar democracy. They proposed working together with the SPD to form a non-dogmatic pro-welfare party on the lines of the British Labour Party or the New Deal Democrats of the USA. This came to nothing: the SPD was not interested in compromising its newly found freedom and there was insufficient backing from the Christian side. The anti-Socialist unity proposal also foundered. Most of its potential Liberal supporters were suspicious of both its cultural and its economic aspects. They feared both that it would be clerically dominated, especially in Catholic areas, and that the influence of the Christian-Social wing, which had the better democratic credentials in the immediate post-war period, would make the party too collectivist and insufficiently distinctive from the Left. For the opposite reason some of the veterans of the *Zentrum* were opposed to any merger plans. They feared that a heterogeneous right-of-centre party would dilute the Christian element, be too pro-capitalist, and, by extending its welcome to Protestants and the religiously non-observant, would bring in too many persons compromised by National Socialism.

Which of these recipes would ultimately prevail would depend on local factors, on the views of influential bodies such as trade unions and above all the churches, and, most of all, on the decisions of the occupation forces who had the power to license. Paradoxically it was the SMAD, which might be thought the least interested of the four in the construction of a competitive party system, that took the initiative. But, as we have seen, the Soviet occupiers came to Germany better prepared with political plans than their Western rivals. On 10 June 1945 they permitted the creation of 'all anti-Fascist parties that aim at . . . solidifying the basis of democracy and civil liberties' as well as of trade unions. The next day the KPD came formally into being, followed shortly by the SPD. More significant for the future shape of German party politics were two further creations: that of an inter-confessional Christian Democratic Union (Christlich Demokratische Union Deutschlands (CDUD)), led by former *Zentrum* politicians, mainly from that party's trade-union and peasant wings, as well as some former Liberals, and a Liberal Democratic Party (Liberaldemokratische Partei Deutschlands (LDPD)), led mainly by former DDP politicians. The Soviet authorities had two motives for these measures. The first was to ensure control over political developments in their own zone, the second to maximize influence over development throughout Germany. The names of the new parties, with a conspicuous 'D' at the end, made it clear that they were to be the nucleus of all-German formations.

The Soviet initiative had two effects. It stimulated German politicians in the Western zones to greater efforts and it forced the Western occupation powers to reconsider their reluctance to countenance organized political activity. In particular they were not willing to recognize the local *Antifa* (anti-Fascist) committees, which they suspected of being Communist-inspired. In the British and US zones, party formations were permitted at the district level in August 1945, and by the turn of the year established at the zonal level. Licensing in the French zone did not begin until December 1945, and the French authorities, anxious to avoid the zones becoming mini-states, insisted on no party organizations beyond the *Land* level. For all these reasons party foundations were more localized and incoherent in the Western zones.

Only the SPD had a pre-1933 network that could be reactivated, and even that was hampered by poor communications, with long-distance travel impossible and even telephoning often difficult. In the British zone the old Catholic *Zentrum* was revived and until the early 1950s achieved some local successes. But even in its old strongholds it never succeeded in mobilizing even half of its former followers. The majority of Catholic political activists from the start preferred the interconfessional road, especially once the Soviet zone foundation pointed in that direction. The only question was—with which partners? In some areas they were former Liberals, especially from the National Liberal wing, in others they included former Conservatives from the DNVP or Protestant activists from the CSVD. In the early stages these foundations bore a number of different names besides Christian Democratic Union or Christian Democratic Party. In Bavaria the new party called itself Christian Social Union, in Baden the Christian Social People's Party. Only at the end of 1945 did the various branches of the new movement, with the exception of that of Bavaria, agree on the name Christlich Demokratische Union (CDU). The uncoordinated initiatives also produced a wide range of policy options. There was considerable disagreement on whether schools should be denominational or interdenominational, but even more on economic policy. The Frankfurt and Cologne branches proclaimed their belief in Christian Socialism and the British zone CDU adopted as late as February 1947 its Ahlen programme which declared that 'the capitalist economic system has failed the German people' and advocated the nationalization of the coal and steel industries. Elsewhere there was greater emphasis on the sanctity of private property. What tipped the balance in favour of Christian Democracy as opposed to the revival of Weimar parties was the support of the churches. After initial hesitations, both the Catholic bishops' conferences and the Synod of the Evangelical Church supported the interdenominational solution.

The emergence of a Liberal force followed a still more uneven pattern. The disintegration of the Liberal camp in the last years of the Weimar Republic and under the Third Reich had been even greater

than that of the Conservative camp. The revival of a Liberal party
organization was fastest in areas where there was a tradition of Liberalism, generally dominated by the DDP, as in the south-western
states of Württemberg and Baden or the Hanseatic cities of Hamburg
and Bremen; where the local CDU was likely to be Catholic dominated
and therefore 'clerical'; or where the CDU had a left-wing economic
programme. Its early nomenclature was as varied as the Christian
Democrats'—sometimes Liberal Democrat, as in the Soviet zone,
sometimes Free Democratic, sometimes Democratic Union. In its
stronghold of Württemberg–Baden, where its leader, Reinhold Maier,
was appointed Prime Minister by the US authorities, it revived its
pre-1918 name of Demokratische Volkspartei. Liberal forces took
longer to unite or to adopt a common name than even Christian
Democrats. A Free Democratic Party (Freie Demokratische Partei
(FDP)) embracing the three Western zones did not come into being
until December 1948. With these licensings the main parameters of
party competition were set. A few minor parties also appeared, mainly
on the Right of the political spectrum. In the British zone these were
the Deutsch-Konservative Partei and a regional party in Lower Saxony,
the Niedersächsische Landespartei (NLP), that evolved into the German Party (Deutsche Partei (DP)). In the US zone it was the populist
Economic Reconstruction Union (Wirtschaftlicher Aufbau-Verein
(WAV)) and the Bavarian Party (Bayernpartei (BP)), dedicated to an
even stronger defence of Bavarian interests than the CSU. The DP
and BP ceased to be effective forces in the early 1960s, the others in
the early 1950s.

One factor that helped to stabilize support for the parties of the
first hour was the adoption of proportional electoral systems. At first
these were supported unconditionally only by the Soviets, out of fear
that the KPD might otherwise be marginalized. The British and US
authorities inclined towards the Anglo-Saxon majoritarian principle
in the hope that this would produce stable majorities. But parts of the
British zone were the only areas that adopted non-proportional systems. In the French and US zones proportional representation was
the norm. In part this was due to the preferences of the German
administrators, who were unfamiliar with any other system, in part
to the unpredictability of outcomes in a still fluid party structure. In

particular the US authorities regarded the newly created municipal and *Land* authorities as consultative, not sovereign. They were anxious to rule by consensus and to avoid both the appearance of favouring one party and the emergence of oppositions that might easily turn into oppositions to occupation policies. Party formation and elections in all four zones meant that the 'supreme authority' of the occupying powers—always an illusion—was at an end. As the Western and Eastern zones embarked on their steadily divergent economic and political paths, occupiers and occupied formed an increasingly close, even though still unequal, partnership.

As in other respects, the SMAD was the first to initiate wide-ranging economic measures. In July 1945 banks and savings institutes were expropriated. In September a land reform began, affecting about one-third of agricultural acreage, in which *Junker* estates were redistributed to smallholders and landless peasants. In October the assets of the German state and of former Nazi functionaries were confiscated; some 25–30 per cent of these went to the Soviet Union as reparations. At least some of these measures, such as the land reform and the proposal to nationalize industrial monopolies, were initially popular. What was less popular was the relentless pursuit of expropriation. By 1948 9,281 enterprises had become 'people's property', ranging from Krupp, Siemens, and AEG to medium and small plants. Such extreme measures would have been impossible to enforce under conditions of open party competition, since even the KPD had declared in 1945 that it was opposed to 'imposing the Soviet system'. However, the freedom of action implied by the licensing of parties did not last long. As early as July 1945 the four parties formed themselves into the 'bloc of anti-Fascist democratic parties' dedicated to a 'firm unitary front' on the principle of unanimity. In April 1946 the SPD of the Soviet zone was pressurized into a fusion with the KPD to form the SED. The only places in the country in which SPD members were able to vote on this proposal were the Western sectors of Berlin: there 62.1 per cent favoured co-operation between the two parties, but only 12.3 per cent fusion. In the Soviet-zone *Landtag* elections of October 1946 the 'bourgeois parties' (CDU and LDPD) managed to poll as many votes as the SED. In Greater Berlin, where the SPD was able to compete against the SED, it got 48.7 per cent against the

SED's 19.8 per cent. These were the last free elections in that part of Germany until 1990. Those SPD, CDU, and LDPD politicians who could no longer put up with the pressures to which they were subjected moved, one by one, to the Western zones.

The speed with which the Soviet authorities transformed the economy of their zone was one symptom of the way in which the Potsdam commitment to German economic unity quickly became a dead letter. But the terms of Potsdam were themselves also a cause of the incipient division, as they made the individual zones the units for the collection of reparations. It was the question of reparations, more than any other, that drove the Eastern and Western occupation authorities apart. But all of this happened within the wider context of deteriorating East–West relations. The installation of Communist regimes in much of Eastern Europe, and Western European fears of a Soviet military threat, were paralleled by a Soviet determination to build up an extensive security belt. Germany, by virtue of its geographical position, became the battleground for this antagonism. Germany was not the cause of the Cold War, but its arena. The more intense the Cold War became, the more both sides were determined to secure an advantage in Germany. The harder they competed in Germany, the fiercer the Cold War became.

The economic and political divisions of Germany went hand in hand. The Potsdam aim of administrative unity could not survive the pursuit of separate policies. The American and British governments concluded at an early stage, in contrast with the Soviets, that they needed to foster a self-sustaining German economy. Dismantling ended in the US zone in May 1946. On 6 September of that year the American Secretary of State James F. Byrnes delivered a speech in Stuttgart that promised Germans the restoration of a normal, peacetime economy and the achievement of self-government. This was the first public offer of an olive-branch to the Germans, and as such had a major symbolic impact. But the policies it outlined had been quietly pursued for some time. The next logical step was to dismantle economic barriers between the zones, at any rate the Western ones. Given French reluctance, that meant a merger of those of Britain and the USA, a step that met not only the increasing difficulties Britain had in financing its occupation, but the British concern to commit the

United States to long-term responsibility for the future of Germany. In December 1946 the two governments agreed to the economic fusion of their zones.

The 'Bi-zone', as it came to be known, was a West German state in embryo. This lay in the logic of its creation, though not in its intention. At the beginning of 1947 neither Britain nor the USA wanted to give up control of its respective zones, neither wanted to exclude France, and neither yet assumed that the breach with the Soviet Union was final. Yet both internal and external factors propelled them towards state-building. The internal factor was the deteriorating economic situation when, after the exceptionally harsh winter of 1946–7, many Germans were near starvation. The external factors were the overall development of US foreign policy and the final collapse of attempts at quadripartite policy-making on Germany. President Truman's speech of 12 March 1947, enunciating the 'Truman Doctrine', painted the world in more starkly bi-polar terms than at any time since the end of the Second World War: the Communist threat was to be resisted wherever it arose. While the immediate impulse to the speech was the situation in Greece and Turkey, the doctrine had clear implications for Germany. The simultaneous failure of the Foreign Ministers' conference in Moscow to agree on Germany gave Britain and the USA the signal to reinforce the institutions of the Bi-zone.

Its development showed the continued interdependence of the economic and the political. Just as the Allied failure to pursue common economic policies led to the political division of Germany, so the attempt to merge the economies of the Western zones required common political institutions, with an increased German political input. At the end of May a bi-zonal Economic Council was created, consisting of delegates from the *Länder* of the two zones in proportion to their electoral strengths: twenty members each from the CDU–CSU and the SPD, four Liberals, three Communists, and five from smaller parties. This narrow majority for the Right was to have far-reaching consequences. But it was once more external as well as internal factors that propelled the Bi-zone to something approaching statehood.

On 5 June 1947 US Secretary of State George Marshall launched the European Recovery Programme (ERP), better known as the

Marshall Plan, to speed up the rehabilitation of Europe's economies. There were conditions attached: the prospective recipients had to agree on a common economic programme and to commit themselves to an open economic order. These conditions the Soviet Union rejected. The Soviet zone and the states of Eastern Europe were therefore excluded from the ERP, but France, and therefore the French zone, were included. When the Organization for European Economic Co-operation (OEEC) was set up to co-ordinate the ERP, the three Western zones were represented in it. This marked the first entry of the Western zones into those supra-national European linkages that were to become their defining characteristic. But this step also showed, more than any preceding one, the end of Germany's status as defeated pariah and underlined the growing interdependence of the West German and neighbouring European economies.

Parallel with this development came the strengthening of the institutions of the Bi-zone. The Economic Council had a permanent seat in Frankfurt, which gave the Bi-zone a shadow capital. In its second enlarged version, which dated from February 1948, it was joined by a *Länderrat*, in which each *Land* had two seats, as a second chamber, and an Administrative Council as a cabinet. None of this amounted to German sovereignty. Policy was still the responsibility of the occupiers. The same applied to other bi-zonal institutions created by the Allies, the Bank deutscher Länder and the Supreme Court (Deutsches Obergericht), which, in their later guises, were to play major roles. But the more German politicians were consulted and the more duties German administrators acquired, the greater their influence became. One of the duties of the Economic Council was to elect departmental directors; one of its choices, the election of Dr Ludwig Erhard as Economic Director, was to have profound long-term consequences. Erhard was an academic economist who had spent the last years of the war in an obscure research institute. Though not a man of the Resistance, he was not a sympathizer with the Nazi regime and in 1944 had drafted a memorandum on the prospects for the German economy after the defeat that he expected. It was to be based on what later became known as the social market economy: maximum competition with a welfare safety net.

Erhard, who owed his position to the narrow right-of-centre

majority in the Economic Council, was the chief interlocutor of the US authorities in the boldest step yet of economic reconstruction, the currency reform of 20 June 1948. The reform abolished the old Reichsmark in the three Western zones and replaced it with the Deutsche Mark (D-Mark) at a conversion rate of 10 : 1. Though the final decision was an American one alone, it necessarily applied not only to the whole of the Bi-zone, but also to the French zone now that it was included in the Marshall Plan and the OEEC. No single measure contributed as much to the future shape of Germany, whether to its political division or to the economic regime of the future FRG. Yet its success depended on the progress that the economies of the Western zones had already made in the preceding three years. What impressed the Allied civilians who arrived in May 1945 were the ruins and the endless trails of refugees. Walter Millis of the *New York Herald Tribune* thought Berlin was 'more like the face of the moon than any city I had ever imagined'. More than anything it was the damage to the housing stock, the breakdown of communications, the dislocation of the population, and the shortage of coal that held up production. Allied bombing had certainly taken its toll of factories, but in the spring of 1945 80 per cent of German industry was in working order. Productive capacity was actually higher at the end of the war than it had been at the beginning of Goering's Four-Year Plan in 1936; many firms had prepared plans for conversion to peace-time production. It was the devastation of the infrastructure, the bureaucratic barriers created by the zonal frontiers, and Allied measures of reparations and demilitarization that were the obstacles to recovery. It was not in 1945 but after the winter of 1946–7 that the economy of the British and US zones reached rock bottom.

Nor was the personnel structure of German industry seriously disrupted. De-Nazification measures were largely restricted to the public sector. Some prominent businessmen were tried for war crimes and the use of slave labour, but in the main the private sector was left alone. One question that remained in limbo for two years was that of nationalization, especially of heavy industry, and here American influence was crucial. The notion that big business had helped Hitler to power and that capitalism had failed the German people was widespread in the aftermath of the war, and support for some measures of public ownership was common, as we have seen, even within the CDU. Britain in particular favoured nationalization of the coal and steel industries in its zone, partly as a means of effective control, partly because it appealed to the Labour government of the day, partly because public opinion in the British zone seemed to favour it—a factor not to be ignored at a time when the Communist Party still had a following in the Ruhr. The SPD was at this stage the strongest party in that zone; all Land Economy Ministers belonged to it and the head of the zonal economic administration was the trade unions' chief theoretician, Viktor Agartz. In December 1945 ownership of the Ruhr coal-mines was lodged in the British Control Commission.

The contrast with the US zone could not have been greater. The USA, like the Soviet Union, was determined to fashion the economy of its zone in its own image, though it did this less by *fiat* than by selective veto. Thus, when the population of Hesse in 1946 voted by 71 per cent in favour of a constitutional provision to empower the *Land* to nationalize, General Lucius D. Clay insisted that any use of this article must await an all-German government. When in 1947 the Hesse government tried to take over the assets of the chemical combine I. G. Farben and to introduce industrial co-determination, Clay vetoed these measures, too. Clay's views on corporate structure were consistent. He was as keen on decartelization as on preventing nationalization: for him they were two sides of one coin. The contrasting approaches of Britain and the USA caused great friction within the Bi-zone. In the end the American view prevailed, and the nationalization even of parts of West German industry disappeared from the agenda. On the day of the currency reform the shops filled with goods as they had not done since before the war. The liberalization of prices that followed killed the black market stone dead. It was the greatest stimulus yet to the economies of the Western zones. Experts are divided on whether the Western zones' recovery would have continued without it, but the currency reform certainly made sense only in the context of an economy already on the mend.

Currency reform also set the seal on the division of Germany and was the biggest step yet towards the establishment of a West German state. Indeed, once the currency was in existence, the adoption of a constitution was almost an anti-climax. As we have seen, differences over reparations and economic management nullified the Potsdam articles at an early stage. The free movement of goods and persons across the Soviet zonal frontier was ended in June 1946, in response to Soviet alarm at the Westward flight of people and property. The SMAD responded to the creation of the bi-zonal Economic Council with the Deutsche Wirtschaftskommission, significantly named so as to apply potentially to the whole of Germany. In March 1948 the Allied Control Council held its last meeting, when the Soviet representative walked out for good. The Western currency reform evoked one in the Soviet zone three days later, but it also led to a major crisis over the control of Berlin. The question was simple: which currency was to prevail in the old capital, divided as it was into four occupation sectors which were separate from the occupation zones? Fearful of the incorporation of Berlin in the economy of the West, the Soviet authorities announced the introduction of their currency for the whole of their city and a ban on passenger traffic between it and the Western zones. The Western allies responded by introducing the D-Mark into their sectors; Berlin, in effect, thereby acquired two economies. By the end of November there were separate Eastern and Western city councils. The Soviet Blockade of West Berlin, during which the USA and Britain flew in over 2 million tons of food, coal, and other supplies, lasted 322 days. When the Soviets lifted the Blockade, the final division of Germany had come a lot nearer.

The Berlin Blockade showed how far relations between the Soviet Union and the West had deteriorated since VE Day. The stationing of American B-29 bombers, capable of carrying atomic bombs, in Britain within days of the beginning of the Blockade demonstrated that risk of war was real. Both sides saw Berlin as a symbol: the West for the containment of Communism, the Soviet Union for its legitimate share in the control of Germany. Each side, watching its antagonist build up its power structure in conjunction with German politicians and administrators, suspected the other of pursuing a long-term, well-planned strategy at its expense. Each side, as we now know, in fact went forward step by step, frequently revising and even reversing decisions once taken. In the West, especially, the need to reconcile the interests of Britain, France, and the USA as well as of the elected politicians of the various parties led to often difficult compromises. From late 1945 onwards Britain and the USA became increasingly convinced that Soviet moves made inter-Allied policy-making impossible. They therefore decided to move ahead independently, which the Soviets interpreted as a plot to divide Germany. The Berlin Blockade was an attempt to prevent this by forcing the West to the negotiating table. Its effect was the opposite of that intended: it merely accelerated a decision that the USA and Britain were already close to reaching, that of establishing a West German state.

A week after the beginning of the Blockade, the three Western Allies presented to the Prime Ministers of the Western *Länder* the 'Frankfurt Documents'—an invitation to proceed with the creation of a West German state, which the Allies had been working on, with Soviet knowledge, for some weeks. In one important sense this set a precedent. It was the first occasion on which German politicians had been invited to participate in the political development of their zones. But it also underlined all the difficulties that such a step entailed. What was on offer was a good deal short of sovereignty: the Allies were to retain substantial residual powers, to be defined in an Occupation Statute. While the USA, and to some extent Britain, would have been willing to go further, France was extremely reluctant to countenance any revived German state, and the fears of Germany's other Western neighbours, Belgium, the Netherlands, and Luxemburg, had also to be considered. On the German side, too, there were dilemmas. While the German politicians welcomed any move towards greater self-government, which they had been pressing for for some time, they were disappointed by the restrictions that would remain. Above all, they were reluctant to accept the odium of participating in the division of Germany into two states, however unavoidable such an outcome might be.

The task of drafting a constitution went to a Parliamentary Council that assembled in Bonn on 1 September 1948—the first occasion on which that provincial university city was the scene of high politics. Its sixty-five members reflected the party strengths of the various *Länder*: twenty-seven each for the SPD and the CDU (whose delegation included eight from the Bavarian CSU), five for the Liberals, two each for the *Zentrum*, the KPD, and the DP of Lower Saxony.

The chairman of the British-zone CDU, Dr Konrad Adenauer, was elected president. Before the Parliamentary Council began its deliberations, the *Land* Prime Ministers met at Koblenz to agree on an agenda and their experts worked out further details at the Bavarian resort of Herrenchiemsee. This procedure demonstrated the primacy of the *Länder* in post-1945 German politics. They were the only units to enjoy the legitimacy of popular election in 1948 and their territories had begun to enlist popular loyalties, despite the haphazard way that some of them had been created. The drafts that emerged from Herrenchiemsee proposed that the new state be called *Bund deutscher Länder* (federation of German *Länder*), to indicate not only the primacy of the sub-national unit, but to leave open the later membership of the Soviet-zone *Länder*. To emphasize the provisional character of any constitutional document, the Mayor of the city-state of Hamburg, Max Brauer, had suggested the term 'basic law' (*Grundgesetz*).

The debates of the Parliamentary Council revealed a much more complex pattern of opinion and interests than its predecessor, the Economic Council. There there had been a straightforward division between the advocates and opponents of a market economy, and the narrow pro-market majority (CDU/CSU, Liberals, and NLP) got its way. In the Parliamentary Council socio-economic issues provided only one cleavage among many. Nor were party differences the sole divisive factor. The conflicting interests of the various *Länder* were as important, with the southern *Länder*, led by Bavaria, favouring decentralization more than those further north. This question cut across the socio-economic party divisions: the Liberals, who were the CDU's allies on economic matters, supported the SPD's more centralizing stance, while the CDU–CSU was divided into northern and southern wings.

Two topics dominated the Council's proceedings: devising the instruments of government and balancing out the claims of organized interests. As the members of the Council—many of them parliamentary veterans of the Weimar Republic—looked back on previous German constitutional experiments, they could find few positive examples to inspire them. They needed to avoid the opportunities for both the totalitarianism of the Third Reich and the incoherence of Weimar. The government they were to establish was to be both limited and stable—twin objectives not easy to reconcile. To ensure this combination of virtues, the Founding Fathers hit on a number of ingenious devices, not all of which turned out to be optimally relevant to later needs. They ensured that it should be difficult to overthrow governments through the 'constructive vote of no confidence' (Article 67): a Chancellor could be forced to resign only if there were a parliamentary majority for a successor. The context for this provision was the type of multi-party parliament that Weimar had experienced. This condition was not to be repeated in the FRG, with the result that the 'constructive vote' has been used only twice, once unsuccessfully in 1972 and once successfully in 1982. They ensured that it should be as difficult as possible to dissolve the lower house of parliament, the Bundestag (Article 68): only if the Bundestag failed for twenty-one days to elect a Chancellor could the President do so. This provision has been used only once, in 1983. Two innovations which have played a major rule in the political life of the FRG were a Bill of Rights and the establishment of a Federal Constitutional Court. The first nineteen Articles of the Basic Law enumerate Basic Rights, including the right to life, freedom of conscience, freedom of speech, and the right to property. One provision that seemed desirable and harmless at the time, though it caused problems later, was the right to political asylum, guaranteed by Article 16. The Basic Law is as significant for what it omitted as for what it included. Its framers distrusted the people as much as the concentration of power. They were burnt children who knew what the fire was like. Their vision was one of disaster-avoidance, not a new heaven and a new earth. In contrast with the provisions of the Weimar Republic, they rejected a directly elected President and popular referendums except on questions of *Land* and local-government boundaries.

The greatest difficulties were caused by the debate on the federal structure. The centralizers, led by the SPD, wanted the second chamber of parliament to be an elected Senate; the majority of the Council preferred the traditional German form of the Bundesrat, to which the governments of the individual *Länder* sent delegates. In this respect they followed the principle of the *Länderrat*, as it had existed in the US zone and then in the bi-zonal Economic Council. At the root of the dispute over federalism was finance, since power over revenue determines power over policy. The Allies as well as the Council appreciated this and finance was the one matter on which they intervened in the Council's activities. They were determined to achieve as decentralized a structure as possible and in the end the Parliamentary Council was forced to compromise. Tax rates were to be fixed uniformly, but where they affected the revenues of the *Länder* they needed the joint approval of both Houses. Taxes were divided between those whose yields went to the federation, those whose yields went to the *Länder*, and those whose yields were to be shared (Articles 105–9).

With this compromise the most difficult part of constitution-making was resolved. But there remained consideration of the claims of the churches, which related mainly to education, and of the trade unions, which related mainly to economic and social policy. The churches, especially the Catholic Church, favoured *Länder* rights, since they suspected a centralized state would be secular and anti-clerical. They also wanted constitutional guarantees of 'parental rights' in education, which was a code for denominational schools. This they did not achieve. All that the Basic Law specified (Article 7) was a right to religious education. But in other respects the Basic Law reflected the influence of the churches—in the privileged position accorded to the family (Article 7) and the right to physical inviolability (Article 2), which has proved to be an obstacle to the liberalization of the abortion laws. The trade unions fared less well. Their demands for the inclusion of economic democracy—that is, co-determination in industry—failed, though they gained much of the substance of this through ordinary legislation later. Their demands for a constitutional provision of the right to strike and for nationalization also failed, though Article 9 guarantees a general freedom of association. The definition of the FRG as 'democratic and social' (Article 20) also went some way towards accommodating them.

The draft that emerged from these deliberations was the outcome of hard bargaining among the parties and the *Länder* and between them and the Allies. After some final brinkmanship an agreed text was adopted on 8 May 1949, four years to the day after Germany's unconditional surrender. The text then went to the *Landtage* for approval. Only Bavaria voted against, on the grounds that it was too centralist, but even Bavaria bowed to the majority. On 23 May, the fourth anniversary of the deposition of the Dönitz government, the Basic Law of the FRG was proclaimed, with Bonn as the provisional capital of the provisional state. That this complex task could have been completed in little over eight months showed that what united the German politicians and the Western Allies was greater than what divided them. Each side had by now too much to lose from deadlock and the resulting delay. Except in the dispute over finance, the Basic Law was the work of the Parliamentary Council. But, though the FRG gave the German people and its politicians considerable policy discretion, the Basic Law was only half of the new state's constitution. The other half was the Occupation Statute, which defined the Allies' continuing powers over foreign and defence policy and, not least, over the industries of the Ruhr. The gradual diminution of these powers, until their final extinction when Germany was unified, is a theme that was to run like a scarlet thread through the FRG's history.

While the Parliamentary Council was active, the SMAD was not idle. A German People's Congress was convened in the Soviet zone in November 1947; it, in turn, led to the formation of a German People's Council in March 1948 to 'fight for the unity of Germany and a just peace treaty'. Though its proclaimed purpose and name were anti-separatist, the creation of departmental executives within it suggests the extent to which the Soviets now regarded an East German state as an option to be contemplated. But the main Soviet-zone developments took place at the party level. Of the 'bourgeois' parties, the LDPD participated in the People's Congress in a subordinate way, while the CDUD refused. Its leaders, Jakob Kaiser and Ernst Lemmer, were thereupon deposed by the Soviet authorities. To dilute the competition still further, two more parties were licensed, the Democratic Farmers' Party (Demokratische Bauernpartei Deutschlands (DBD)) and the National Democratic Party (Nationaldemokratische Partei Deutschlands (NDPD)), the latter to recruit former small-time Nazis. The major change, however, took place within the SED, which dropped the pretence that it was an even-handed fusion of Communists and Social Democrats and proclaimed itself in January 1949 to be 'a new type of party, i.e. a fighting party of Marxism–Leninism'. With that the pre-conditions for a Soviet-type East German state were in place. On 7 October the People's Council transformed itself into a Provisional People's Chamber and proclaimed the constitution of the GDR, the text of which had been negotiated by the SED leadership in Moscow.

By the time this happened the FRG was firmly in place. One final decision that the Parliamentary Council had to make was on the electoral system. Here, too, the outcome was predetermined by earlier developments. The law adopted by the Council reflected its party composition, which in turn reflected the composition of the *Landtage*, which in turn derived from the decisions made by the Allies about electoral systems in 1946–7. By now the CDU–CSU was sufficiently confident of its position, or at least of its ability to form electoral alliances, to favour a change to the Anglo-American simple-majority system, a change that the US authorities supported. But for this scheme there was no majority support in the Council. Instead the Council adopted a proportional system with three qualifications: 60 per cent of the seats in the Bundestag were to be filled by simple majority in individual constituencies, the remainder from compensatory lists. To be entitled to seats a party needed to gain at least 5 per cent of the votes in any one *Land* or to win at least one constituency. All the USA achieved was to ensure that this system was instituted by simple statute and not enshrined in the Basic Law. The first Bundestag election took place on 14 August. It gave the CDU–CSU 31 per cent of the vote, the SPD 29.2 per cent, the FDP 11.9 per cent, the KPD 5.7 per cent, and the remaining parties, all of them right of centre, 22.2 per cent. The Bundestag convened on 7 September. On the 12th it elected Theodor Heuss as the Republic's first President and on the 15th it elected Konrad Adenauer Chancellor and head of government— by one vote. A new era had begun.

3 The Adenauer Era

We have no doubts that in accordance with our origins and
our convictions we belong to the Western European world.
(Konrad Adenauer, 20 September 1949)

FIVE days after being elected Chancellor, Adenauer presented his
cabinet. It was a three-party 'small coalition' of the Right, consisting
of the CDU–CSU, the FDP, and the small, north German DP. The
new government had a parliamentary majority of fourteen. Its appointment was a turning-point not only constitutionally, but ideologically.
Anyone gazing into the German crystal ball in the spring of 1945
might well have forecast the division of the country into Soviet and
Western spheres, perhaps even into separate states. He would have
been much less likely to anticipate the intact survival of the capitalist
system, let alone its unprecedented efflorescence. There would have
been many reasons for such an assumption, connected as much with
the general climate of opinion as with specific German circumstances.
The Soviet contribution to Allied victory and the achievements of
European resistance movements did much to raise the prestige of
Communist parties. Through most of Europe the first post-war elections brought a swing to the Left, even if not necessarily towards
Communist parties. Some nationalization and an extension of the
welfare state were the norm. Given the—presumed—role of big business in bringing down the Weimar Republic and, at the least, its
comfortable coexistence with the regime of the Third Reich, it seemed
only too plausible that Germany would follow a similar path. Most of
the writers and intellectuals who came to prominence in the aftermath
of the war assumed that the fulfilment of democracy required Socialism of some kind, however vaguely defined.

What applied in the realm of ideas applied even more strongly
to political parties. No party had emerged with greater hopes from the
ashes of the Third Reich than the Social Democrats. They alone had
voted against special powers for Hitler in 1933, they alone had been

anti-Nazis from the first to the last hour; equally, they now resisted the inveiglements of the Communists. Their leader, Kurt Schumacher, had survived ten years in a Nazi concentration camp, minus an arm and with impaired eyesight. They assumed that the experience of Nazism would turn Germans towards democracy and better control of capitalism. They assumed further that the pauperization of the vast majority of the population would attract them to Socialism and that equal resentment of the occupation regimes would attract them to an independent neutrality.

All these assumptions, as it turned out, rested on serious miscalculations. Weimar had done nothing to encourage faith in parliamentary institutions. The experience of National Socialism had merely heightened disgust with all politics. Hitler, many Germans thought, was not so much the antithesis of democracy as the product of its excesses. Socialism they saw not as the antithesis of Nazism, but as a continuation of the regimentation, ration-queues, and favouritism of the Third Reich—and, now, of the Soviet zone. They might be pauperized, but they did not despair of a return of bourgeois decencies. And much as they might dislike and resent American, British, and French occupation, these feelings were as nothing compared with their fear and hatred of Soviet Communism. What Germans longed for was a return to privacy, family, inner peace, and public morality; the beneficiaries of these longings were not Kurt Schumacher's crusade, but the churches. Despite their chequered records under Hitler, they were virtually the only institutions trusted by both occupiers and occupied. This did not guarantee a united ecclesiastical front: the historical divisions between Lutheranism and Rome ran too deep for that, as did the genuine conflicts of principle within Protestantism. Like Schumacher they feared social breakdown and saw the risk of Bolshevization; their recipe, which was rewarded with greater success, was the interdenominational CDU and the favourable Basic Law.

Though Germans reacted to the experience of Nazism in a conservative way, and though the social structure of at least the Western zones remained more stable than many had anticipated, this conservatism was different from what it had been before 1933. The most revolutionary consequence of the Second World War was the destruction of Prussia. This had begun before 1945. While many Prussian conservatives, whatever their distaste for the Nazis' vulgarity, had at least tolerated Hitler's coming to power, it was the old aristocracy that led the July Plot of 1944 against him and that felt the full fury of his vengeance. After 1945 the Eastern part of Prussia was occupied—*de facto* annexed—by Poland, and in the Soviet zone the Junker estates were expropriated. The territorial and economic basis of the Prussian oligarchy that had dominated the German army and significant parts of the civilian administration was gone. The geographical distribution of the population had also changed radically, as millions of refugees and expellees streamed westwards. And yet, despite all this, the social structure of the Western zones changed rather little. There were two reasons for that: the failure of de-Nazification and the absence of socialization.

Cleansing German public life of the infection of National Socialism was the declared aim of all the victor powers. The climax of this reckoning with the fallen regime came at the International Military Tribunal at Nuremberg in 1946, where those major Nazi leaders who survived were put on trial for their crimes against humanity. Other trials of functionaries of the Gestapo, the SS, and officials or industrialists involved in deportations, the employment of slave labour, or genocide took place in the individual zones, but to investigate the political pasts of millions of citizens proved self-defeating. The US administration tried hardest, with a questionnaire of several pages, the answers to which could lead to dismissal, fines, or imprisonment. In Hesse one public servant in three was suspended from employment under this procedure, almost all of them to be reinstated. The whole exercise became discredited. Almost every German knew of cases in which some harmless opportunist had been harassed, while a big fish had escaped. In any case, private industry and the professions were largely exempt from the purges. There was a further reason, other than exhaustion on the part of victors, why mass de-Nazification was abandoned. If occupiers and occupied were to need each other more than either had imagined in 1945, the pressure to let bygones be bygones would become irresistible. Thus, apart from a few spectacularly guilty war criminals and a fairly effective purge of schools, the personnel of the bureaucracy, the judiciary, universities, and the private economy differed little in 1949 from 1945. Real democratization would have to await a generational change.

This social stabilization was one factor that favoured the conservative tendencies in the population. The other was the recovery of the economy on a private-enterprise basis. We have already seen that recovery was well under way by the time of the currency reform, further stimulated by the Marshall Plan and special aid that channelled $3 billion into Germany; and that the US administration, headed by General Clay, was determined to inhibit any steps towards Socialism or collectivism. Whether matters would have developed very differently without Clay's intervention must be an open question. Popular anti-capitalism, as it existed in the early years, was primarily directed at coal and heavy industry, not against private enterprise as such. The manner of the currency reform, however, certainly reinforced the restorative trend in society. While cash holdings were converted at the rate of 10 : 1, shares were converted at the rate of 1 : 1, thereby confirming the existing distribution of wealth and the existing ownership structure in the economy. This measure was far from universally popular. The currency reform was intended to be disinflationary and the liberalization of prices and wages widened the gap between the two. The bitterness of the trade unions at this blow to living standards culminated in a twenty-four-hour strike by nine million workers on 12 November 1948. But by the summer of 1949 the benefits of the reform were beginning to trickle through and the first green shoots of the 'economic miracle' further deradicalized opinion.

All these developments did not merely halt the advance of the SPD, which had emerged as the party with the best prospects in the early *Landtag* elections; more importantly, they strengthened the right wing of the CDU at the expense of the left. The principal spokesman of the CDU Right was Dr Adenauer, who had been Lord Mayor of Cologne from 1917 to 1933 and again in 1945, and who had, after his removal from office by the British, devoted himself to building up the CDU in the British zone. His election as Chancellor was the culmination of his efforts at weaning the new party from flirtations with collectivism, but the decisive shift had begun earlier. While the CDU Left remained influential in some *Land* governments, the CDU delegation in the bi-zonal Economic Council allied itself with the Free Democrats. It was this coalition that steered policy towards price and wage liberalization and elected Ludwig Erhard as Economic Director, while the SPD went into opposition. It was in Frankfurt, not Bonn, that the party alignment that dominated the first two decades of the FRG emerged.

Adenauer was determined to perpetuate this alignment for reasons of both economic and foreign policy, but he had to face strong opposition in his own party. The CDU Left, though now in a minority, had not given up. It was led by Jakob Kaiser, who had been one of the founders of the Soviet-sponsored CDU in Berlin, and Karl Arnold, Prime Minister of North Rhine–Westphalia, where there was a strong Catholic trade-union movement and working-class CDU vote. They opposed Adenauer's polarizing strategy on both general and specific grounds. They believed in consensus politics, especially at this still early stage of Germany's democratic development, and that meant 'great coalitions' with the SPD. These had been the initial model in most of the Western *Länder* and remained so in some of them even after the foundation of the FRG—in the south-west, in Baden–Württemberg, until 1960. But they also feared that the type of right-of-centre coalition Adenauer insisted on, and in which Ludwig Erhard was Minister for the Economy, would be too pro-capitalist and too indifferent to the possibilities of rescuing German political unity.

There was, however, another reason why Adenauer got his way: the SPD was not interested in a Great Coalition either. In economic policy they had made this clear as long ago as 1947–8, when they fought for, and lost, control of the bi-zone's Economic Council. In 1949 they were still far from convinced that the social-market economy would be the basis of the FRG's future and were confident that the poverty and unemployment, which were undeniably two of the concomitants of the currency reform and of price liberalization, would reward them with victory at the next election. In foreign policy they were in a greater dilemma. They campaigned as the party of national unity partly because their old strongholds were in the Soviet zone; in the Western *Länder* they risked being outvoted. But they also stressed national unity because they had always favoured centralized political structures and because they had to live down past denigration as lacking in patriotism. This strategy was particularly that of their federal chairman, Kurt Schumacher. He and Adenauer were playing the same game according to the same rules, but from opposite ends of the field. However, no one in West German politics was more strongly anti-Communist than Schumacher. The SPD's insoluble difficulty was that, as long as German unity was apparently available only on Soviet terms, there was no alternative to the Western option and to a division of Germany that might well be long term. Schumacher died in 1952, but the national policy of the SPD remained largely unchanged until the end of the decade. However, at the *Land* level, many of the SPD leaders, like those of the CDU, were pragmatists, pursuing accommodation and practising the art of the possible. With the conventions of *Land* politics well established by 1949, the FRG evolved a dual political system, with parties bearing the same label operating with different priorities and coalition strategies at the federal and sub-federal levels.

If the evolution of the Western zones in the immediate post-war period made possible the victory of the Adenauer coalition in 1949, Adenauer's domination of the FRG during its first fourteen years set its political course irreversibly. This was true in its international alignment as well as its domestic structure. In his foreign policy Adenauer had three aims: to gain freedom of action from Allied tutelage, to integrate the FRG into a democratic Western Europe, and to bring about the re-unification of Germany. To achieve all three objectives required a delicate balancing act. Integration in Western Europe meant above all establishing a partnership with France and a reconciliation between these 'hereditary enemies' after three wars in three generations. Yet this could not be brought about without respecting France's security needs, and that in turn meant slow progress in the quest for sovereignty. Above all, integration with the West had a military as well as a political and economic dimension and was therefore likely to deepen rather than end the division of Germany. Thus re-unification necessarily became a long-term objective, to be subordinated to the reconstruction and security of the FRG. Adenauer was always convinced that the Communist system would ultimately fail, though he might not live to see the failure. In his scenario the unification of Europe on a Western basis would have to be the pre-condition of a united Germany. For that reason, as we shall see, he was at no stage interested in a special deal with the Soviet Union, however tempting its conditions. His attitude towards Communism was that of the wartime Allies towards Germany: unconditional surrender.

While German national unity was thus indefinitely postponed, Western integration and West German sovereignty were pursued with both urgency and success. The highest priority had—if only for domestic political reasons—to be that of ending the FRG's dual constitution, which subjected it to the Basic Law, on the one hand, and the Occupation Statute, on the other. In the early period of the FRG its legislation still required Allied counter-signatures. It was not until 1951 that it was allowed to have a Foreign Minister, a post to which Adenauer appointed himself. A first step towards emancipation came with the Petersberg Agreement of November 1949, in which the Allies agreed to an end of industrial dismantling and admitted the FRG to membership of the Ruhr Authority. Dissatisfied with the terms of this agreement, Kurt Schumacher accused Adenauer of being 'the Chancellor of the Allies'; the charge misfired in a way that tells us much about the state of West German public opinion. No doubt Germans resented the remaining prerogatives of the Allies. But, at the height of the Cold War, five months after the outbreak of the Korean War and with the consolidation of the GDR as a single-party state, the prospect of full sovereignty without the Allied protective umbrella was not enticing. Under these circumstances there were worse fates than being governed by the Chancellor of the Allies.

The FRG's first major step towards European integration was economic. It took the form of the Schuman Plan, launched by the French Foreign Minister, Robert Schuman, for the integration of the iron and steel industries of France, Italy, the Benelux states (Belgium, Netherlands, and Luxemburg), and West Germany. The European Coal and Steel Community (ECSC) not only opened up economic opportunities; it also offered the FRG a further chance of co-operation on a basis of equality and a further step towards international rehabilitation. For a country in which the idea of the traditional nation-state was discredited, the European arena presented a much better opening for the realization of national interests than the search for sovereignty. The SPD opposed the Schuman Plan: they argued that it pulled the FRG further away from the prospect of German unity towards a Western Europe that was predominantly Catholic, capitalist, and conservative. But the ECSC was in the logic of Western co-operation that had begun with the Marshall Plan and the Western zones' inclusion in the OECD and it pointed the way to the more ambitious EEC of 1957.

The controversy over the ECSC was as nothing compared with that over the next step in integration, the proposal that the FRG contribute militarily to Western defence. It was the biggest crisis the young republic had yet had to face and one of the biggest in its whole history. As with so many steps in the origin and development of the FRG, it had an external as well as an internal impulse. To face the Soviet military threat NATO had been founded in 1949, but initially its conventional military component was minimal. The situation changed with the outbreak of the Korean War in June 1950. This not only seemed to provide further evidence of aggressive Communist intentions, but directed US military preoccupations from Europe to Asia. A West German contribution to NATO, which would no doubt have been on the cards sooner or later, now became urgent. For Adenauer, who had never worn a uniform or fired a shot in anger, this was the biggest opportunity yet for equality of status in the Western camp.

Conscious of his neighbours' potential misgivings, Adenauer offered a West German contribution to a multinational force, but progress towards the acceptance even of this was slow and delicate. What emerged was the proposal for a European Defence Community (EDC); this, with a concomitant ending of the state of occupation, was enshrined in the Paris–Bonn accords of 1952. It was at this stage that Stalin, with only a few months to live, played his final card. Anxious to prevent West German rearmament, he offered a united, neutral, and unoccupied Germany. Was he genuinely prepared to evacuate the GDR, with its strategic and economic potential, in return for US disengagement? The prize would have been great, but so would the price. Though Churchill, now once more Prime Minister of Britain, was tempted to consider the offer and even Adenauer hesitated, the Western powers were not really interested. They were by now committed to 'negotiation from strength', and a West German defence contribution was essential to that. This commitment became all the stronger with the appointment of John Foster Dulles as US Secretary of State, following the election of Dwight D. Eisenhower to the Presidency in 1952. To the existing policy of 'containment', he added that of 'roll-back', though only the first of these was ever implemented. Nothing illustrated Western caution better than the response to the workers' uprising in East Berlin on 17 June 1953, which quickly spread to other parts of the GDR and was put down only by Soviet military intervention. The temptation to take advantage of this temporary power vacuum was resisted. Just as the neutralization of Germany was an unacceptable risk, so were adventures. What mattered to both Adenauer and Dulles was consolidation.

When German rearmament did come, it was not in the form first planned. Britain declined to have anything to do with the EDC and the French Parliament rejected French participation in it. What replaced the EDC was formal West German membership of NATO. It came into force on 8 May 1955, the tenth anniversary of unconditional surrender, and gave the FRG the ending of the Occupation Statute and virtual sovereignty in domestic and foreign policy. In return, the FRG agreed to refrain from the manufacture of ABC weapons and from changing existing frontiers by force. The major West German concession to France concerned the Saar territory: its population was to vote on a new statute that was to 'Europeanize' it, with strong economic links to France. But the referendum rejected the statute. Instead, the Saar rejoined the FRG on 1 January 1957 as a new *Land*, the first to do so under the provisions of Article 23 of the Basic Law. With this accession Germany's Western frontiers were finally settled and the basis laid for the Franco-German partnership that for Adenauer was second only in importance to the special relationship with USA.

Domestically the question of German rearmament was even more difficult than it had been diplomatically. With each step towards the FRG's Western integration, the division of Germany grew deeper. The military integration created the real risk that Germans might have to fire on Germans. Above all, there was the irony that Germans, having only so recently been lectured on the wickedness of militarism, were now once more to bear arms and to do so compulsorily. It was this prospect that called into being the first significant political mass mobilization in post-1945 Germany. This was the *Paulskirche* movement, named after the Frankfurt church in which the protesters had drawn up their manifesto, which consisted of a coalition of Social Democrats, trade unionists, and Protestant clergy and laity. It was also responsible for a split in the CDU. As early as 1952 Adenauer's Minister of the Interior, Gustav Heinemann, had resigned in protest against the prospect of rearmament. He briefly led his own splinter party, which gained little support, and then joined the SPD, eventually becoming the third President of the FRG. The *Paulskirche* movement failed in its objective. The Bundestag accepted the necessary treaties and Parliament passed the amendment to the Basic Law that permitted the establishment of defence forces (Article 87*a*). But these disputes showed that defence policy was the most divisive issue in German domestic politics, and would be so again in the 1980s and 1990s. Indeed, the divisions showed themselves again in 1958, after Adenauer had indicated that he wanted nuclear weapons for the *Bundeswehr*. This provoked a new mass protest with the slogan 'struggle against nuclear death'.

The ease with which this policy revolution was able to clear the parliamentary hurdles showed Adenauer's mastery of electoral politics, for under him the West German party system was transformed. The 1949 Bundestag election had produced a result that was transitional between a party system inherited from the Weimar Republic and the one that was to become characteristic of post-war Germany. Although the two main parties, CDU–CSU and SPD, won 60 per cent of the votes between them—more than at any election under Weimar or the Empire—a total of ten parties gained representation. The years immediately following threatened an even greater fragmentation. In 1950 a party to represent the interests of refugees and victims of de-Nazification, the League of Expellees and those Deprived of their Rights, commonly known as the Refugee Party (Bund der Heimatvertriebenen und Entrechteten (BHE)), was formed. It achieved spectacular successes in some *Landtag* elections and won 5.9 per cent of the votes in the 1953 Bundestag election. Even more disturbing was the rise of a neo-Nazi party, the Socialist Reich Party (Sozialistische Reichspartei (SRP)), led by Major-General Ernst Remer, whose unit had crushed the revolt against Hitler in July 1944. It won 11 per cent in a *Landtag* election in Lower Saxony in 1951, but was banned by the Federal Constitutional Court in 1952 as a threat to the liberal-democratic order.

In spite of these developments, the 1953 Bundestag election produced a result unprecedented in German party history—a landslide in favour of the CDU, which won 45.2 per cent of the vote and was only one seat short of an absolute majority. At the next election in 1957 Adenauer triumphed in a way that has not been equalled since, with 50.2 per cent. Some minor changes in the electoral law may have contributed to this result. For 1953 the 5-per-cent hurdle was raised from the *Land* to the federal level and for 1957 the number of constituencies to be won outright was raised from one to three. But the main reason for the decline of the minor parties was that this was what voters wanted. The Communist Party, which had scraped into the first Bundestag, was reduced to 2.2 per cent in 1953 and suffered the SRP's fate at the hands of the Constitutional Court in 1956. The Bavarian Party, which had its base in only one *Land*, was a victim of the change in the 5-per-cent rule and failed to get elected in 1953. The Refugee Party also failed to clear the 5-per-cent hurdle in 1957, though it survived in a number of *Landtage* until the mid-1960s. Two other parties survived temporarily only because the CDU 'lent' them enough constituency seats—the *Zentrum* in 1953 and the DP in 1957. The only non-Socialist party other than the CDU and CSU to survive the 1950s by its own efforts was the FDP, but it, too, lived dangerously.

Although the CDU scarcely needed the support of other parties in the Bundestag, Adenauer continued to rule with as wide a coalition as possible, determined to exclude only the SPD from power. His main reason for this lay in the need to get his military policy ratified. Amendments to the Basic Law require two-thirds majorities; they also require the assent of the Bundesrat, which reflects the party constellations in the *Land* coalitions. Once the Basic Law was amended, these coalition partners could be safely dispensed with and Adenauer reverted to a scheme that had always been popular with the CDU, that of replacing proportional representation with an Anglo-American simple-majority system. The FDP retaliated to this threat to its existence by withdrawing its support from the CDU-led cabinet in North Rhine–Westphalia and installing an SPD Prime Minister. This, in turn, led to a split in the FDP's Bundestag delegation: the bulk of the party decided to leave the coalition, but the FDP ministers refused to do so. There were, of course, issues other than electoral reform at stake between the CDU and the FDP. Personal relations between Adenauer and the FDP chairman, Thomas Dehler, were bad, reflecting different approaches to the question of German unity as well as to educational and cultural policies, with the FDP representing a predominantly anti-clerical constituency. The FDP survived the crisis with 7.7 per cent of the vote in 1957, its lowest share yet. What this crisis illustrated was the strength and weakness of the third party in the German political system. It is the FDP's function to be a coalition partner: between 1949 and 1995 it has been out of office for only eight years. It spent twenty-four years in coalition with the CDU and thirteen with the SPD. There was no doubt that during the Adenauer period the FDP was closer to the CDU than to the SPD, if only because of the SPD's collectivist economic policy. But this made it all the more necessary for the FDP to emphasize such distinctiveness as it possessed. In politics as in business a partner is also a competitor, an ally is also a rival.

None of this detracted from the scale of Adenauer's electoral triumphs. In the eight years between 1949 and 1957 the CDU's support doubled from 7.4 million to 15 million votes. The growth came from the supporters of smaller parties and from previous non-voters. The SPD meanwhile stagnated at around 30 per cent. What were the causes of this success? Support for the government's foreign policy, which put security above national unity, was no doubt a factor. But the biggest contribution came from the economic record. True, for Adenauer foreign policy came first, but to pursue this he needed a secure domestic base and that meant turning an uprooted and demoralized population into a new community. One in five of the West German population was a refugee; millions of others had lost their homes and possessions. When Adenauer took office unemployment was running at 9.5 per cent. In the course of the 1950s an average annual growth rate of 7.5 per cent more than doubled the gross domestic product of the FRG and all but eliminated unemployment.

Any success on this scale requires a combination of good management and good luck. The good management began with the Allied currency reform and Erhard's price liberalization. But these measures would not have done the trick without a number of other factors, though the exact contribution of each of these remains a matter of dispute. The first was Marshall Aid. Another was the relatively favourable structure of German industry, with its emphasis on modern manufacturing methods, to which must be added the benefits of postwar reconstruction. A major stimulus came from the Korean War boom, which boosted German exports. But the greatest structural advantage came from the labour surplus, constantly fed by the stream of refugees who continued to emigrate from the GDR, even after the main flow of expellees from further East had dried up. By keeping wages depressed they gave German products an increasingly sharp competitive edge, which meant that, on the basis of the exchange rate fixed in 1948 at 4.20 DM to the US dollar, the Deutsche Mark was increasingly undervalued. The value of the currency was further enhanced by West German monetary policy. The central bank, the Bank deutscher Länder, created by the Allies in 1948, was transformed in 1957 into the Bundesbank, with a statutory obligation to maintain a stable currency and with complete formal discretion over the money supply and interest rates. In 1952 the FRG registered a foreign trade surplus for the first time, a record that has been maintained uninterruptedly ever since. By the end of the decade the economic miracle, as it came to be known, had brought most Germans modest—and in some cases substantial—affluence and created the formidable export machine with which we have become familiar. Ludwig Erhard's slogan of 'prosperity for all' was close to being realized, even though the prosperity was far from being equally distributed.

Though the economic miracle helped to maintain social peace, it also needed social peace as a pre-condition. This was the joint achievement of the government and the trade unions. The market economy was always meant to have a social component. Those who privately—even secretly—elaborated its ideology in the late 1930s and early 1940s were aware that one of the appeals of National Socialism lay in its promise of social justice after the hardships of the Depression. They were also aware that economies based on competition lead to inequality which, if pressed beyond a certain point, poses a risk to a market economy's legitimacy. Above all they were aware that Germany was Europe's oldest welfare state, its social insurance schemes dating back to Bismarck's legislation of the 1880s. The way to acclimatize Germans to a civil society based on a market economy was to reassure them that some of their traditional expectations of the state would remain intact.

In securing social peace the trade unions were key players. As we saw in the debate on the Basic Law, they did not have that strong a hand to play in the post-war years. They had been destroyed by Hitler and, under the occupation regime, had to watch their step. It was only in 1949 that the sixteen trade unions, one for each of the major sectors of the economy, formed themselves into the German Trade Union Federation (Deutscher Gewerkschaftsbund (DGB)). But, in contrast with their predecessors in the Weimar Republic, they reconstructed themselves on a unitary basis, free from ideological divisions, and this enabled them to help shape the FRG's industrial relations. Moreover, Adenauer was anxious not to pick a fight with them. His quarrel was with the SPD, and the greater the distance he could put between the opposition, with which many union leaders sympathized, and the unions' interests, the better he would be pleased. The first test of this relationship came when the Ruhr industries reverted to German ownership in 1951. Would the principle of co-determination (*Mitbestimmung*) introduced by the British, that gave workers' representatives half the seats on the supervisory boards, remain in force? In response to union pressure the government agreed to this, but in all firms outside the coal and steel sectors unions achieved only one-third representation.

These measures fitted the general emerging pattern of industrial relations in the FRG, that of juridification. Just as employees have a say in corporate strategy through co-determination, so they have a say in plant working conditions through the works council (*Betriebsrat*). In both cases the law merely specifies that there shall be workers' representatives; *de facto* the great majority of these are union nominees. In return for this power-sharing, labour is subject to considerable constraints. A wide range of disputes can be settled by labour courts; while disputes are being heard, or as long as a valid contract is in force, workers are required to abstain from strike action. All strikes require a three-to-one majority in a ballot. The effect of these measures was to give labour a recognized place within the existing system. Co-determination was a victory, but a victory at the expense of a separate political programme. It meant the abandonment not only of national-ization, but of the class struggle. From the early 1950s onwards the unions' role was that of maximizing their members' benefits from the re-established market economy. The supra-partisan nature of the DGB also affected its place in the political sphere. The majority of union members vote for the SPD and the great majority of union officials belong to the SPD, sometimes in prominent positions. But there is also a sizeable CDU-inclined component and all CDU-led cabinets have contained at least one trade-union representative. That means that, on the one hand, it is difficult to mobilize the DGB for partisan campaigns, while, on the other, it is difficult for Conservative govern-ments in Germany to reduce union powers or welfare provisions in the way that governments of the Right have done elsewhere during the 1980s.

If workers' rights were one part of the social component in the market economy, welfare was the other. Some of the government's redistributive measures were a response to a temporary crisis—for example, the 1952 law on burden-sharing—designed to compensate war victims of various kinds. Others, such as the introduction of family allowances, were the direct outcome of Catholic social theory. But the more general expansion of the welfare state was part of a wider strategy. It was not only designed to integrate the population in the new order by giving them a share of the growing economy; it had—for Adenauer at least—a more specific purpose. The FRG was, in his view, to be a showpiece. It was to demonstrate to the population of the GDR that capitalism could deliver better welfare than Social-ism, and to demonstrate to its own population that the SPD had no monopoly of social concern. This policy culminated in 1957 in a universal old age pension linked to the general rise in incomes. The CDU's absolute majority in 1957 was no doubt an acknowledgement of this calculation.

By 1957 the FRG had acquired all the features by which it came to be recognized. It was firmly and institutionally anchored in the West. It was a front-line state facing the Iron Curtain and the Soviet bloc. It had a market economy with a distinctive and increasingly exemplary social component. One final step needed to be taken to put the seal on the Europeanization of the FRG. It came with the Treaty of Rome in 1957, in which the six members of the ECSC formed the EEC, popularly known as the Common Market, the forerunner of today's EU. Absorbing the FRG into a wider unit satisfied the aspirations of many post-war Germans. 'Europe' was a welcome substitute for the discredited notion of a nation-state and Article 24 of the Basic Law empowered the FRG 'to transfer sovereign rights to international institutions'. Such moves also had the advantage of assuaging the fears and suspicions of its neighbours.

The 1957 election brought Adenauer to the apogee of his power, but it also raised questions about the quality of West German democracy. Critics of Adenauer's role talked of the evolution of 'chancellor democracy' (*Kanzlerdemokratie*). They saw the democratic process reduced to a series of plebiscites in favour of the governmental incumbent, something far removed from genuine popular self-government. It is undeniable that Adenauer, whose personality had been formed before the First World War, was not the most conciliatory of statesmen and that he frequently behaved in a paternalistic or authoritarian way. Yet as part of the political learning process chancellor democracy had its points. Under the Weimar Republic and the Empire, polling day had been an opportunity to affirm an ideological allegiance. Under chancellor democracy it became a way of choosing a responsible government. Adenauer symbolized this rationale of the electoral process by combining governmental with party office. When he became Chancellor he was no more than chairman of the British-zone CDU. Opinion polls showed that he was unknown to half the population. The first national congress of the CDU did not take place until 1950, a year after the first Bundestag election. It was on that occasion that Adenauer was elected its national chairman. Even after that the party's organization remained rudimentary and it was not until 1957 that the CDU decided to form a joint parliamentary grouping with the Bavarian CSU.

One problem that the young republic faced was that of the German past. A regime like that of the Third Reich cannot rely on terror alone. It needs enthusiasts and true believers, even if those are only a small minority. It needs a much larger number who are prepared to support, or at least accept, significant portions of its ideology. Above all, it needs collusion—from opportunists, careerists, moral cowards, and informers, as well as from the millions of persons in official positions who helped to maintain the regime simply by routine performance of their duties. For six out of its twelve years the Third Reich was at war, which made it all the more difficult for those in uniform to distinguish between simple patriotic duty and active support for the regime's ideology. Those who governed the FRG had, therefore, to tread a careful line between a clear dissociation from the past and imposing collective guilt on the bulk of the population.

There is no reason to doubt the sincerity of the leading politicians' disavowal of National Socialism, nor of their commitment to democracy. Adenauer in particular was anxious to make his peace with the survivors of Germany's Jewish community and did so through a generous restitution agreement for both individuals and the state of Israel. In other respects the tendency was to draw a veil over the past. De-Nazification and war-crimes trials, which had largely come to an end even under Allied occupation, were not resumed. In the personnel of the civil service, the judiciary, and the universities there was almost complete continuity with previous regimes. Some appointments to high positions were distinctly controversial, as much outside the country as inside: in particular that of the State Secretary in the Chancellor's office, Dr Hans Globke, who had drafted the official commentary on the Nuremberg Laws. Few of these relics of the National Socialist regime were a danger to the state; they adapted readily enough to the new rules of the game. But as a signal of the moral content of the new order they were not inspiring or encouraging. Nor was a great deal done by way of education. The Third Reich did not feature much in school or university syllabuses. The resistance to Hitler was treated perfunctorily and the families of the 1944 conspirators had difficulties in securing pensions. The government calculated, no doubt correctly, that raking over the past was not one of the citizens' priorities. If a new consensus was to be created, it would have to embrace both the sheep and the goats. There would be a price to pay for this pragmatism in the 1960s, but in the 1950s it bought domestic peace and quiet. In any case, Germany's political leaders had a constructive as well as a defensive agenda. For Adenauer, nationalism was an obsolete sentiment: part of his mission was to liberate his compatriots from this inherited liability. By integrating the FRG in the democratic West and by slowly building up a domestic democratic order, he and his colleagues hoped that the bad dreams of the past would fade. This did not mean that Germans were to lose national pride. There was nothing to stop them from admiring their poets and their mountains, the revived economy and their sporting heroes; what was important was to depoliticize this patriotism. In that respect the exercise was largely successful.

In riding to his triumph in 1957 Adenauer had outflanked his two principal rivals—externally this meant the GDR, domestically the SPD. Both now prepared to make up lost ground. The GDR had been one of the first objects of the FRG's newly found freedom of action. West German governments regarded the GDR as illegitimate, lacking in popular backing, and resting on Soviet force. They insisted that they and they alone were entitled to speak for the whole German people, the so-called 'claim to sole representation' (*Alleinvertretungsanspruch*). The practical expression of this was the Hallstein Doctrine, that threatened breach of diplomatic relations with any state—the Soviet Union excepted—that recognized the GDR. In contesting this claim the GDR had to rely on Soviet support, and the Soviet Union had actually accorded full sovereignty to the GDR in 1954, some months before the Paris accords with the FRG came into force. There remained nevertheless two thorns in the East German flesh. The first was the never-ceasing westward flow of refugees. Between 1949 and 1961 the GDR lost 2.7 million people in this way, to which should be added another million between 1945 and 1949. The second was the enclave of West Berlin in the heart of the territory of the GDR. Indeed the two were connected, for West Berlin was the escape-hatch for migrants.

To remove both these thorns Stalin's successor Nikita Khrushchev proposed radical measures to the Western powers in 1958: an end to the four-power control of Berlin, which was in any case now a dead letter; a demilitarized 'free city' of West Berlin; and transfer of Soviet responsibilities for Berlin to the GDR. If the West did not agree, the Soviet Union would sign a separate peace treaty with the GDR. Since West Berlin was a symbol of Western prestige and honour, such demands were unacceptable, though Britain and the

USA did toy with compromise formulas. In the end Khrushchev's threat imposed the solution. Alarmed by the prospect of a peace treaty that would finally seal off their state, East Germans fled in unprecedented numbers—47,000 alone in the first twelve days of August 1961. On the 13th the Soviets responded by building a wall to separate East from West Berlin. Morally this event was a defeat. Politically it was an act of defiance: the GDR was determined to survive, whatever the cost. But it was also a major setback for Adenauer. His calculation had been that, if the West stood firm, the East would have to accept its terms.

Domestically Adenauer's third term was marked by a reformation in the SPD. Its third successive defeat left it no choice but to rethink its role in West German politics and to learn the lesson of the CDU's success. The CDU had been innovative not only in the type of campaign it fought, but in the type of party it was. The strength of its appeal lay precisely in the weakness of its organization, which meant that it was not dominated by apparatchiks, and in its newness, which meant that it was not overburdened with the ideological baggage of previous generations. It was deliberately designed to be a people's party (*Volkspartei*), not tied to a particular interest or section of the population. The contrast with the SPD could not have been greater. The SPD's programme dated from 1925; in its organizational structure it resumed where it had left off in 1933. To belong to the SPD was to choose a way of life, in which meetings, social life, and leisure activities merged. By 1949 the party had recruited three-quarters of a million members, one for every ten of its voters: in some areas, like Hamburg, the ratio was closer to one in five. It was a party of the committed, many of whom had suffered in the Nazi years. But none of that helped it escape from its 30-per-cent ghetto. As the years passed, it acquired the reputation of a party that always said no. It had opposed the currency reform and the turn to a market economy with warnings of hardship and social injustice; but in the long run too many Germans had done well out of this policy for the warnings to be remembered. It had opposed the ECSC and rearmament even in the guise of the EDC, on the grounds that this would deepen the division of Germany; but it did not reveal how it would meet the FRG's security needs. On the other hand, where the SPD wielded political power, in city and *Land* governments, it was capable of acting quite pragmatically, and the conversion of the trade unions to the world as it existed set an example that it was difficult to ignore. Indeed, the evocations of Marx and the class struggle had begun to sound hollow even during the Weimar Republic.

It was, therefore, not too difficult to reformulate the party's principles in a way that increasingly corresponded with its practice. The process culminated at the Bad Godesberg congress in 1959 in which the delegates replaced exclusive inspiration by Marxism with an allegiance to Christian ethics, humanism, and classical philosophy. More specifically it accepted the principle of the market economy, admittedly with some qualifications: 'as much competition as possible, as much planning as necessary'. The new policies were the work of a new generation, many of whom were influenced by their experience of British, US, or Scandinavian politics during their exile. The main 'revisionists' were Fritz Erler, Carlo Schmid, Willi Eichler (who had spent the war in Britain), Willy Brandt (who had spent the Nazi period in Sweden and Norway), and an ex-Communist, Herbert Wehner. A year after Godesberg, Wehner went even further, accepted the FRG's membership of NATO, and offered to pursue a bi-partisan foreign policy. The basis for the SPD's transformation into a *Volkspartei* was laid. But the SPD also now acknowledged the conventions of chancellor democracy. For the 1961 Bundestag election it nominated the Governing Mayor of West Berlin, Willy Brandt, as chancellor candidate.

The shock of the Berlin Wall five weeks before polling day, combined with the modernization of the SPD, meant that the CDU–CSU could not hope to retain its absolute majority in 1961. For the first time the gap between the two main parties narrowed. The CDU–CSU went down 4.9 per cent to 45.3 per cent, the SPD went up 4.4 per cent to 36.2 per cent. Adenauer remained Chancellor for another two years, but the Adenauer era was effectively over.

4 The Second Foundation of the Federal Republic

The chances of liberal democracy in a German society have never been as great as they are in the German Federal Republic . . . authoritarianism of the traditional kind has become impossible in German society.

(Ralf Dahrendorf, *Democracy and Society in Germany* (1965))

The structure of our state rests on fear of the people, on distrust of the people. The distrust towards parties, government and politicians, to which the people would in turn be obligated, does not manifest itself sufficiently or effectively.

(Karl Jaspers, *Wohin treibt die Bundesrepublik?* (1966))

THE 1950s were a decade of reconstruction in Western Germany, not of reform. The priority for both government and citizens was a return to normality, though, as we have seen, the normality they achieved was by no means the same as any in the German past. By 1961 there was a reasonably stable party system which permitted a chance of a peaceful alternation of power, and a widely accepted form of constitutional government. Anti-system parties faced public rejection, and would have done so even if they had not been banned under Article 21(2) of the Basic Law. Special-interest parties, like the Refugee Party, were in decline, as were regional parties such as the Bavarian Party and the DP. The FRG had adopted a market economy that provided prosperity for most of its citizens, even if not, as Erhard had proclaimed, for all. In the words of Fritz René Allemann's influential book of 1956, Bonn was not Weimar. Above all, the search for international recognition and equality of status had made giant steps forward. True, the victor powers retained some reserve powers; true, the path to international recognition that the Federal Republic had chosen involved the abandonment of traditional state sovereignty. But in return for this it had gained increasing influence within the arenas in which it operated, notably NATO and the EEC.

None of this had been achieved without controversy. All who had brought a definite agenda to the building of a post-Hitler Germany were forced to compromise, and compromise brings disappointment. Most West Germans accepted the division of their country as the price of security, but the question of national unity remained a domestic political issue. Most West Germans accepted the loss of territories to the East as the price of defeat, but a vocal expellee lobby remained an electoral force and the question of the final recognition of the Oder–Neiße frontier with Poland continued to sour the FRG's foreign relations. Most West Germans accepted and even welcomed the flourishing market economy, but some Socialist utopians remained both inside and outside the SPD; above all there was discontent with some of the resulting inequalities. Most West Germans accepted the welfare state as it had been expanded in the 1950s, but its extent was controversial, especially among the ranks of Adenauer's own supporters; there were those within the CDU and especially the FDP who feared that future costs had not been taken sufficiently into account. The same doubts applied even more to co-determination, which the coalition had enacted against the better judgement of some of its members, including Erhard.

Though the general direction of West German politics was by now fixed, not all options were foreclosed and not all questions had been settled. Above all there were doubts about the quality of political and cultural life. The FRG of the 1950s was a provincial and conformist place. With the downgrading of Berlin it lacked a creative metropolis like Paris and London, where literature, art, scholarship, and government mingled. Munich, Cologne, or Hamburg, for all the excellence of their facilities, were no match for those world-cities. A list of notable West German novels, plays, films, paintings, sculptures, or musical compositions from the FRG's first decade would have been short. The same applied to scientific research. In part these defects were a legacy of the anti-modernism and repressive atmosphere of the Third Reich, in part they were due to the haemorrhage caused by the intellectual emigration of the 1930s. But they were also a reflection of the materialistic perspective of a generation for whom economic reconstruction came first and last. Those who dissented from these values during the 1950s were a small minority, but their turn came in the 1960s. Unreformed institutions and an unmastered past were to become an issue in a way that they had not been since 1949. Before that could happen Adenauer had to leave the stage. The decline of the CDU–CSU vote in the 1961 election was a warning to the 85-year-old Chancellor, but one that he would have preferred to ignore. There were, however, signs that he was beginning to lose his touch. His first major miscalculation came in 1959, over the succession to the Federal Presidency, once Theodor Heuss had completed his second five-year term. Adenauer and the CDU proposed Ludwig Erhard for this position, but he, sensing that he did not have the CDU's and CSU's full support, insisted on a unanimous nomination. When this was not forthcoming, he withdrew, whereupon Adenauer proposed himself. That was a major mistake, since he evidently assumed that he could turn the dignified office to which Heuss had lent considerable prestige into one of executive power of the kind General de Gaulle had in mind for the Fifth French Republic. When the CDU parliamentary group responded to this move by proposing Erhard for the Chancellorship, Adenauer withdrew his presidential candidature: while he respected Erhard's judgement in economic policy, he had no confidence in his ability to conduct foreign policy or provide national leadership. The outcome of this episode was that the obscure Agriculture Minister, Heinrich Lübke, became President and that the first doubts began to appear about Adenauer's continued grip on affairs.

The second miscalculation arose out of the building of the Berlin Wall, when he evidently did not register the traumatic effect on public opinion of this event. For two days he failed to visit West Berlin; when he finally went, he was booed. The electoral check that the CDU suffered meant that Adenauer had to revert to a coalition with the Free Democrats, which involved a further limitation of his power. This became relevant in the third mistake the government committed, which became known as the *Spiegel* affair. In October 1962 the news magazine *Der Spiegel*, well known for its muck-raking, published a report on a NATO exercise that alleged serious defects in the West's military capacity. Leading members of the *Spiegel*'s staff were thereupon arrested—some of them as far away as Spain—and charged with treason. At the centre of the storm over this incident was the Defence Minister, the Bavarian Franz-Josef Strauß, widely suspected, then as later, of harbouring an unsuitably authoritarian temperament. These suspicions were confirmed when he gave misleading answers to questions in the Bundestag and by the end of 1962 the FDP had secured his resignation. Less than a year later Adenauer, too, went. His successor was Ludwig Erhard. The *Spiegel* affair symbolized the end of the Adenauer era in another way. It was the harbinger of a decade-long questioning of the West German power structure.

Before leaving office Adenauer set one final seal on his foreign-policy achievements, the Franco-German Treaty of Friendship of 1963, known as the Elysée Accord. In one sense there was nothing surprising about this treaty; it could be interpreted as one more step in the direction of Franco-German reconciliation, which had already been symbolized by the creation of the EEC. With the resolution of the Saar question in 1957, the last of the direct conflicts between the two states had been removed. Adenauer had always placed great emphasis on a partnership with France; the Elysée Accord initiated and institutionalized the frequent summit meetings between the French and West German heads of government, for which there was no parallel between any other European states. France's new ruler, President de Gaulle, had a rather different motive for seeking out the FRG. He was determined to reduce the influence of Britain and the USA on European affairs and in pursuit of this aim had offered the FRG rather stronger support at the time of the Berlin crisis than had the USA.

Yet from the German point of view the Elysée Accord was based on a misunderstanding. The partnership with France could not be a substitute for the US nuclear umbrella, however much Adenauer might distrust the moves toward *détente* that President Kennedy had initiated—moves that were temporarily interrupted, but ultimately accelerated, by the Cuban missile crisis that coincided with the *Spiegel* affair. In other respects, de Gaulle's and the FRG's agendas diverged. De Gaulle had vetoed the British application to join the EEC and he rejected the principle of majority voting by the European Commission, thereby securing a veto power for any one member state. He withdrew France from the joint military command of NATO and pursued the development of an independent French nuclear capability. This policy appealed strongly to Franz-Josef Strauß, who hoped for a West German integration into this strategic concept. But with Strauß's and then Adenauer's departure, the attractions of a strong strategic link with France faded. Erhard and his Foreign Minister Gerhard Schröder were 'Atlanticists', who were reluctant to abandon the primacy of the West German–American relationship.

The Erhard government turned out to be an interlude and not a very happy one. Neither in the economy nor in foreign relations was the administration successful, although Erhard had no difficulty in securing re-election in September 1965. Erhard's first misfortune was that economic growth rates continued to decline from the record levels of the 1950s. In the first half of the 1960s they averaged 3.4 per cent, but it was not until 1967 that the West German economy experienced its first year of negative growth. Nevertheless, voter dissatisfaction with this performance showed itself in June 1966 in elections in the FRG's biggest *Land*, North Rhine–Westphalia, up to then a CDU stronghold. The SPD won 49.5 per cent of the vote and missed an absolute majority by two seats. In December of that year the SPD formed a 'small coalition' in North Rhine–Westphalia with the FDP. But by then the Erhard government was no more. On 27 October the FDP ministers resigned from the coalition and at the end of November Erhard followed them. The occasion for the government's collapse was disagreement over the budget deficit: Erhard wanted to raise taxes, the FDP to cut expenditure. But the underlying reason was that the government had run its course. Above all, Erhard had failed in his negotiations with the USA. Having set out to obtain an increased US contribution to the cost of NATO and some sharing in NATO's nuclear capability, he got neither. Yet it would be wrong to dismiss the Erhard government as lacking in achievements. It initiated a rethinking of relations with the East, and outside government circles a new ideological agenda was emerging. Both these developments matured under the Great Coalition that followed Erhard's departure.

On 1 December a new government was formed under Kurt-Georg Kiesinger of the CDU, with the SPD as a not very junior partner. Willy Brandt became Vice-Chancellor and Foreign Minister; Karl Schiller, Minister for the Economy. It was the SPD's first participation in a national German government since 1930. Both parties had tactical reasons for this move. Those of the CDU were short term: to recover its lost prestige by sharing the responsibility for government and to prevent a small coalition between the SPD and FDP. Those of the SPD were long term: to complete the move towards political respectability begun at Bad Godesberg and to convince sceptics once and for all that it was a capable and responsible administrator. The Great Coalition was popular and opinion polls showed that it was many Germans' preferred form of government. This was only partly due to the economic recovery engineered by Schiller's Keynesian policies, which brought growth back to 7.5 per cent in 1969. The more decisive reasons were cultural. Much as the German party system had changed since the early years of the FRG and much as voters had learned to choose between competing aspirants to executive office, there was a strong residual aversion to public conflict and a desire to have policy made in an objective, consensual, non-partisan way. Many public commentators, who had hoped for a linear development of West German politics in an Anglo-Saxon direction, thought the resort to a government of national unity a regression. In an article ominously entitled 'Wird Bonn doch Weimar?' ('Will Bonn become Weimar after all?') the distinguished political scientist Karl-Dietrich Bracher argued that 'democracy appears to be acceptable to the Germans when it ensures prosperity for an equally a-political and anti-Communist affluent society, and when the government establishes itself above the parties and their despised "horse-trading" compromises'.

Those who disliked the Great Coalition did so for three reasons: that it would encourage secret government, that it would marginalize legitimate opposition, and that it would result in policy inertia. The first of these fears was not realized. Though there were regular informal meetings at the Chancellor's country home between party leaders, some of whom were not members of the cabinet, their conclusions had no binding force. The Great Coalition did not imitate the Weimar practice, or the post-1945 Austrian practice, of 'coalition pacts' drawn up by non-accountable caucuses. Politics, including the politics of disagreement, continued to be public. The marginalization of opposition did occur, as will be discussed below. Policy inertia, however, was not initially a very serious problem, though this tells us nothing about the merits of the measures passed or not passed. The most important domestic item was the Emergency Powers Law, which was designed to give the FRG government powers that had originally been the prerogative of the occupation powers. In opposition the SPD had always voted against such a measure; in coalition it ensured that any implementation would require the prior approval of the Bundestag. Nevertheless, this law was highly controversial and was one of those most strongly opposed by the extra-parliamentary Left. A proposal to which the SPD had originally agreed, but about which it then got cold feet, was the CDU's old plan to change the electoral system. While there was at no stage agreement on what scheme was to replace the status quo, the effect would have been to disadvantage the FDP. This was unpopular, given the general public preference for coalition government; it also became less and less attractive to the SPD, who feared that it would exclude them from power and who wished to keep open a bridge to the FDP. Electoral reform was first postponed and, after the change of government in 1969, shelved. Since then it has not been an issue.

In foreign policy the inclusion of the SPD brought more positive results, though here, too, it was a question of accelerating trends already initiated before 1966. The building of the Berlin Wall required a reassessment of relations with the GDR; the East German state was clearly going to be around for some time to come and could no longer simply be ignored. The slow *détente* that followed the resolution of the Cuban missile crisis made a more flexible approach to the rest of the Eastern bloc possible. The first tentative steps in this direction were in fact taken by Gerhard Schröder, who began to hint that the FRG needed to define its own state interests irrespective of its long-term obligation to speak for East Germans, too. This meant accepting, even while deploring, the presence of Communist states to the East as part of the world order. The most explicit statement of this revised concept came from a Social Democrat, Egon Bahr, who was later to become head of foreign-policy planning under Brandt and was for more than twenty years a leading SPD player in relations with the East. In a public lecture in July 1963 he launched the concept of change through *rapprochement* (*Wandel durch Annäherung*), that of 'overcoming the status quo by not changing the status quo in the short term'. To this formulation he added the suggestion that Germans were uniquely placed to take an initiative in this matter.

Bahr's statement broke two taboos. It suggested that the FRG should think in terms of direct, bilateral relations with the GDR and that the time had come for the FRG to draw up its own agenda of foreign-policy priorities. Others had thought this, but no one in the mainstream of politics had said it out loud. It was in foreign affairs, more than any other policy area, that the partners of the Great Coalition came together. Both the CDU and the SPD had moved towards Atlanticism, the CDU from Adenauer's and Strauß's flirtation with Gaullism, the SPD from the neutralism of the 1950s. Both had begun rethinking their attitudes to the East. In part the FRG's hand was forced in these matters by changes in the world constellation. The 1960s saw an acceleration in decolonization and a proliferation of newly independent states, mainly in Africa and Asia, many of which came together in a 'non-aligned bloc'. Though some of these states were better disposed than others to the Soviet Union, few were inclined to have their foreign relations dictated by an inter-German quarrel. Their very existence, therefore, was a challenge to the Hallstein doctrine, a fact that was dramatically illustrated when Egypt established diplomatic relations in May 1965 with the GDR and the FRG did not retaliate. The contradiction was resolved only when, later that year, the FRG established diplomatic relations with Israel, which led the great majority of Arab states, including Egypt, to break off relations with Bonn. A similar problem arose when Cambodia recognized the GDR in 1969. Though the FRG restricted itself to calling this an 'unfriendly act', that was enough for Cambodia to break off relations. The difficulties of maintaining the credibility of the Hallstein doctrine in Europe were further emphasized when the FRG extended diplomatic recognition to Romania, which also had diplomatic relations with the GDR, though it was at this time emphasizing its relative independence from Soviet foreign policy.

The logic of this new attitude towards the Communist East was that the time had come to accept the status quo; what followed from that was that the FRG should extend diplomatic recognition to the GDR. But the time for that was not yet ripe. Much as the partners in the Great Coalition were agreed on many of the principles of West

German foreign policy, recognition of the GDR was anathema to the right wing of the CDU and above all to the CSU. This particular step would have to await a change of government. What did happen was a subtle change in political semantics. Up to the late 1960s one of the taboos of West German politics had consisted of not calling the GDR by its official name. Most of the media either referred to it as 'the so-called GDR', or put the initials in quotation marks. Politicians and official publications called it the Soviet zone of occupation (Sowjetische Besatzungszone or SBZ for short), or the Eastern zone, or simply *die Zone*. It was, therefore, an innovation for Brandt first to refer to 'the other part of Germany' as a state and then to call it the GDR outright. It was not only coalition disagreements that prevented the next step from being taken. The GDR reciprocated by increasing its demands and the whole concept of *détente* was threatened when the armies of the Warsaw Pact crushed the Prague Spring in August 1968.

If some of the assumptions of West German foreign policy were being slowly revised in the course of the 1960s, many of the assumptions of its domestic policy were being radically challenged. For this there were structural as well as contingent reasons. The contingent reason was that the existence of the Great Coalition marginalized opposition. The parliamentary opposition consisted of the FDP, with forty-nine seats out of 496. The real opposition was increasingly to be found on the streets. It is difficult to believe that the new challenges from the Left and, to a lesser extent, the Right would not have emerged anyway, Great Coalition or no Great Coalition. The intellectual preparation for both was under way before 1966, but the explosion would not have come so soon, nor have been so intense, but for the atmosphere created by the Great Coalition.

The strength of the Adenauer era had been its ability to promise and proclaim stability. 'No experiments' had been the guarantee to West Germans that Bonn was neither Weimar nor the Third Reich. Yet in many ways 'no experiments' was a pretence. The first fifteen years of the FRG were a huge experiment. A stable parliamentary democracy, a growing constitutional consensus, a crisis-free market economy, and firm integration in the West were major innovations in Germany: a combination of all four was unheard of. The FRG in 1965 was a very different place from the Western zones of 1945 and not only in physical appearance. It was this change that led Liberal optimists like Ralf Dahrendorf (quoted at the head of this chapter) to believe that his compatriots had irrevocably joined the West and, by extension, the modern world. German democracy might be imperfect, but it was incomparably better than anything that had gone before.

Yet there were dissenters from this judgement who drew the opposite conclusion from the same evidence. They saw the liberal constitutionalism of the FRG as a fig-leaf that disguised the way authoritarianism and conformity continued to dominate public life. They pointed to the continuity of personnel in education, the public service, and the economy after 1945, to the overriding anti-Communist consensus that narrowed the range of political debate, to the remilitarization of the state that came with rearmament, and above all to the failure to come to terms with German guilt for the Third Reich and its crimes. During the 1950s the writers and intellectuals who thought like this were lone voices. The bulk of the population were too preoccupied with mending their personal lives to listen; they were too close to the years of the Third Reich to want to be reminded of their, or their families' and friends', involvement in it. By the mid-1960s the climate of opinion had begun to change. Affluence brought its familiar discontents. The reconstruction years were over and personal horizons could begin to widen. At the same time many feared that the scope for dissent was narrowing, the closer the SPD moved to the CDU. The formation of the Great Coalition seemed the final step in the forging of an anti-pluralist cartel. As long as the SPD at least paid lip-service to Marxism, advocates of radical change could shelter in it. After Bad Godesberg this was no longer so. The FRG's leading Marxist political scientist, Wolfgang Abendroth, was expelled from the party and its student organization, Sozialdemokratische Studentschaft (SDS), was disaffiliated.

It was not only the economic and political environment in the FRG that changed. There was demographic change, too. A younger age group were less willing to accept their parents' conspiracies of silence. A number of events combined to stimulate these sceptical and, in the end, rebellious attitudes. One such event was the so-called Auschwitz Trial, the prosecution and conviction in 1963–5 of seventeen former overseers and guards at the Auschwitz extermination camp. After more than a decade of inaction, the West German authorities had decided to take up the cases left unfinished by the Allies; the publicity that the trial generated raised once more the question of what the role of individuals had been under the Third Reich, and how many more men and women, like the seventeen in the dock, were quietly living in the FRG. One outcome of the trial was a parliamentary battle to extend the statute of limitations, which, under existing German law, restricted prosecutions to twenty years after the alleged event. In the end an exception was agreed for Nazi crimes, though there were misgivings about tampering with the rule of law, even in a cause as worthy as this. The trials and the limitations debate reopened what has become a permanent component of the German public agenda: the question of overcoming the past, which further widened the gap between the wartime and post-war generations. The repression of the past was one of the causes of the 1960s rebellion; the Great Coalition and the emergency legislation were others. For those conscious of the continuing democratic deficit of the FRG, these interconnected events were further proof of a reversion to the bad old habits of German politics. It was not some teenage revolutionary but the octogenarian philosopher Karl Jaspers who outlined the scenario: 'From the party oligarchy to the authoritarian state; from the authoritarian state to dictatorship; from dictatorship to war.'

At least as strong a factor as any of these were events outside Germany and outside Europe. The single most important one was the war in Vietnam, which became the main mobilizer of the New Left in the developed world. In West Germany in particular it polarized the images of the USA. More than any other Western state the USA had been the godfather of the FRG; more than any other the USA had been its role model, admired by Right and Left for different reasons—for its individual freedoms, whether political or economic, its effective federal structure, its egalitarian social philosophy, and as the home of the New Deal and the Marshall Plan. The industrial reconstruction of the FRG borrowed from American methods of management; its effect was increasingly to turn the citizen into an American-style consumer. This admiration—or acceptance—of the American model remained, and has remained, widespread. What was new was its converse, the militant rejection. Up to the mid-1960s anti-Americanism had been the province of the disgruntled Right: for them America was too crass, too vulgar, too materialist, too Jewish, too non-white. Now the USA emerged as the oppressor of the Third World, whether directly, as in Vietnam, or indirectly through its dictatorial clients in Latin America or in the person of the Shah of Iran.

Alongside this rejection of the USA came the rejection of inherited structures at home: in the family, in politics, and above all in education. Hence the centre of the New Left rebellion was in the universities. West German students had a real grievance. Their numbers had multiplied, but facilities had not kept pace. Above all the structures of higher education had hardly changed since before the First World War, with professorial hierarchies in command and little personal contact between teachers and taught. Paradoxically, one of the universities to take the lead in the student movement was the Free University of Berlin, which had been founded in 1952, largely with US money, to accommodate exiles from the venerable Humboldt University, now in East Berlin and under Communist control. Because West Berlin was not part of the FRG, conscription did not apply there: it was, therefore, particularly attractive to non-conformist youth. Equally paradoxically, much of the student movement's ideology was imported from the USA. Campus revolts had begun with the Free Speech movement at Berkeley, California, and spread across the continent to Columbia University. The rationale for giving students and intellectuals a vanguard role had also been provided by the German emigrants to the USA of the so-called Frankfurt School, principally Theodor Adorno and Herbert Marcuse, who argued that under modern capitalism the working class had been bought off by welfare and affluence and was, therefore, no longer able to perform its emancipatory role. Younger German followers of this school, in particular the social theorist Jürgen Habermas, reimported these ideas into West Germany. The dominant component of the first phase of this movement was a non-violent utopian anarchism. In this respect it differed little from its US or French analogues, though the survival in West Germany of older authoritarian structures gave it a better defined target. What distinguished it in political method was a contempt for parliamentary conventions. It believed in the street demonstration, the leaflet war, and the sit-in. It proclaimed itself to be the Extra-Parliamentary Opposition (Außerparlamentarische Opposition (APO)).

Before long, however, the movement fragmented. The West Berlin atmosphere, student protest, and anti-Americanism came together on 2 June 1967, when a theology student, Benno Ohnesorg, was fatally wounded by the police during a demonstration against a visit by the Shah. The indignation at this incident ignited student militancy throughout the FRG; it was further inflamed when one of the student leaders, Rudi Dutschke, was paralysed by an assassination attempt in April 1968. One consequence of this escalation was the encouragement of violence among the protesters. If, as the extreme wing argued, violence was the only means at the disposal of the existing order, violence was justified in opposing it. It was from these roots that the terrorism of the 1970s and 1980s sprang. A more immediate consequence was the breakdown of order in the universities, with occupations of administration buildings and the disruption of lectures and seminars. Some universities have not recovered to this day from the resulting polarization.

The radicalization of politics under the Great Coalition happened predominantly on the Left, but the Right was not untouched by it. It would have been surprising if the politics of resentment had not surfaced from time to time in the FRG in the form of cyclical surges of neo-Nazism. This had happened in the early 1950s in the brief irruption of the Socialist Reich Party and to a lesser extent in 1959–61 when one of its successors, the Deutsche Reichspartei (DRP), polled over 5 per cent in *Landtag* elections. Activists of the Far Right were not restricted to these fringe parties. They were to be found in the DP, the Refugee Party, the CSU, and even the FDP. Nor were their activities purely electoral; the late 1950s saw a rash of acts of vandalism against synagogues and Jewish cemeteries. To revitalize the various declining parties and politically homeless individuals, the National Democratic Party (Nationaldemokratische Partei Deutschlands (NPD)) was formed in 1964. Its foundation, like the early stages of the APO, therefore antedated the formation of the Great Coalition, though, like the APO, it clearly benefited from it.

The NPD's primary appeal was to the disgruntled remnants of the old far Right and to unintegrated expellees. But its following was more heterogeneous than that of any of its predecessors and it was electorally more successful. Between 1966 and 1968 it secured election to seven *Landtage* and peaked at 9.8 per cent in Baden-Württemberg in 1968. Many of its new voters were CDU or CSU supporters who disapproved of their party's coalition with the 'Reds', but the NPD also gained former SPD votes from victims of the recession. The programme of the NPD was largely negative—a rejection of all that had happened in and to Germany since 1945: not only its division, but its internationalization—economic as well as political—and the loss of the Eastern territories. It certainly disapproved of any coming-to-terms with the past: Germans needed 'a true picture of their history', not 'the glorification of treason'. There were also the first signs of what was to become a major theme in the 1980s and 1990s—namely, resentment at immigrants. How many supporters the NPD recruited on the basis of its manifestos, and how many by tapping ill-defined discontent, is difficult to say. The speed with which it declined—by 1972 its electoral support had shrunk to 0.6 per cent—suggests that its appeal, though broad, was shallow. It included ex-Nazis and neo-Nazis among its leaders and followers, and above all among its publicists. But in the general profile of its supporters it was the first post-Nazi party of the extreme Right, a bridge between unalloyed neo-Nazism and the later Republican Party, which had its ups and downs in the 1980s and 1990s.

Although both the NPD and the APO as organizations remained consigned to the fringes and excluded from the FRG consensus, their agenda had an impact on mainstream politics and contributed to the increasing difficulties of the Great Coalition. The CDU saw the growth of the NPD as a warning not to go too far in the direction of the SPD, especially as far as approaches to the East were concerned. There clearly was a hard-line anti-Communist segment of West German public opinion which, even if not in the majority, could not be ignored by the CDU. On the other hand, at least some of what the APO was saying found an echo in broader sections of German society and contributed to a transformation of public expectations and quite substantial innovations in party programmes. These dealt, on the one hand, with policy towards the East, or *Ostpolitik* as it came to be known, and, on the other, with domestic reform under the general heading of democratization.

The divergences within the Coalition on *Ostpolitik* demonstrated again the extent to which foreign affairs dominated the politics of the

FRG and could determine the fates of governments. Half-way through the life of the Coalition, in 1968, two events occurred that seemed at first to impede the progress of *Ostpolitik*. The first was the Soviet crushing of the Prague Spring and the proclamation of the 'Brezhnev doctrine', i.e. of the limited sovereignty of states within the Soviet sphere of influence. The second was the election of the Republican Richard Nixon to the Presidency of the USA. Nixon had risen to prominence on the basis of anti-Communist rhetoric and was closely associated with McCarthyism: his occupancy of the White House therefore seemed to spell a halt to *détente*.

As it turned out, neither of these misgivings was justified. Soviet policy, it was increasingly evident, was concerned with security, not expansion. As with previous rebellions against Soviet rule, whether in Berlin in 1953 or Hungary in 1956, the Soviet Union's priority was the defence of its perimeter, not its extension. With each successful defence of the perimeter, including the building of the Berlin Wall, Soviet confidence grew, especially since the West signalled that it was disinclined to interfere with oppression provided that it was restricted to the other side of the Iron Curtain. With the restoration of its authority in Czechoslovakia, the Soviet Union was more, not less, ready to take up new negotiations, if they could lead to further Western acknowledgement of the permanence of the post-1945 settlement. Nor did the election of Nixon signal a return to the attitudes of the Cold War. While the USA's immediate preoccupations were in Asia— reconciliation with Communist China and as graceful a withdrawal as possible from Vietnam—the new administration showed itself favourable to accelerating *détente*. Nixon's national security adviser, Henry Kissinger, was as security conscious as Brezhnev, but more flexible in seeking ways of reducing friction. Those who, like Brandt and Bahr, wanted to go further in *Ostpolitik* therefore soon recovered their nerve. Nerve was needed, since the only meaningful next steps could be diplomatic recognition of the GDR and final acceptance of the Oder– Neiße frontier of Poland.

In domestic politics, too, the gap between the coalition partners began to widen. The message of democratization, even if interpreted differently from the APO, was penetrating into the SPD. In some respects the SPD managed to enact its reforms through the Coalition.

The Criminal Law Amendment Act of 1969 was largely the work of the SPD Minister of Justice, Adenauer's former colleague Gustav Heinemann. It emphasized rehabilitation rather than retribution as the aim of punishment, and decriminalized blasphemy, adultery, and homosexual acts between adults. Nevertheless, the SPD began to fear that the constraints of the Coalition would delay further reform and would try the patience of their potential supporters in the country.

What accelerated SPD rethinking about the shape of government as the 1969 Bundestag election approached was the transformation of the FDP. Nothing stimulates internal questioning in a party like consignment to the opposition benches. What had been true of the SPD in the 1950s applied to the FDP after 1966. Its congress in 1968 marked not only a change in leadership but also a response to new electoral demands. The new leader, Walter Scheel, was less closely associated than his predecessor, Erich Mende, with the nationalist, socially conservative wing of the party that had its base among the older age groups in Protestant small towns and villages. A number of other figures associated with the radical-democratic wing, such as Hildegard Hamm-Brücher and the sociologist Ralf Dahrendorf, advanced rapidly in the hierarchy. The party adopted a programme of institutional reforms, in particular in justice and education. In foreign affairs it called for the abandonment of the Hallstein doctrine and direct negotiations with the GDR. In its way the internal revolution in the FDP was as important for the development of the party system as the establishment of the CDU as a people's party in the 1950s and the reform of the SPD in the early 1960s. It made possible the construction of an alternative to the twenty-year dominance of the CDU.

As the 1969 election drew near, the attraction of the FDP as a coalition partner for the SPD increased. The SPD's abandonment of electoral reform was one asset in this *rapprochement*; the SPD–FDP *Land* coalitions in North Rhine–Westphalia and, a year later, in Bremen, were a second. But the biggest step came in March 1969, when the presidential electoral college, consisting of all Bundestag members and an equal number representing the *Landtage*, met to elect a successor to President Lübke. The CDU, with 482 college votes, nominated the former Foreign Minister, Gerhard Schröder; the SPD, with 449 votes, Gustav Heinemann. The twenty-two NPD members decided to support Schröder. The decision was therefore in the hands of the FDP. Their vote in favour of Heinemann was the clearest signal yet of the possibility of a realignment. Heinemann himself, the first and so far only SPD nominee to occupy the presidency, called it a partial change of power ('ein Stück Machtwechsel'). The FDP was far from unanimous about the course to take. At least some *Land* organizations were uneasy about the party's leftward trend and there were fierce battles over the composition of candidates' lists for the Bundestag election. A number of *Landtag* deputies switched to the CDU and twelve FDP members of the presidential electoral college, including Erich Mende, refused to vote for Heinemann. It was by no means certain that the FDP vote in the country would hold up.

The FDP proclaimed throughout the election campaign that it was open to all sides. But the closer polling day came, the more obvious it was that the SPD and FDP would prefer a coalition with each other if the parliamentary arithmetic permitted it. As CDU leaders began to hint that they would not contemplate another Great Coalition, SPD leaders reciprocated. The more intensely the coalition partners competed with each other, the less they could keep the issues that separated them out of the campaign. All the questions that had preoccupied the Coalition for months, if not years, were now debated in the open. This was true of the revaluation of the D-Mark, which was supported by the Economy Minister, Karl Schiller, but opposed by the Finance Minister, Franz-Josef Strauß, of *Ostpolitik*, and of the judicial code.

The electors provided for a small but decisive shift. The CDU's vote was virtually unchanged at 46.1 per cent, but the SPD almost closed the gap and was now only 3.4 per cent behind. The FDP survived by the skin of its teeth at 5.8 per cent. The NPD won 4.3 per cent and therefore no seats. Within five days of the result being announced, Brandt and Scheel had agreed on the formation of a left–centre coalition and President Heinemann nominated Willy Brandt for the Chancellorship. Another piece of *Machtwechsel* had happened. And yet it very nearly had not happened. Altogether nearly thirty-three million votes were cast. Had the CDU–CSU gained only 400,000 more votes, it would have achieved an absolute majority. Had the NPD gained only 230,000 more, it would have been entitled to twenty-five seats and a renewed Great Coalition would have been inescapable. Had the FDP gained only 270,000 fewer votes, it, too, would have been excluded from the Bundestag.

The mandate for change, if that is what it was, was a narrow one. The parties that formed the new government had three more seats than in the previous Bundestag, giving them a majority of twelve; the party that moved into opposition had three fewer. A continuation of the Great Coalition would have been perfectly feasible, just as an SPD–FDP coalition would have been (just) possible before 1969. Superficially what happened in 1969 was a switch of coalition partners of the kind that is familiar in multi-party systems. Just as the SPD had replaced the FDP in 1966, so the FDP had now replaced the CDU. The political alternation in 1969 was not complete, because the FRG does not have single-party governments, but it was significant. It reflected a change of political mood, in which an alternation was widely anticipated. For the first time in twenty years almost half the German electorate voted for parties that offered adventure rather than caution. The CDU repeated its hitherto successful strategy with another safety-first slogan ('safely into the Seventies'), which was countered by the SPD's 'seeking new ways'. No election is ever decided by one single issue, but if any predominated in this one it was the question of relations with the East. It was an irony that foreign policy, the midwife of the Great Coalition, had become the grounds for divorce.

The experience of the 1960s underlined the unpredictability of West German politics. Behind the veneer of stability there was a pattern of constant and at times rapid change. Who would have predicted in 1949 that Konrad Adenauer would still be Chancellor ten years later, sitting on an absolute parliamentary majority? Who would have predicted on the day the Berlin Wall was built that at the end of the decade Willy Brandt would be Chancellor with a mandate to normalize relations with the GDR? The change of climate in the FRG in the mid-1960s was sudden, even if not total. A period of consolidation and complacency gave way to a phase of questioning and a search for innovation. A generation preoccupied with repairing the ravages of war yielded to one more conscious of missed opportunities and superannuated taboos. Not all the demands for change were carefully thought out or well considered. Some made for a more open society of wider opportunities, less deference, and a greater range of ideas. Others were naïve, destructive, and nihilistic. Nor did everything change. The bases of the FRG's constitutional order, the market economy and allegiance to the West, remained in place and survived all challenges. But enough of the assumptions and procedures of public life changed between 1965 and 1969 to justify our calling this transition the second foundation of the FRG.

5 The Other Germany

All the great progressive ideas that the German people has
ever produced, the legacy of all struggles for a realm of peace
and social security, of human dignity and fraternity, are being
realized in the German Democratic Republic.

(Theses proclaimed by the Central Committee of the SED
on the twentieth anniversary of the GDR, 24 January 1969)

THE pre-history and development of the GDR were in many respects
a mirror image of those of the FRG. At the end of the war both the
Soviet occupying powers and the politicians closest to them found a
number of options open to them, of which the creation of a separate
East German state was by no means the most obvious or the most
desirable. The victorious but exhausted Soviet Union had two overwhelming priorities at this stage—military security and economic re-
cuperation. How these were to be secured would depend on two
factors not fully under the control of the Soviet leadership—relations
with its former Allies in the West and political opinion in its own
zone. While the four victor powers were agreed on the total disarmament of Germany, it took them some time to evaluate how much they
had to fear from each other. And while they initially regarded the
German population as subjects to be moulded by their will, they
discovered before long that they would need the help of local politicians, and that this help would entail an increasing dependence on
them as well as the need to mobilize the population in support of their
policies.

In May 1945 Stalin knew what he wanted to achieve, but there
is no evidence that he had at that stage a fully worked-out strategy on
how to achieve it. He was convinced that he needed a security perimeter and was determined that this should include Poland, Czechoslovakia, and Hungary, despite the assurances he had given about
respecting democratic processes in those countries. But whether that
perimeter would also include some or all of the two militarily occupied states of Germany and Austria was less clear. A Germany and

Austria wholly within the Soviet sphere would obviously be unacceptable to the Western powers. A demilitarized, neutral Germany or Austria as a guaranteed buffer between emerging blocs might be acceptable to both sides. That is how the Austrian question was solved in 1955. In return for Russian withdrawal the West had to abandon the opportunity of incorporating Austria in its own defence perimeter, even though that 'perpetually neutral' Austria was ideologically and economically firmly affiliated to the West.

In Germany too much was at stake for such a solution to be viable. For Britain and the USA a neutral Germany, as offered more than once by Stalin, looked too much like a vacuum that could be filled from the East. Above all, as we have seen, the economic structures of the Anglo-American and Soviet zones began to diverge so radically that the prospect of a single German political unit became more and more remote. It was at this stage that differences of priority between the Soviet leadership and their German subordinates became crucial. Whatever the final political shape of Germany, the Soviets were determined to maximize their influence in it, and for this they needed trustworthy representatives on the spot. The KPD was the obvious candidate for this role, but, like most Communist parties, it was faction-ridden; from Moscow's point of view the group round Walter Ulbricht in Berlin was the most reliable. But even Ulbricht did not invariably see eye to eye with his masters, at least as far as timing and tactics were concerned. True, in any serious dispute Moscow had the last word. Nothing could happen unless Moscow approved and anything that Moscow decided would in the end be implemented. But the final outcomes were often the result of debate and dispute in which the local knowledge of the KPD—and later the SED—could exercise some influence.

Above all the KPD leadership were conscious of the limited appeal of their party under conditions of free competition. This led them initially to be more cautious than the SMAD in turning the Soviet zone into a 'people's democracy'. The KPD's first proclamation promised 'the completion of the bourgeois-democratic transformation that was begun in 1848' in the form of a democratic parliamentary republic. All other moves in the early years were aimed at compensating for this weakness. These included the forcible fusion of the SPD into the

SED and the creation of various mass organizations, such as the Federation of Free Trade Unions (Freier Deutscher Gewerkschaftsbund (FDGB)), Free German Youth (Freie Deutsche Jugend (FDJ)), and the Democratic Women's League (Demokratischer Frauenbund Deutschlands (DFD)). But once it became clear that the KPD or the SED was unlikely to be successful in free all-German elections, Ulbricht became convinced that the formation of a Socialist state in the Soviet zone was preferable to any demilitarized neutrality for the whole of Germany. In this respect, too, the strategies of East and West were mirror-images. For each of them the division of Germany was a second-best choice. Each intended, once division was unavoidable, that its state would be a shop-window for its favoured political and economic order; each assumed that it would act as a magnet for the discontented population of the other state. Much that might at first sight seem to be purely domestic politics should also be understood as a message aimed directly across the border. In the Soviet zone that was true of the early economic reforms, of later social institutions like the universally available kindergartens or the support given to the arts, and above all of the anti-Fascist rhetoric and the peace propaganda. The same was true, as we have seen, not only of the free elections and the consumer affluence of the FRG, but of the expansion of its welfare state.

In this competition the Soviet zone and the GDR began with some advantages as well as obvious drawbacks. The overwhelming drawback was the association of the KPD with the Soviet occupation forces. The traditional German tendency to regard the Slav peoples as inferior had been reinforced by wartime propaganda, and the overwhelmingly anti-Communist tone of National Socialist ideology had had its effect. The population's worst fears were confirmed at the end of the war, when the arrival of the Soviet army was accompanied by rape and looting on a massive scale. Even after discipline was restored, the Soviet reparations and dismantling policy, however justified it might have been by the damage inflicted by the German occupiers on the USSR, was a further cause of popular hostility. However much the population of the Soviet zone might have welcomed the end of the war and of the Third Reich, most of them did not regard the Red Army as liberators. Against that the KPD and its allies were able to call on some positive factors. The area of the Soviet zone had throughout the twentieth century been a stronghold of the Left, including, in the years before 1933, the KPD. In the last completely free pre-Nazi election, that of November 1932, the Left had won 46 per cent of the vote there, of which 21 per cent had gone to the KPD, well above the national average. The Nazi persecution of German Communists, more severe than that of any other political opponents, enhanced their standing among opponents of Nazism; some SPD members and officials advocated closer collaboration, and a few of them outright organizational unity with the KPD.

At least some of the early economic measures taken by the SMAD were popular. That was true of the land reform that redistributed the Junker estates to peasants and landless farm labourers, of equal pay for women, and even of the nationalization measures that were initially aimed only at the property of Nazi officials and war criminals. The more thoroughgoing de-Nazification, no doubt motivated by the desire to clear the administration for the KPD's own nominees, nevertheless appealed to many who were disillusioned with the laxity of the purges in the Western zones. An impressive number of creative artists and scholars who had been in exile during the Nazi period chose to return to the Soviet zone or the GDR, rather than the West, including the writers Arnold Zweig, Heinrich Mann, Stefan Heym, and Bertolt Brecht, the graphic artist John Heartfield, the composer Hanns Eisler, and the philosopher Ernst Bloch. All of these developments helped the claim of the GDR to represent 'the better Germany'; if this claim did not gain significant sympathy for the GDR among West Germans after 1949, it did manage to dampen or inhibit criticism from those who were unhappy with developments in the West. If in the end the Soviet zone and the GDR lost the propaganda war, it was because these considerable initial advantages were soon subordinated to other ends.

As a division of Germany became more and more likely, the Soviets and the SED leadership had to make two decisions. The first was whether to establish a separate state on the territory of the Soviet zone, the second—if the answer to the first was 'yes'—was what kind of state. On the first question the Soviets soon had little choice. Once the Western Allies had decided on the currency reform, with the concomitant division of Berlin and the preparations for the Parliamentary Council, there was no point in not going ahead with an East German state. What was less obvious was whether it was at this stage in the Soviet interest to turn this state into a 'people's democracy', i.e. a single-party state with a collectivized economy, which is what the SED leadership favoured. For Stalin, tactics were subordinate to strategy and the strategy was to secure the military withdrawal of the USA from Europe, beginning with Germany. When the Berlin Blockade failed in this objective, the need to establish a secure Communist base in Germany became more pressing. This was the context in which the Stalinization of the Soviet zone began in earnest.

The first formal step in this process was the proclamation of the SED as an orthodox Marxist–Leninist party. That development applied not only to its ideology but to its organization. At the head of the party was the Politburo, which exercised power through its apparatus, headed by the Party Secretariat. That made the SED's General Secretary, Walter Ulbricht, the most powerful political figure in the state. Once the GDR was in being, its institutions were adapted to the requirements of absolute political control. Article 6 of the constitution made hate campaigns against the institutions of the republic a punishable offence, a provision that could in time be turned against any form of dissent. In February 1950 a Ministry of State Security (Staatssicherheit (Stasi)) was created on the Soviet model. In December 1951 a further Soviet device was imported, the establishment of a *nomenklatura*, which enabled the state—and through it the party—to control the appointment and promotion of all employees in the public sector, whether administrative or economic. In 1952 the five *Länder* that had been established at the end of the Second World War were abolished; with them the last meaningful units of sub-national political power disappeared. Parties other than the SED continued to exist, though increasingly in the shadow of the state party. Indeed they survived until the collapse of the GDR. They were, however, steadily deprived of an independent role. In 1950 the four bourgeois parties, the CDU, the LDP, and the two later formations, the DBD and the NDPD, together with the SED-dominated mass organizations and the SED itself, were formed into the 'National Front of Democratic Germany'. This National Front presented a single list for the 1950 election to the Volkskammer. In a turn-out of 98 per cent it gained 99.7 per cent of the votes—another assimilation to Soviet practice.

Hand in hand with the political collectivization of the GDR went the economic collectivization, in pursuit of which the 1952 Congress of the SED proclaimed the beginnings of the 'construction of Socialism'. In fact, this process was by then well advanced, although the constitution had guaranteed the rights of property and of freedom of association. As early as 1948 the private sector accounted for only 39 per cent of the gross domestic product. Nevertheless, when the GDR came into being there was still a significant independent bourgeoisie, a factor that would sooner or later prove an obstacle to the creation of a 'people's democracy'. Once the GDR was in being, assimilation to the Soviet model accelerated. The first five-year plan was launched in 1950 and in the same year the GDR became a member of the Council for Mutual Economic Assistance (CMEA, better known as COMECON), the Soviet-sponsored body for co-ordinating the economies of Eastern Europe. By the end of 1951 the public sector already accounted for 79 per cent of industrial production.

The economic reconstruction of the GDR was impressive: by the end of 1952 production stood at 108 per cent of the 1936 level. Compared with the FRG's 143 per cent this did not look too favourable; on the other hand, the GDR had received no Marshall Aid and had suffered far greater dismantling than the Western zones. The rebuilding of the GDR against these odds therefore became a source of considerable pride to its citizens, even of those who had no sympathy with their regime and were fully aware of the way the regime mismanaged its resources. Indeed the principal defect of the GDR's economic development lay in its dependence on Soviet direction. Investment was concentrated on heavy industry, for which the GDR's resources were ill suited, at the expense of consumer goods. Though certain basic services, like housing, public transport, and domestic fuel, were—and remained—heavily subsidized, most consumer items were—and remained—scarce, expensive, and of poor quality. Moreover, the targets in the Five-Year Plan were unrealistic, so that the regime found itself obliged to resort to more and more authoritarian methods. The only short-term solution to the economic shortcomings was to raise the working norms, i.e. to make people work more for the same pay. It was this decision that created the first major crisis for the regime, a challenge to its legitimacy from which it never fully recovered—the workers' uprising of 17 June 1953.

Like many of the crucial events in both the German states, it had an international as well as a local context. The external impulse was the death of Stalin on 5 March. His successors, led by Georgi Malenkov as General Secretary of the Communist Party of the Soviet Union (CPSU), were inclined towards a more moderate and less terror-reliant set of policies, which reopened the always latent conflict between the hard-line Ulbricht and the Soviet leadership. Above all, the change of guard in Moscow encouraged Ulbricht's opponents in the SED to press for economic concessions to the population. The 'new course' announced on 11 June went some way towards these, but the raised norms were not rescinded. On 17 June the building workers in the new prestige boulevard of East Berlin, the Stalinallee, went on strike and were rapidly followed by similar actions in over 250 localities, involving more than 300,000 workers. More significantly, the strikers' demands quickly escalated to include free elections: what had begun as a protest against working conditions developed into a rebellion against the state. Whether the rising would have developed into a full-scale revolution if it had been allowed to run its course is impossible to say. Given the political overtones of the strike movement, the Soviet authorities decided on swift repression; tanks moved in and by 19 June the rising was over. It was the first workers' uprising against self-proclaimed workers' states in Eastern Europe, but not the last: Poland, Hungary, and Czechoslovakia were to follow.

Little as the new Soviet leadership loved Ulbricht and much as it sympathized with his opponents in the party, it could not allow him to be overthrown by popular pressure. The immediate impact of 17 June, therefore, was a mixture of economic relaxation and political repression. The 'new course' was confirmed. Prices of a wide range of goods were lowered and more resources were made available for consumer goods, measures that were helped by the ending of Soviet demands for reparations. Ulbricht's opponents were purged from the Central Committee of the SED and large numbers of subordinate officials were dismissed. Harsh prison sentences and seven death sentences were imposed on the leaders of the rising. Moreover, once

Ulbricht's control was reasserted, the 'new course' was abandoned. The second Five-Year Plan, announced in 1955, once more favoured heavy industry.

The events of 17 June and their aftermath illustrated a number of dilemmas inherent in the structure of the GDR, which the leadership was never able to resolve. The highest priority of the regime was the maintenance of power, if necessary by the use of force. Repressive measures against the minority of active opponents caused no compunction. However, the humiliation of needing to hold down the whole of the population by military means, and especially by the military means of a foreign power, was, if at all possible, to be avoided. In the search for greater legitimacy, or at least more secure authority, the regime had a number of choices, all of which it pursued at one time or another. Some of them yielded limited success, others did not, though, as the ultimate collapse of the GDR showed, the fundamental problems proved to be insoluble.

The main choices before the regime were economic, ideological, and diplomatic, with considerable overlaps between them. The economic choices were, on the one hand, between the continued emphasis on heavy industry and the satisfaction of consumer demands, and, on the other hand, between centralized planning and a diffusion of managerial responsibility. The privileged position of heavy industry reflected the lack of such an industrial base in the area of the GDR which, before 1945, had concentrated on the manufacture of finished products. But it also reflected the leadership's antiquated notion of what constituted economic progress. Above all, it reflected the requirements of the CMEA, compliance with which would strengthen the GDR's bargaining hand within the Soviet bloc. This meant that, in the absence of an effective price mechanism or of reliable cost accounting, those responsible for planning the economy had no means of discovering the true structure of demand. The fact that most of the GDR's foreign trade was with the less developed economies of the CMEA also meant that the GDR economy was shielded from the discipline of the world market. Of this the regime was well aware: the trouble was that all exits from this undesirable situation had political drawbacks. To tolerate a significant private sector that might respond to market signals would not only mean conceding that the principle of central planning was defective; worse, it would entail cultivating a class that was potentially hostile to the state. The GDR was to be the first German Workers' and Peasants' State. There was no place in it for a petty bourgeoisie. An alternative palliative for the inflexibilities of central planning was a decentralized public sector, with higher managerial autonomy at the plant or industry level. But this, too, had its risks. It could lead to the emergence of a technocratic class with assumptions and priorities different from those of the Politburo. The purpose of centralized planning was not merely to ensure maximum economic advantage, but also to ensure political control over the economic process. Managerial pluralism would necessarily undermine the achievement of this aim.

In determining the role of ideology in the consolidation of the state the regime faced similar problems. The generation of KPD veterans who dominated the SED in the early years of the GDR were convinced Marxist–Leninists. They had memories of the political struggles of the Weimar Republic, and under the Third Reich they had suffered at best exile, at worst imprisonment and torture. The establishment of the GDR they regarded as the culmination of their anti-Fascist struggle and the institutional expression of the German revolutionary tradition. Those of the SED's leaders who came from the SPD and who were not purged in the early 1950s could at least take comfort in shared Marxist values even if they had misgivings about the dictatorial methods. The regime could also at this stage count on the loyalty of those party members and citizens who were conscious of the region's left-wing traditions or who found the GDR, warts and all, preferable to an FRG in which capitalism had been restored and the Third Reich swept under the carpet. The trouble was that these sources of support were not enough to sustain the regime. The GDR had one fatal birth defect: the power its rulers exercised was illegitimate. Therefore, when the 17 June rising demonstrated the lack of legitimacy, no easy answer suggested itself. Repression removed the symptom, but did not cure the disease. A campaign of consciousness-raising followed, with more careful recruitment to the party and its cadres and with intensified indoctrination. But there was no guarantee that this would make the legitimacy deficit go away. That left a further option to be pursued—namely, a downgrading of ideology. Instead, the regime would concentrate on a modestly satisfactory standard of living, with job security and subsidized essentials, what Hungarians later termed 'goulash Socialism', in the hope that the population would then forget that they were living in a state in which they did not really want to live. If acclamation was not available, then the absence of rejection would do.

In this search for minimum levels of acceptance, foreign policy played a role. The regime could claim to stand for peace and *détente*, insisting that it was the West that had initiated the division of Germany and escalated the arms race. It could also claim to stand for reconciliation with Germany's Eastern neighbours by recognizing the Oder–Neiße frontier with Poland. The second of these propositions gained a better hearing than the first. Most East Germans, even those who were refugees from further East, became reconciled to the post-1945 frontiers. After unification they were surprised to find that in the FRG the German–Polish frontier was still an issue. The peace propaganda had a less certain impact. East Germans were aware of the growing militarization of their own state, even before the creation of the National People's Army (Nationale Volksarmee (NVA)) in 1956. The most this line of argument could achieve was to create an indifferent neutrality in the minds of East German citizens, in which both sides were held equally to blame for the competitive rearmament.

The biggest difficulty that the regime faced in this respect was posed by the question of German unity. Officially the GDR remained committed to this objective, though it evaded the response that Western negotiators invariably made to its offers—namely, the insistence on free all-German elections. The more the social systems of the two Germanies diverged, the more the GDR turned into a people's democracy in economic as well as political structure, the more difficult it became to envisage a basis on which the two states might be amalgamated. Nikita Khrushchev, by now First Secretary of the CPSU, underlined this difficulty in 1955 when he declared that German unification would be possible only if the Socialist achievements of the GDR were preserved. Soviet recognition of the GDR as a sovereign state in that year, the GDR's membership of the Warsaw Pact, and the establishment of diplomatic relations between Moscow and the FRG confirmed that the 'two–states theory' of the German Question was now official Soviet policy.

The different variants of economic, ideological, and diplomatic options were all tried at different times after the crushing of the 1953 rising, with varying success. For these purposes it is simplest to divide the political development of the GDR into three phases: (i) from 1953 to the building of the Berlin Wall in 1961, (ii) from 1961 to the removal of Walter Ulbricht from the First Secretaryship of the SED in 1971, and (iii) the period of Ulbricht's successor, Erich Honecker.

The first period was marked by the completion of the transformation of the GDR into a people's democracy. The wind of change blowing from Moscow left Ulbricht unimpressed. For the Soviet Union's satellite states, and in particular for his own, he saw nothing but trouble in the process of de-Stalinization. His worst fears were confirmed by the strikes in Poland and the Hungarian uprising that followed Khrushchev's denunciation of Stalin at the XX Congress of the CPSU in February 1956. However, the failure to reform after 1953 did not remove all challenges to the regime. While working-class opposition was partly cowed and partly bought off, intellectual dissent grew; it thereby illustrated the ambiguous role of the official ideology in integrating those whom it most counted on for support. The dissenters, too, considered themselves Socialists and Marxists; their quarrel was with the regime's interpretation of its proclaimed ideals. The manifesto of the group round the philosopher Wolfgang Harich insisted, 'We want to remain in the position of Marxism–Leninism. But we want to get away from Stalinism . . . in a reunited Germany there must not be a restoration of capitalism.' The Harich group were arrested in 1957 and sentenced to long terms of imprisonment. Other dissenters, most notably the philosopher Ernst Bloch, decided to emigrate to the FRG. Others still, like the physicist Robert Havemann, continued to be tolerated, only to be disciplined later. Opposition within the party leadership was dealt with equally ruthlessly. Those in the Central Committee round Karl Schirdewan who favoured a less hard-line policy were purged in 1958, though they remained free to pursue non-political administrative tasks.

With industry and trade largely in the hands of the state, what remained to ensure complete political control of the economy was the collectivization of agriculture and artisan businesses. The land reform undertaken by the Soviets had created half a million peasant proprietors, and of all the economic measures taken in this part of Germany that was the one that was most positively received. The agricultural collectives (Landwirtschaftliche Produktionsgenossenschaften (LPGs)) set up in 1952 were initially voluntary and those peasants with the least viable holdings were content to join them. From 1959 onwards, however, the pressures on peasants to join the LPGs intensified, often in the form of physical coercion or arrests. Most peasants had little choice but to bow to these pressures; by 1961 90 per cent of agricultural production was collectivized. But there was a price to be paid for this campaign to change the social structure of the GDR. Following the rise in living standards, symbolized by the end of all food rationing in 1958, the number of refugees to the West had fallen steadily, from 279,189 in 1956 to 143,917 in 1959. After that the decline in the growth rates of the economy, which led to the abandonment of the second Five-Year Plan, as well as the collectivization measures, reversed the trend, and with the escalation of the Berlin crisis in 1961 the trend became a flood. Its culmination, as we saw in Chapter 3, was the building of the Berlin Wall.

The building of the Wall, for all the obloquy that it brought, gave the regime a breathing space, but also faced it with new obligations. With the construction of a 'Socialist society' and a single-party state largely complete, the regime now had to concentrate on the practical problem of raising living standards. In that respect the turn of the decade would have marked a caesura in the development of the GDR even without the building of the Wall. But while the Wall presented the regime with a captive population, it also removed the safety valve of emigration. If another 17 June were to be avoided, the regime would have to offer both material and political benefits. At first the opposite happened; following the building of the Wall there was a new wave of repression, accompanied by the introduction of military conscription. The Wall, originally restricted to Berlin, was extended to cover the whole length of the GDR's frontier, with a mined 'death strip' as a glacis. Guards had shoot-to-kill orders. Between 1961 and 1989 over six hundred East Germans met their deaths while trying to escape from the GDR. However, the progressive de-Stalinization of the USSR under Khrushchev meant that the GDR could not drag its feet indefinitely. If the Soviet economist Yevsei Liberman could insist that profitability was the only valid test of productivity and the works of Solzhenitsyn could be openly on sale in Moscow, as was the case in the early 1960s, it was difficult for the GDR to resist similar liberalization. Certainly greater variety in literary production came to be tolerated; critical works like Christa Wolf's *Der geteilte Himmel* and Stefan Heym's *Die Papiere des Andreas Lenz* appeared, and more Western authors became available. But the most important change was in the methods of economic management.

The New Economic System announced in June 1963 was made possible by the security provided by the Wall, but it was also the outcome of the social changes of the previous fifteen years. If the regime were to abandon terror as a primary means of control, it needed to replace it with the political neutralization of the population and the satisfaction of its material needs. But material demands, too, were undergoing change. As the anti-Fascist idealism of the founding years faded and the phase of basic reconstruction ended, individual citizens wanted greater private satisfactions, whether for careers, possessions, or leisure. A major change in the social structure had been the growth of educational opportunities and the emergence of a new intelligentsia, which, on the one hand, was wooed by the regime and, on the other hand, demanded a less marginal status in decision-making. A society of this type is not so easily governed by primitive coercion.

The New Economic System was associated with two members of the Central Committee, Erich Apel and Günter Mittag. Apel was an engineer by training, rather than a typical career apparatchik, which was in itself significant. The new system was based on greater autonomy for individual enterprises, whether in borrowing for investment, procurement, or targeting of customers, as well as a more refined incentive structure in prices, profits, wages, and bonuses. The economic benefits of these reforms were undeniable. As productivity grew, so did private affluence. Ordinary East Germans were rewarded with more consumer durables and a shorter working week. But the political risks were equally undeniable. When Apel and Mittag called for decision-making on the basis of 'a high degree of expert knowledge' as opposed to 'arbitrary directives . . . [and] excessive frequency of further corrective measures' they were challenging one of the essential premises of SED rule—the party's claim to a monopoly of information and wisdom. The same challenge was implied by the

greater literary freedom. What emerged was a battle between claim-
ants for influence on the future shape of the GDR—between what
one scholar has termed the 'strategic clique' (i.e. the party leadership)
and the 'institutionalized counter-élite'. The strategic clique's dilemma
was that it willed the counter-élite's ends but could not tolerate its
means. It wished to incorporate the population into the system, which
entailed a more depoliticized approach, but it could not face abandon-
ing the *raison d'être* of its power, the claim to ideological control. It
was, therefore, not long before the strategic clique counter-attacked,
encouraged by the fall of Khrushchev in Moscow in 1964 and his
replacement by the less reform-minded Leonid Brezhnev. The second
phase of the New Economic System, introduced in 1965, was distinctly less liberal than the first. A new trade treaty with the USSR in
1965 tied the GDR's foreign trade more firmly than before to the
East, quite contrary to the intentions of the economic liberalizers. On
the day that the treaty was signed Apel committed suicide.

The economic counter-attack went hand in hand with a cultural
one. At the end of 1965 Erich Honecker, by now regarded as Ulbricht's
heir apparent, delivered a strong attack on unorthodox writers and
thinkers, singling out the song-writer Wolf Biermann, the novelist
Stefan Heym, and the scientist Robert Havemann. Indeed Havemann,
who had avoided overt persecution in the 1950s, had already been
dismissed the year before from his teaching post at the Humboldt
University and expelled from the party. Yet the strategic clique's
counter-offensive could not achieve complete success. Too much had
changed in East German society and the expectations of the population,
and these changes were reflected in the leadership composition of the
party. In 1963 40 per cent of Central Committee members and candidates were graduates, compared with 30 per cent in 1953. The number
of those recruited from technical occupations quadrupled over the
same ten-year period. Half the new members in 1963 had joined the
KPD or SED in 1945 or later; their political experience excluded the
earlier periods of struggle. Slowly but inexorably the new educated,
technocratic middle class was taking over control of the party. Indeed,
in many ways this intelligentsia became the regime's favoured and
most loyal stratum in society, as is shown by the membership and
electoral following of the SED's successor, the Party of Democratic

Socialism, in the 1990s. Those not in this privileged position continued their withdrawal into private, a-political life. The GDR developed a *Nischengesellschaft*, a society of nooks and recesses, in which its citizens concentrated on family, friends, and hobbies. Social solidarity was devoted not to the pursuit of the officially proclaimed utopia, but to mutual help in overcoming or circumventing the frustrations imposed by an over-zealous state or administered shortages.

The economic progress of the 1960s and the more relaxed regime in Moscow meant that the GDR was no longer a pure colony. Its economy was the second largest in the CMEA and its exposed strategic position meant that the Soviet Union needed it as much as the other way round. Within the limitations of the Soviet bloc the GDR had become a state in its own right which was slowly developing its own foreign relations. Ulbricht's state visit to Egypt in 1965, a state visit by President Tito of Yugoslavia in the same year, and a trickle of diplomatic recognitions, mainly from the Third World, were encouraging signs of this. But the main foreign-policy preoccupation remained relations with the other German state. The retirement of Adenauer, the first signs of a more open-minded assessment of relations with the East by Erhard's Foreign Minister, Gerhard Schröder, and finally the appointment of Willy Brandt as Foreign Minister in the Great Coalition were all signs that the GDR might begin to emerge from its isolation. But no one was quicker than Ulbricht to recognize that such a process brought its dangers and to appreciate the subversive potential of Egon Bahr's formula of 'change through *rapprochement*'. The more friendly the noises of West German politicians became, the more strongly they hinted at recognition of the GDR, the more urgent it became to insulate the population against the blandishments of the West. Delimitation (*Abgrenzung*) was the best defence against the ill effects of *détente*. The first major signs of this new approach came in 1968, with the adoption of a new criminal code and a new constitution. In dealing with ordinary crimes the new code reflected the more humane assumptions of the 1960s, compared with earlier periods. In dealing with political offences, 'especially assaults on peace, on the sovereignty of the German Democratic Republic and on the Workers' and Peasants' State', it remained unrelievedly harsh, retaining for extreme cases the death penalty, though this was never imposed in the remaining twenty-two years of the GDR. The true significance of the new code, however, lay in the breach of German legal unity. There were now not only two states, but two legal systems. The new constitution equally confirmed the two-state theory of inter-German relations. 'The German Democratic Republic is a Socialist state of the German nation,' it stated. 'The economy of the German Democratic Republic rests on the Socialist ownership of the means of production.'

The election of the Brandt–Scheel government in the FRG raised both the hopes and the fears of the GDR regime—hopes for steps towards full recognition, fears for the consequences of more intimate contacts. Nor was the regime master of its timetable, since pressure from the Soviet Union to take advantage of the opportunities for *détente* now intensified. Brandt had taken an initiative by offering unconditional negotiations to Poland soon after becoming Chancellor, which culminated in diplomatic recognition at the end of 1970. Even more importantly West German–Soviet negotiations began in Moscow early in 1970. Talks among the victor powers resulted in the Four-Power Agreement on the status of Berlin of September 1971 (discussed in detail in the next chapter). Ulbricht viewed all these developments with deep suspicion, so much so that Moscow decided that the time had come to depose him. In May 1971, then aged nearly 78, he was succeeded by Erich Honecker as First Secretary of the SED. By then bilateral negotiations between the two German states were well under way, though in a way that confirmed the GDR leadership's fears as well as its hopes. An official visit by Brandt to Erfurt in Eastern Germany in March 1970 was certainly a triumph for the GDR's attempts to secure treatment as an equal. But the crowds that welcomed the West German Chancellor with chants of 'Willy, Willy' showed only too clearly where the true political allegiance of the GDR population lay. In terms of the GDR's inter-German agenda, the negotiations that followed were a complete success. In the Basic Treaty signed on 12 December 1972 the two German states recognized each other's sovereignty; in September 1973 the two states were admitted to membership of the United Nations. The Hallstein doctrine was dead and the GDR could now pursue normal relations with all states—including, in 1974, the USA.

None of these momentous developments, however satisfactory in foreign-policy terms, solved the GDR's continuing domestic difficulties. External recognition did nothing to legitimize the state in the eyes of the population. Indeed, reinforcements of the delimitation policy probably had the opposite effect. In the amended constitution of 1974 all reference to the German nation disappeared. The GDR was simply defined as 'a Socialist state of workers and peasants'. The 1976 programme of the SED similarly omitted the commitment of the 1963 programme to 'overcoming the division of the German nation brought about by German and foreign imperialists'. Yet the various treaties and agreements of 1971–2 made the Iron Curtain more, not less porous. Communications between the two Germanies revived. Telephone links between East and West Berlin, severed at the time that the Wall was built, were restored. Family visits to the GDR multiplied until by 1980 there were two million of these per year. Even the taboo on viewing West German television was gradually lifted, so that by the 1980s the vast majority of the population 'emigrated' every evening to watch the news programmes from the other side, and those remote areas that failed to receive them were considered disadvantaged. Though the GDR was now among the top ten industrial states in the world and had the highest living standards of the Soviet bloc, the gap between it and the FRG was widening, not narrowing; the new opportunities for contact merely made this ever more evident. In the post-recognition GDR, squaring the circle of control and participation was more difficult than ever. Some significant concessions were made to particular groups. There was more attention to women's rights, in particular by the legalization of abortion on demand in 1972, and to the claims of youth and the churches by the institution of an alternative non-military form of national service. But discontent increased rather than diminished in the course of the 1970s, as memories of the heroic reconstruction period dimmed and the continuing hardships of everyday life were resented more strongly. To combat the discontent, Honecker reverted to his earlier instincts of tighter thought-control and found a scapegoat in dissident writers and artists. In 1976 Wolf Biermann was deprived of his citizenship while on a tour of the FRG; he was followed the next year by some of the most prominent East German writers, including Reiner Kunze and Jurek Becker. Others, like Günter Kunert and Rolf Schneider, left of their own accord, while those who stayed, like Stefan Heym, were subjected to greater restrictions. Rudolf Bahro's democratic Socialist manifesto *Die Alternative* could be published only in the FRG, a crime for which the author was sentenced to eight years, commuted a year later by the permission to emigrate. In the light of these repressive measures it proved to be a liability that the GDR had been a signatory of the 1975 Helsinki Final Act of the Conference on Security and Co-operation in Europe (CSCE) and even more so that the regime had published the text of the agreement in the press. The attraction of this agreement was that it was a further international legitimation of the GDR and, with its emphasis on the inviolability of frontiers, a guarantee of the post-1945 geography of Europe. That the Final Act also guaranteed the human rights of all citizens of the signatory states seemed only a minor disadvantage: one more empty gesture in this direction could make little difference in the eyes of the GDR regime. It did make a difference, however, and Helsinki monitoring committees became a focus of dissent as time went on.

The GDR embarked on the 1980s—the last decade of its existence, as it turned out—in the same uneasy stability that had characterized it since the building of the Wall. By now a recognized member of the international community, it was still tied to the Soviet Union by treaty, trade patterns, and geopolitical reality. The various attempts at economic reform had failed to satisfy the population, though the GDR was exempt from the acute discontent that was to be found, for instance, in Poland. The SED's repeated claims to an unchallengeable leadership role, and the effective crushing of any dissent within the SED, prevented the emergence of a counter-élite and thus made any significant opening of the political system impossible. When the GDR finally collapsed in the autumn of 1989, it was easy enough to point to all the systemic weaknesses we have mentioned as an explanation. In 1980 virtually nobody forecast or expected such a collapse.

6 *Ostpolitik*

> That the path of the German nation parted, that it could no
> longer be followed in the form of a united state, may be felt
> as tragic by some, by many—we cannot act as if it has not
> happened.
>
> (Willy Brandt, Erfurt, 19 March 1970)

THE 1960s were the decade of the FRG's adolescence, when many of
the assumptions on which it was founded were questioned. The 1970s
were the decade of its maturity, when it ceased to be a provisional
state and when those who led it were increasingly men and women
who had entered politics after 1945. The theory of provisionality
remained. The constitution was still called the Basic Law and the
aspiration to re-unification remained in its preamble. But by the time
Willy Brandt became Chancellor the FRG had outlasted both the
Weimar Republic and the French Fourth Republic. While some observers inside and outside Germany were worried about its stability,
few doubted that it had come to stay. And, precisely because it had so
obviously come to stay, the FRG's new rulers were convinced that the
time had come to rethink their state's domestic order and foreign
relations.

As always, these reassessments did not begin overnight and
many of the impulses came from outside Germany. Student radicalism may have had more lasting effects in the FRG than elsewhere, but
it was no more widespread or violent than in the USA, France, or
Italy. The younger generation in the USA had the Vietnam War, in
which they might be personally involved, as a direct incentive to
rebel. In France the revolt of 1968, which coincided—as it did not in
the FRG—with working-class militancy and a general strike, threatened the survival of de Gaulle's presidency and, indeed, the state.
The use of '1968' as shorthand for the climax for the New Left's
challenge to established authority is more properly applied to France
than to the FRG, where there was no single apogee on this scale.
True, 1968 was the year in which the Emergency Laws were passed

and in which the attempt on Rudi Dutschke's life took place, but in its application to the FRG it is still more of a metaphor than an exact description.

The same factors apply to the much more momentous changes in German foreign policy: the assumption of direct relations with the states of the Communist East, in particular the GDR, and a reorientation towards Eastern neighbours that went by the name of *Ostpolitik*. The framework of this was the general development of *détente*, of which the FRG was both an initiator and the chief beneficiary. *Détente* was the child of the nuclear stalemate between the superpowers and of the gradual stabilization of their strategic spheres, at any rate in Europe. With the building of the Berlin Wall, the demarcation between the blocs was complete and Berlin gradually ceased to be the occasion of crises. The rest of Western Europe was secure under the American nuclear umbrella. The Soviet rulers had more to fear from their own populations than from NATO; therefore, once the GDR was sealed off and Czechoslovak dissidence crushed, they, too, could afford to relax. Moreover, there was at least some linkage between conflicts outside Europe and the European strategic climate. The peaceful resolution of the Cuban missile crisis in 1962 helped both the US and the Soviet administrations to return to the slow unfreezing of the Cold War that had hesitantly begun after the death of Stalin. Conflicts elsewhere had little effect on developments in Europe. Both sides were determined to keep the Vietnam War a side-show and the surrogate wars that the superpowers fought in the Middle East remained equally insulated. The global climate was, therefore, favourable to an easing of tension along the European front line, if that was what the European participants wished to bring about.

By 1969 that is precisely what enough of them did want. As is usual in such cases, they did so from motives that were complementary, but far from identical. As far as the FRG is concerned, its initiatives between 1969 and 1972 are a perfect illustration of the delicate combination of dependence and autonomy, of supra-national integration and semi-sovereignty that characterized the FRG from the day of its foundation. Above all, these initiatives emphasized once more the centrality of foreign policy to the politics of the FRG and the extent to which it thereby became not only the object of other states' decisions, but also the possessor of unique opportunities. For the Western Allies, the creation of the FRG was a foreign-policy decision; for the West German politicians who participated in it, it was proof of their dependence on the foreign-policy decisions of others and of the price to be paid for security. From then on the FRG's statesmen had to pursue twin objectives: as much security as necessary, as much autonomy as possible. The outstanding master of this two-track strategy was Adenauer, who understood from an early stage that by maximizing his usefulness—indeed his indispensability—to his Western patrons he could also maximize his freedom of action. This formula applied above all to a policy area necessarily closer to his concerns than to any of his diplomatic partners or allies: *Deutschlandpolitik*—that is to say, the whole complex of questions concerned with the future of a divided Germany.

Deutschlandpolitik consisted of multiple options. It could involve hard-line anti-Communism in order to isolate the GDR and force the Soviets into concessions. It could involve playing for time, on the assumption that sooner or later the inherent weaknesses of the Communist system would deliver it into the hands of the West. It could also involve a set of temptations and offers to either the GDR or Moscow, in the hope that one or both would settle for the status quo on the West's rather than their own terms. Above all, *Deutschlandpolitik* contained the potential of a double game. The FRG's security needs, as well as its credibility as a reliable partner, demanded loyalty to the Western alliance. *Deutschlandpolitik* demanded, above all, loyalty to the special relationship with Washington. But it also demanded an open line to Moscow, for without Moscow there could be no movement in the German question.

Within the limits imposed by an alliance with the West, Adenauer was quite prepared to define his own priorities. More than once that meant a more confrontational line towards Moscow than that preferred by Washington or London. That was true, as we saw, in 1952, when, in contrast with Churchill, Adenauer rejected Stalin's offer of neutrality; it was true again at the height of the Berlin crisis in 1958–60, when he preferred unconditional French support to the more flexible attitude of the USA. On the other hand, Adenauer never rejected the idea of a dialogue with Moscow, if only because he saw little point in a dialogue with the GDR. Why talk to the monkey when there is an organ-grinder? He showed this by personally travelling to Moscow in October 1955 in order to open diplomatic relations with the Soviet Union. There was a specifically German element to these negotiations: to secure the return of the remaining prisoners-of-war in Soviet hands. But there was a broader purpose, too. It was to make sure that there could be no repetition of the 1945 Potsdam conference, when others had determined the fate of Germany. Formal relations with the Soviet Union were a piece of pre-emptive diplomacy, a declaration that the FRG needed to have a foot in the East as well as the West, however little the East might be willing to offer for the time being.

At this stage no one used the term 'Ostpolitik' to describe this opening to the East, if only because before 1945 the word had had expansionist connotations. There is nevertheless a case for saying that West German *Ostpolitik* began on the day on which Adenauer visited Moscow, although the term itself is irrevocably associated with Willy Brandt's Chancellorship. The maturing of Brandt's concept of *Ostpolitik* also stretched over many years and cannot be separated from his nine-year term as Governing Mayor of West Berlin (1957–66). He had to bear the brunt of the crisis that followed the building of the Wall. Like Adenauer, he was dismayed at the feebleness of the Anglo-American reaction, but drew the opposite conclusion from it. He concluded firstly that the time had come for West German initiatives and secondly that these should be directed at the GDR as well as its Soviet masters. The first small step in this direction—and small steps were, as he himself repeatedly stressed, an essential part of his strategy—came with the 1963 agreement to permit family reunions across the Wall over the Christmas and New Year holiday. Parallel tentative steps were being taken, as we have seen, by Erhard's CDU Foreign Minister, Gerhard Schröder, and bigger steps once the Great Coalition was in place. What we saw between 1966 and 1969 was proto-*Ostpolitik*, with both the SPD and CDU thinking aloud and testing the water. However, given the differences between the partners of the Great Coalition, concrete steps had to wait until there was a change of government.

Both the Soviet Union and its satellites, including the GDR, also had an interest in a revised West German attitude towards them. The common feature of their expectations of the West was a final and unconditional recognition of the post-1945 geography of East–Central Europe. For Poland that meant acceptance of the Oder–Neiße frontier, which only France among the Western Allies had so far recognized. For Czechoslovakia that meant final West German repudiation of the 1938 Munich agreement that had reduced Czechoslovakia to an indefensible rump. For the GDR that meant recognition as a sovereign state on an equal footing with the FRG. For the entire Communist bloc it meant the end of the Hallstein doctrine, which, by insisting that the FRG was the only legitimate German state, gravely inhibited the foreign relations of those states that recognized the GDR. As long as both sides clung to their irreconcilable positions, no progress was possible. A number of conditions needed to be satisfied before movement could begin. The first was the passage of time, which would convince both sides that their maximum programme was no longer achievable. The fraying of the Hallstein doctrine that we observed in Chapter 4 was one symptom of this. The second was the realization on both sides that they had more to gain than to lose from *détente*. The third was that there should be agreement among each of the superpowers and their respective allies on the steps to be taken. This was more critical on the Western side, where there was a greater degree of equality between the partners of the alliance, but even within the Soviet bloc some differences of interest existed, particularly between the Soviet Union and the GDR as long as Ulbricht was in charge.

The Brandt–Scheel government, therefore, certainly benefited from its electoral mandate and it took the decisive initiatives. But in other respects its existence was as much a symptom as a cause of the changed world environment. It benefited from the slow thaw of the 1960s, from the greater self-confidence of the Soviet Union, and, above all, from a US administration also committed to *détente*, even if it defined *détente* slightly differently, given its Asian as well as its European priorities. It could not have acted as it did against a US veto or a stone-walling Soviet Union, but neither could it afford to stand still while the superpowers were moving towards each other. Brandt and Scheel therefore had the good fortune to inherit a window of opportunity, but it is to their credit that they took advantage of it. Moreover, the timing and the directions in which they took advantage of it underscored the degree to which West German policy-makers now had discretion in these matters and the extent to which they could expand that discretion.

Brandt's timetable revealed not only the order of importance that he attached to the FRG's Eastern neighbours, but also the ascending order of difficulty that he foresaw in the various negotiations: Moscow first, Warsaw second, East Berlin third. Putting Moscow first recognized, as Adenauer had done fourteen years earlier, that Moscow held the key to any *Ostpolitik*. If the negotiations with Moscow were successful, the others would, with luck, run smoothly; if not, there was little point in trying anything else. The negotiations in Moscow took up the first half of 1970. At this stage of *Ostpolitik* the FRG needed to make opening concessions in the hope of reaping benefits later. Even before the Moscow talks had begun, the FRG had reassured the Soviet side by signing the Nuclear Non-Proliferation Treaty. Early in 1970 it signed an agreement to supply pipelines that would enable the Soviet Union to export natural gas to Western Europe, a step that involved some risks, since it provoked the disapproval of the USA. But the most difficult part of the negotiations was semantic. What exactly was it that each side was to promise the other? The Soviets wanted nothing less than unqualified recognition of their empire in Eastern Europe. The West Germans wanted to avoid any final settlement short of a comprehensive peace treaty and to maintain their commitment to German re-unification, however remote that prospect might now be. Above all, they had to bear in mind that it was not they, but the four victor powers, three of whom were their allies, that could dispose of the future of Germany. In the battle over words they managed to reduce 'unalterable' frontiers to 'inviolable' and to accept the GDR as an equal partner in German–German relations without according it the status of a sovereign foreign state. To underline the last point the German team handed the Soviets a 'Letter on German Unity' that reiterated the German people's claim to 'unity in free self-determination'.

The Moscow Treaty, signed on 12 August 1970, formed the basis of the other Eastern treaties that followed in the next three years.

It went a long way to recognizing the Soviet Union as the guardian of the political order in Eastern Europe, a step that accorded with West German strategy, but did not please the Soviet Union's satellites: the first stage of the FRG's guarantees to Poland and the GDR were contained in a treaty with Moscow, not in treaties with them. The Moscow Treaty made sense only if it were to be followed by bilateral agreements with the FRG's immediate Eastern neighbours and if these were supplemented by guarantees by the Western Allies of the FRG's legitimate claims on the East. It is true, as Brandt himself pointed out, that he had given away nothing in Moscow that was not already lost. But there was West German public opinion to consider, not to mention Polish and Czech pride.

In fact, the Moscow negotiations, though a necessary start, were part of a much more extensive linkage. Less than four months after the Moscow Treaty an agreement was signed in Warsaw between the FRG and Poland. It repeated the West German guarantee of the Oder–Neiße frontier, though still subject to final confirmation in a peace treaty. In the event, that final confirmation did not come until after German unification. The very fact that a treaty between the FRG and Poland dealt with the frontier between Poland and the GDR was a tacit recognition that the FRG was a legitimate spokesman for all Germans. In other respects the FRG got less than it hoped for. It wanted freedom of emigration for the remaining ethnic Germans in the Polish Western (formerly German) provinces. In the following five years some 60,000 of the applicants got exit permits. Though there was, and is, no unanimity about the number of ethnic Germans in Poland, the 60,000 were only a fraction of those entitled. Only in 1975 was there a settlement of the emigration question in the framework of the Helsinki Final Act. Brandt's successor, Helmut Schmidt, secured exit permits for 125,000 ethnic Germans in return for a DM 1.3 billion contribution towards pensions for Polish war victims. Relations between the two states were more delicate than those with any other neighbours, weighed down by ineradicable resentments on both sides. Poles remembered the unprovoked German aggression that unleashed the Second World War, the unparalleled brutality of the German occupation, and the deportations of slave labour; Germans remembered the seizure of territory in 1945 and the expulsion, under inhuman conditions, of its population. If Brandt's visit to Warsaw is now remembered for anything, it is for his spontaneous act of kneeling at the site of the Jewish Ghetto. It had, strictly speaking, nothing to do with German–Polish reconciliation, but it had everything to do with holding out an olive-branch to former victims.

The *quid pro quo* for the West German approaches to Moscow and Warsaw was the Four-Power Agreement on Berlin of September 1971. Here the Soviet concessions were greater than those of the West. On the one hand, the Soviets secured confirmation that West Berlin, though economically integrated with the FRG, was not a part of it, and that sittings of the FRG's parliament or the presidential electoral college would no longer take place there. On the other hand, they accepted that the FRG might act as West Berlin's diplomatic representative. More importantly, they agreed to unhindered civilian traffic between the FRG and West Berlin.

The Berlin Agreement was important in a number of ways, not just in its substance. It demonstrated the significance of Berlin in Great Power relations and as an earnest of Soviet goodwill: with the 1971 agreement Berlin ceased to be a Cold War flashpoint. It demonstrated the leverage the FRG government had on Western and Soviet policy, for Brandt had made it clear that without a Berlin deal the Moscow and Warsaw treaties would not pass the West German domestic political test. Berlin showed how far the politics of Germany had moved from Potsdam, when the victors could decide all and Germans nothing. Finally it demonstrated the interdependence of Great Power and German politics. *Détente* made the progress it did because both sides wanted it and needed it. It could operate in a number of arenas—in South-East Asia, in the Middle East, or in arms limitations. But unless it also operated in Germany, by removing the German and Berlin questions from the agenda of Great Power disputes, the remainder would be no more than a series of partial and peripheral deals.

The climax of *Ostpolitik*, however, was still to come, though it was a well-prepared climax and, by the time it happened, a well-rehearsed one. Much of the substance of German–German relations had been resolved at Moscow and in the Four-Power Agreement, but the GDR could not be excluded entirely as an actor in the process of *rapprochement*. Contacts between the two governments had been grow-ing even before the appointment of Brandt as Chancellor. Brandt's spectacular visit to Erfurt has already been mentioned. The return visit of the GDR's Prime Minister, Willi Stoph, though less spectacu-lar, was no less significant. Even the Four-Power Agreement could be implemented only by a bilateral transit agreement, signed in Decem-ber 1971, and by a fully-fledged treaty, signed in May 1972—the first treaty of any kind between the two states. All these preliminary moves culminated in the Basic Treaty between the two German states. Helped by all the preliminary steps already taken, helped above all by the Soviet Union's anxiety to crown *détente*, as shown by the removal of Ulbricht from leadership of the SED, it took less than five months to arrive at an agreed text, which was promulgated on 8 November 1972.

In outline it gave both sides what they wanted. It gave the GDR a formal relationship with the FRG and the acknowledgement that there were now two German states. It gave the USSR a further acknowledgement of its suzerainty in the areas it had claimed at the end of the Second World War. The FRG, on the other hand, was able to restrict itself to recognizing the independence of the GDR, but not its full sovereignty. The two states were to exchange 'permanent representations', not embassies. The FRG continued to maintain that there was no separate GDR citizenship and that the GDR was not, as Brandt had already insisted at Erfurt, a foreign country. In other respects the Basic Treaty was vague. Both sides claimed to want a 'normalization' of relations, but had conflicting and contradictory notions of normality. The FRG hoped to open up frontiers and to facilitate contacts and communications, whether at the level of the family or of the mass media. That is what Western normality con-sisted of. The GDR insisted on non-interference in its internal affairs: the status of civil liberties in the GDR was not the FRG's business. That is how normality was understood in the East. Those articles of the Basic Treaty that dealt with freedom of movement were therefore open-ended. They consisted of undertakings by the GDR, not guar-antees. The GDR understood the Basic Treaty as a repudiation of German unity. In its constitutional amendments and the adoption of a separate legal code, it had aimed, as we saw in Chapter 5, at under-lining its separateness. 'Delimitation' was well under way by 1972; the

Basic Treaty merely made its extension more urgent. The Brandt government, on the other hand, saw the Basic Treaty as a substitute for German unity, as an opportunity for rescuing the idea of a single German nation within the framework of two states, of puncturing the Iron Curtain, while recognizing that it could not be removed in its entirety. It took this view not merely because those were its genuine convictions, but because to do so was a domestic political necessity in the Bundestag.

The relative haste with which the Basic Treaty was drawn up had to do not only with the tempo of *détente*; it was dictated by the ticking of the domestic political clock. Foreign policy was always, as we have seen, domestic politics in both parts of Germany, *Deutschlandpolitik* doubly so. The narrow parliamentary majority of the Brandt government made the whole of *Ostpolitik* a high-risk operation. Public opinion was already polarized on its merits. The government's successive commitments touched some of the most sensitive nerves in German political consciousness: anything that looked like the final abandonment of the lost territories of the East and anything that looked like the acceptance of the final division of Germany would merely accentuate opposition to it. As a result, by the time the Basic Treaty was ready for signature the government had lost its majority.

Polarized partisanship was not the norm in post-war West German politics. The popularity of the Great Coalition was proof of the German yearning for harmony. The SPD had realized by 1959 that its own polarizing attitudes were self-defeating and Adenauer had to overcome considerable opposition within the CDU to his single-minded strategy. The CDU was therefore in a dilemma after the 1969 election. In its twenty years of power it had benefited from the increasingly consensual tone in parliamentary life and the give-and-take of coalition government. It could not claim that Brandt's *Ostpolitik* was a radical departure from precedent; it had its roots, after all, in the admittedly more tentative initiatives of Schröder and Kiesinger. It therefore had within its ranks senior members who were at least qualified supporters of what was happening.

What tipped the CDU and its sibling the CSU into outright opposition was anger at having lost the election—or, rather, a refusal to admit that they had lost it. The CDU–CSU had emerged as the largest party in 1969 with 46 per cent of the vote. They had not even been consulted on the formation of a government, but were out-flanked by a Brandt–Scheel–Heinemann collusion. They were deprived of office, they believed, not by electoral rejection, but by parliamentary intrigue. This conviction was their main incentive for threatening, in the words of their parliamentary leader, Rainer Barzel, 'four times 365 days' opposition'. In addition, parties that have just lost power tend to move from the political centre to the ideological periphery in the hope of sharpening their appeal and recovering their morale. That meant that, once the CDU–CSU realized that it was consigned, however temporarily, to opposition, the intransigence of Franz-Josef Strauß won out over more moderate voices, including those of the future President, Richard von Weizsäcker. Moreover, the sense of betrayal at the FDP's joining the SPD favoured the revival of the old strategy of driving the FDP out of politics, by breaking up CDU–FDP *Land* coalitions wherever possible. Since the FDP had barely survived in 1969 and was dropping below 5 per cent in one *Landtag* election after another, the chances of achieving this were high.

What helped the opposition in its offensive was the disintegration of Brandt's majority; what hindered it was its own indecisiveness. When the Moscow and Warsaw treaties came up for ratification in the Bundestag, most CDU and CSU deputies abstained. More ominously for the government, the votes in favour numbered only 248, exactly half the Bundestag membership. What had happened was that four FDP and two SPD had defected to the opposition. Parliament was now deadlocked. Even before the votes on the treaties, the opposition had decided to challenge the government by moving a 'constructive vote of no confidence' under Article 67 of the Basic Law—that is, proposing Barzel as an alternative head of government. To general surprise the motion failed by two votes, as did an attempt to defeat the budget the next day. Two opposition deputies, it emerged later, had been bribed. It was in the course of the breathing space provided by these two failed votes that the Basic Treaty became West German domestic politics. Brandt calculated that, if it could be concluded by the autumn, he could risk an election, given the known popularity of *Ostpolitik*. With the initialling of the Basic Treaty in sight, Brandt contrived to lose a vote of confidence in the Bundestag by persuading his cabinet ministers to abstain and President Heinemann dissolved the Bundestag. Polling day was set for 19 November 1972. It was a single-issue election and indeed a single-personality election. Brandt was by this time not only the hero of Erfurt and the Warsaw ghetto, but the Nobel Peace Laureate, an ideal accolade in the eyes of a population hungry for international approval. The election result was a triumph for Brandt. With 45.8 per cent of the vote, the SPD for the first time outvoted the CDU in a federal election. The FDP recovered to 8.4 per cent. The CDU fell to 44.9 per cent, its lowest score since 1949. The Basic Treaty passed the Bundestag on 21 December. On 18 September 1973 the FRG and the GDR were admitted as members of the United Nations.

A 54 per cent vote for the government parties in a record turn-out of 91 per cent was an unambiguous endorsement of *Ostpolitik* and a personal triumph for Brandt. But it also marked a turning-point in West German constitutional conventions. We have seen that under Chancellor democracy West German elections had moved from being sectarian competitions to a choice between aspirants to executive power. Until 1972, however, there had still been limits to the voters' ability to choose. They could identify one of the two major parties with an incumbent Chancellor or his challenger, but the formation of a coalition was a matter for the parties after the election. Even in 1969, as we have seen, several coalition possibilities were open. In 1972 they were not. So dependent were the FDP and SPD on each other after the alternation of power, so closely were they associated with *Ostpolitik*, so much did their joint fates depend on the Bundestag votes of 1972 and the election fought on that issue, that they announced in advance that they would govern together if their mandate were renewed. In 1972 electors could vote not only for or against a Chancellor, but for or against a government. The convention of announcing a coalition preference in advance has continued since then. The changed role of the FDP in government completed its transformation into a 'social–liberal' party. In the Freiburg Theses, adopted in March 1972, it committed itself to the 'democratization of society' and the 'reform of capitalism'. Coalition with Social Democracy also brought about a change in the FDP electorate. Between 1965 and 1972 the proportion of self-employed among FDP supporters dropped from 33 per cent to

11 per cent, while the proportion of white-collar employees rose from 46 per cent to 66 per cent. The FDP voters' preference for the 'social–liberal' coalition was shown most strongly by the tactical ticket-splitting that the West German double ballot permitted. Of those who gave their list vote to the FDP, 53 per cent gave their constituency vote to an SPD candidate as being best placed to defeat the CDU.

With the Brandt–Scheel coalition's victory, the programme of *Ostpolitik* was largely complete. Only two items of unfinished business remained. The first was a treaty with Czechoslovakia, signed on 11 December 1973 and ratified by the Bundestag on 10 July 1974. It accepted the Czech demand that the Munich Agreement of 1938, already repudiated by all its other signatories, be declared null and void. But the other Czech demand, that all transactions carried out during the German occupation of Czechoslovakia between 1938 and 1945 be declared invalid, failed. The Czechoslovak government also promised to facilitate the emigration of the remaining ethnic Germans, but the implementation of this undertaking proved no easier than those made by the other East European states. The second item was domestic and judicial. It concerned the question whether the Basic Treaty breached the constitutional commitment to working for national unification. The CSU government of Bavaria claimed that this was so and took its case to the Federal Constitutional Court. The Court, however, rejected this plea, ruling that the Treaty was not 'a treaty of partition'. The Brandt government's careful attention to semantics had paid off.

The successes in *Ostpolitik* all but exhausted the government's energies. The remaining eighteen months of Brandt's Chancellorship were an anti-climax. They showed that the coalition's foreign-policy consensus did not necessarily extend to domestic politics, that Brandt's inspirational idealism was not matched by administrative skills, and that reformist impulses can outrun limited resources. That is not how it had seemed in the immediate aftermath of the 1969 election. The new government was the government of *Ostpolitik*, but it was not only the government of *Ostpolitik*. Brandt's programmatic speech to the Bundestag devoted more attention to domestic than to foreign policy, above all to the extension of democracy: 'We want to dare more democracy . . . We have not arrived at the end of our democracy, we are only just getting going.' This call reflected not only the mood of the new-style, rejuvenated FDP, but also that of many Germans who had begun to show their impatience with the traditions of their society. It was also the cause of most of the government's difficulties and frustrations, which contrasted markedly with its diplomatic success. The government's reform programme covered four main areas —education, the economy, industrial relations, and civil liberties. In education, as in so many concerns, the agenda in the FRG resembled that of most other Western countries, but the pressures were more intense, and the perfectionist criteria that are a characteristic of German culture were more likely to invite disillusionment. The agenda was twofold—an extension of opportunity and an extension of participation. The expansion of higher education in the 1960s was a response not only to the needs of a modern economy for more qualified persons, but to a qualitative change in career expectations. Where schools and universities had traditionally—in Germany as elsewhere— served to stabilize social structures, they now became on a massive scale instruments of social mobility. In the first place this was so through the sheer increase in the number of pupils and students. Even in the five years 1965–70 numbers in *Gymnasien* (i.e. selective academic high schools) doubled and the number of university students, already on the increase before then, rose by a further quarter. *Per capita* expenditure on all forms of education doubled. But reformers of the Left demanded more: first, the abolition of the distinction between strictly academic and vocational education; secondly, a redistribution of power within all educational institutions, in other words 'daring more democracy'. At the level of higher education this was attempted through the 'framework law' of 1971 that set out new, participatory structures for universities. At the level of secondary education it was attempted by the universalization of comprehensive schools (*Gesamtschulen*). Both, in their initial form, stumbled on the hurdle of federalism. Education in all its many forms is the prerogative of the *Länder*, as it had been under the Weimar Republic and the Empire; the principle of cultural sovereignty (*Kulturhoheit*) was jealously guarded by them. Though the Basic Law had been amended in 1969 to make higher education one of a number of common concerns of federation and *Länder*, the government's proposal failed to win the support of enough *Länder* in the Bundesrat and it had in the end (i.e. in 1975) to content itself with a much diluted law. So, too, the school proposal was rejected by CDU–CSU-governed *Länder*, as a result of which educational policy become doubly divisive. The *Länder* now comprised two categories, defined by party control, one that went over to comprehensive schools ('group A') and one that did not ('group B'). Moreover, each *Land* passed its own university reform law, giving now more, now less power to junior lecturers, students, and subordinate staff in academic appointments and syllabuses. None of this made schools and universities less of a battleground between Left and Right. Each side appreciated only too well that ownership of the means of education could determine the composition of the next generation's élite and its dominant ideology.

While the SPD and FDP were in broad agreement in educational matters, they differed when it came to industrial relations. The FDP was reformist, but not collectivist. For the SPD, and especially its trade-union constituency, 'daring more democracy' involved an extension of industrial co-determination. The SPD's original intention of extending the partial arrangements dating from Adenauer's legislation to all large firms was stalled by the FDP's opposition. A compromise law had to wait until 1976: while all firms with over 2,000 employees were to have equal representation for shareholders and employees on the supervisory board, senior managers became a separate constituency within the employee side.

The problem of co-determination reflected a wider dissensus on macro-economic policy, though as much within the SPD as between the coalition partners. Reforms cost money. This was true of the expansion of educational opportunities; it was true even more of the extension of pension rights, over and above the provisions of Adenauer's 1957 law, on which the coalition agreed in 1972; it was true also of the often generously appointed public amenities that *Länder* and municipalities embarked on. It was the specific intention of the SPD to extend the private affluence of the FRG to collective affluence through the better provision of public goods. Since the government had taken office at the height of the Schiller boom, this rise in public expenditure did not at first seem to cause much concern. But the boom did not last, and for much of its term of office the government was in the grip of a fiscal crisis as well as, towards the end of its term, an incipient inflationary crisis. The two most ardent advocates in the cabinet of financial stringency were the Minister of Finance, Alex Möller, and the Minister of the Economy, Karl Schiller, both of the SPD. When Möller failed to persuade his cabinet colleagues to stabilize their spending programme in May 1971, he resigned. In his place Brandt appointed Schiller, who at this stage still believed in Keynesian expansionism, to hold both the Finance and the Economy ministries. The following year Schiller was converted to Möller's view and actually succeeded in securing cuts in the budget, but he was by this time so unpopular and isolated within the cabinet that he resigned in July 1972 and indeed soon afterwards left the SPD. His successor as dual manager of finance and the economy was the Defence Minister, Helmut Schmidt. After the election, which had strengthened the FDP, the two posts were again divided; the Economy Ministry went to the FDP, whose fief it has remained.

Schmidt, another reformed expansionist, and his new Economy colleague, Hans Friderichs, now had to battle not only against demands for expenditure but against inflationary pressures. In part these were caused by the size of the public debt, which increased by 42 per cent in nominal terms between 1969 and 1973, in part by large wage settlements, especially in the public sector. But the FRG was also the victim of two external events which hit it harder than most of its partners. The first was the collapse of the Bretton Woods system of fixed exchange rates, caused when the US government uncoupled the dollar from the price of gold in 1971. The second was the outbreak of the 'Yom Kippur war' in October 1973, which was followed by the oil shock in which the Organization of Petroleum Exporting Countries (OPEC) banned exports to pro-Israeli states and imposed a sixfold increase in the price of crude oil. The floating of the dollar released large, unregulated capital flows, for which the D-Mark, thanks to its strength, was an attractive haven and which thereby became one of the causes of inflation. Other Western states besides the FRG were hit by the oil embargo, but the FRG and Japan alone among the major economies had no significant domestic or guaranteed oil and natural gas resources. The economy, more than any other factor, clouded the rest of Brandt's Chancellorship and contributed to his reputation for poor management. By the time he resigned, growth was perilously close to zero, inflation had more than tripled to 7 per cent, and unemployment was edging towards the million mark for the first time since the 1950s.

One final problem bedevilled the Brandt government and indeed those that succeeded it: civil liberties and law and order. 'Daring more democracy' entailed an extension of civil liberties. The reforms in education and industrial relations were an important part of this programme. Women's rights were another, including liberalization of the abortion law. Here was a matter on which the coalition could agree and the outcome was the Abortion Law Reform Act of 1974 which legalized abortion on demand in the first twelve weeks of pregnancy. This Act was short-lived, since the Federal Constitutional Court found that it contravened the Basic Law's protection of 'the right to life' and 'the inviolability of the person'. It was, therefore, replaced with a more restrictive reform, permitting abortion on medical grounds only—which made it a matter of finding the right doctor.

Much more intractable was the question of political extremism. For the first twenty years of the FRG's life the threat of political extremism had come from the Right. It came in the form of neo-Nazi parties, of pro-Nazi or anti-Semitic vandalism, or of far-Right sympathizers in the public service, whether in the judiciary or in education. What the FRG did not have to face was political violence or terrorism. In the 1970s this changed. It was one of the outcomes of the radicalization of the 1960s and the APO. Most APO members wanted reform, however far-reaching, rather than revolution. Violence, when it happened, took the form of riots rather than urban guerrilla warfare. The arson attacks on department stores as a protest against consumerism seemed at the time very much the exception. But, once the first cohort of APO members had graduated, the challenge they posed took on a different dimension. Brandt's aim was to mobilize their enthusiasm and integrate them into his reformist crusade. But even in so far as he succeeded in doing this he fashioned a rod for his own back. What he called integration the APO called 'the long march through the institutions'. The institutions targeted were in the public sector—education, the social services, the civil service in general—but also the media. They included above all the various sections of the SPD, especially the Young Socialists (Juso), and local government in large cities, which was largely SPD dominated. At precisely the time when the SPD was reaping the electoral benefit of having de-ideologized itself at Bad Godesberg, a new generation of activists was trying to reconvert it to Marxism. They increasingly influenced the proceedings of SPD congresses and, rather more significantly, began to provide a new generation of SPD politicians. Of the 1972 intake of SPD Bundestag deputies, approximately fifty belonged to the New Left.

Coping with nonconformists is the perennial problem of political parties. Coping with them in the public service is a different matter, especially when nonconformity turns to violence. Although the main wave of terrorism falls into the post-Brandt period, urban guerrilla violence began in the early 1970s. Its international ramifications were brought out by the massacre of Israeli athletes by Arab gunmen at the Munich Olympics in 1972. The authorities' dilemma arose out of the difficulty in drawing a line between the small minority of violent revolutionaries and those whose loyalty to the constitution could not be taken for granted. The difficult trade-off between permitting public servants ordinary civil liberties and ensuring their loyalty to the state is common to all liberal democracies. It is all the more acutely felt in Germany, where there are memories of the Weimar Republic, in which many public servants were out of sympathy with the democratic values of the constitution and some were openly hostile to them, and of the Third Reich, in which many public servants complied with the illegalities of the regime, or with infringements of human rights in the name of legality. The authorities in the FRG tried to come to terms with this difficulty through the so-called 'Decree on Extremists' (*Radikalenerlaß*) of 1972, which was not a decree at all, but a set of guidelines agreed between the federal government and the *Länder*.

The wording of the Decree differed little from that of the Civil Service Law of 1953, which demanded that civil servants must unconditionally support 'the liberal-democratic basic order' (*freiheitliche demokratische Grundordnung (FDGO)*). But the Decree amplified this by enjoining widespread screenings of applicants and existing officeholders, and defining 'well-grounded suspicions' of political disloyalty as grounds for disqualification from employment. In the course of the

1970s some 2,250 persons were denied employment under the terms of the Decree, another 2,100 were disciplined, and 256 were dismissed. Of those barred or dismissed a substantial number won appeals in the courts. Given the size of the German public service, which employs some 17 per cent of the labour force (3.7 million civil servants and others in 1972, 4.5 million in 1984), these numbers seem trivial. Yet the number of screenings was huge—some 3.5 million— and involved a formidable surveillance apparatus. As a result the whole process became increasingly contested both at home and abroad. Its opponents claimed, not without justice, that the investigators did not distinguish between hard-core Maoists and petitioners against nuclear power, that as a result any kind of nonconformist behaviour was indiscriminately stigmatized, and that association with the Left was judged more severely than that with the Right. To discredit it they christened it a bar on professional careers (*Berufsverbot*). Outside Germany the impact of the Decree was even more unfavourable. Those inclined to suppose that the old state authoritarianism was far from dead found their suspicions confirmed. The *Berufsverbot* in its fully-fledged form was fairly short-lived. Though the Federal Constitutional Court endorsed it in principle, deadlock between the two houses of parliament meant that the relevant legislation was never passed. From 1976 onwards the SPD-governed *Länder* slowly disengaged themselves from the requirements of the Decree and by the 1980s it was, though never formally rescinded, a dead letter.

The attempt to defend democracy through the curtailment of civil liberties was the most acute of the moral dilemmas the Brandt government faced. It reappeared in a different form under his successor, Helmut Schmidt. It symbolized the misfortunes that dogged much of the government's domestic initiatives and, though the SPD and FDP did not always see eye to eye, it was yet another of the issues on which the main differences arose within the SPD. These had to do not only with policies, whether over the *Berufsverbot* or the budget, but increasingly with Brandt's administrative failings. Once *Ostpolitik* was signed and sealed, Brandt's immediate lieutenants became restive. Both the SPD's Bundestag floor leader, Herbert Wehner, and its deputy chairman, the Finance Minister Helmut Schmidt, began to hint publicly that it was time for Brandt to go.

Brandt resigned on 6 May 1974, but for a reason that his antagonists had not anticipated, namely the arrest of one of his leading aides, Günter Guillaume, as a GDR agent. His successor was Helmut Schmidt. At the same time President Heinemann's term of office came to an end and Brandt's ally, the FDP leader Walter Scheel, became the new Head of State. Within the cabinet the former Minister of the Interior, Hans-Dietrich Genscher, became Schmidt's Foreign Minister and Vice-Chancellor, as well as Scheel's successor as Chairman of the FDP. The change of guard marked a caesura of both style and outlook. Brandt and Heinemann were moralists, didactic rather than instrumental in their approach. As representatives of the 'other Germany' they established a degree of goodwill abroad without which the foreign-policy revolution of 1969–72 would have been more difficult to achieve. The men who moved up were pragmatic administrators, more attuned to managing the limited possibilities that the colder economic climate was offering. Schmidt's cabinet contained five trade unionists, compared with two in Brandt's, showing a swing towards the Right within the SPD, and Genscher was a man of the centre rather than a committed reformer.

The Brandt Chancellorship brought about a greater change in the FRG's status and structure than any other five-year span in its history. In 1969 it was tentatively embarking on foreign-policy initiatives; in 1974 it was as autonomous an actor on the European and world stages as any middle-ranking power. It had regulated its relationships with its Eastern neighbours and embarked on a direct, even if somewhat distant, partnership with the Soviet Union. Leonid Brezhnev's state visit to Bonn in May 1973 demonstrated the fruits of *Ostpolitik*. In its domestic politics, too, the FRG that Brandt bequeathed differed substantially from the one he had inherited. He presided over the first German government in half a century with a mandate to liberalize. That his government was only partially successful in this respect is another matter. That it happened at all was a sure sign that the majority of West Germans had left the assumptions and anxieties of post-war emergency behind. A numerous critical intelligentsia had emerged as a new factor in politics and would remain so.

The departure from office of Brandt and Heinemann coincided with the twenty-fifth birthday of the FRG. That the remaining years before unification were calmer and more predictable, that the FRG was not only stable, but became a byword for stability, was due to the foundations built by Adenauer and Erhard and reinforced, in his idiosyncratic way, by Brandt.

7 *Modell Deutschland*

> It is admitted as a general principle that moderation and the
> mean are always best.
>
> (Aristotle, *Politics* 1295b)

HELMUT SCHMIDT, the Federal Republic's fifth Chancellor, from
1974 to 1982, inherited a mixed legacy. He led a state that was self-
confident and respected, but remained subject to domestic and foreign challenges. Above all, the breach in the ideological consensus that
had begun in the later 1960s and that Brandt had been unable to close,
continued to inhibit policy-making and ultimately led to Schmidt's
fall.

The first asset that Schmidt inherited was an improved relationship with the FRG's Eastern neighbours. Thanks to Brandt's work,
the image of Bonn as a revanchist bunker faded, and though relations
with the states of the Eastern bloc remained strained, they were no
longer confrontational. For the time being *détente* had got as far as it
could go; Schmidt's and Genscher's priorities were to consolidate the
gains of *Ostpolitik*, not to embark on new initiatives. The one important further step that the FRG was involved in, the Conference on
Security and Co-operation in Europe (CSCE), it was careful to interpret as consolidation, not innovation. The text adopted at the conclusion of the CSCE—the Helsinki Final Act, for short—consisted of
three 'baskets'. Basket One dealt with security and disarmament on
the basis of 'mutual respect for sovereignty and equality'. This was a
further Soviet attempt to secure an international agreement to perpetuate the post-1945 frontiers of, and spheres of influence in,
Europe, including the division of Europe. The chief benefit to Bonn
of this basket was that it reinforced the Four-Power Agreement on
Berlin. Basket Two dealt with increased economic and technological
co-operation. This promised immediate benefits to the countries of
the Eastern bloc, whose governments were increasingly anxious about
the modernization gap opening between themselves and the West.

But it also suited the now-established West German strategy of 'penetrating' the East in order to bind it into an irreversible network of interdependence. Basket Three dealt with human rights. It was initially greeted with indifference in the East and some cynicism in the West, but in its incremental encouragement of dissident groups it proved decisive in sealing the fate of the Communist world. It demonstrated by 1989 that Soviet rulers had more to fear from their own populations than from the entire nuclear arsenal of NATO.

The less favourable legacy bequeathed to Schmidt was the state of the world economy. When he took office, the FRG was on the verge of recession, faced with both rising unemployment and rising inflation. It suffered the consequence of Brandt's spending spree and the oil shock, but the effects of the oil shock were worse in most other major Western economies. The FRG's temporary discomfiture was quite compatible with its increasing relative economic strength. The altered strategic constellation that resulted from *détente* and the long-term emergence of the FRG as an economic giant affected both the scope and the direction of West German policy initiatives. No one was better aware of this than the new Chancellor and no one better prepared for the altered requirements of his office than he. He had held successively the Defence, Finance, and Economy portfolios under Brandt. He had acquired an expert understanding of the academic literature on all three topics and the ability to adapt their contents to policy requirements. He was a problem-solver at a time when the FRG's problems were more complex than at any previous time, but also when the opportunity of contributing to their solution was better than ever before.

The key to Schmidt's thinking was the concept of security. Up to 1969 West German security needs had been one-dimensional. In the context of the Cold War they were military-strategic. As *Ostpolitik* developed, *détente* and an East–West partnership took their place beside the need to maintain the strategic equilibrium. In 1974 and the years that followed, the threats to currency stability and energy supplies further enlarged the dimensions of West German security concerns. It was to these that the Schmidt government turned first in both the domestic and the international contexts.

If the method was problem-solving, the objective was stability—

stability, more than anything else, in currency terms. Even in the last year of the Brandt government the fight against inflation had taken on greater priority. Now, with the oil shocks fuelling world-wide inflation, it became the overriding objective. The key to this, in Schmidt's eyes, lay in monetary policy and exchange-rate policy; in the pursuit of this an institution that had up to then remained in the background, the Bundesbank, moved to the centre of the stage. The Bundesbank had been established in 1957 with a simple remit, to ensure the stability of the currency by regulating the money supply and interest rates and to do so without formal regard to the political wishes of the government of the day. As long as the industrial peace of the reconstruction years lasted, as long as the capital–labour partnership gave trade unions an incentive to keep wage demands moderate, as long as fixed exchange rates kept capital flows to manageable proportions, the Bundesbank could act discreetly and uncontroversially, sheltering behind an image of objective wisdom and technical expertise. Public confrontations between it and the government of the day, as on the question of D-Mark revaluations between 1958 and 1961, or on the question of controlling capital holdings by foreigners in 1972, were very much the exception. The Bank's job was to secure a framework within which the agents of the various social forces could act autonomously and co-operatively. Once uninterrupted growth gave way to economic turbulence its decisions became more controversial; once exchange rates began to float its role as guardian of the currency made it an international actor.

The Bundesbank has had, and retains, a privileged position in the ranks of German policy-makers and has increasingly become a model for other states, or unions of states, seeking to take the making of monetary policy out of the hands of politicians. But it has always had a limited agenda and it has never been the only actor on the policy stage. It can set monetary targets and determine interest rates. It can, like all central banks, intervene in the foreign-exchange markets and thereby affect the exchange rate. But it cannot make treaties, like those affecting European integration, or enter into international agreements, like those that set up the European Monetary System (EMS) (discussed below), which might well affect or even cancel out its efforts. Moreover, the Bundesbank does not have a monopoly in the financial advice to the government. In 1963 a Council of Expert Advisers (*Sachverständigenrat*) was set up; in 1967 the Economy Minister, Karl Schiller, anxious to give the federal government a greater role in steering the economy, set up two further bodies, a Financial Planning Council and an Economic Trends Council, though both were short-lived. In response to the recession of 1966–7, but also in response to his ideological inclinations, Schiller moved towards consensual macro-economic planning in the form of the Concerted Action, which was designed to co-ordinate the aims and assumptions of the government, academic experts, organized labour, employers, the *Länder*, and the municipalities. Under the Brandt government there was an even greater trend towards central planning, helped by the creation of a federal Ministry of Research and Technology.

There were, however, strict limits to this state intervention. There was no prospect of centralized indicative planning on the French model, in which the state possessed many of the levers of industrial investment and location; nor of rigid corporatism of the kind practised in Austria or Sweden, in which agreements on prices and wages between the principal interest groups were virtually binding on the negotiating partners and on the state. No West German government ever lost sight of the principles on which the social market economy was based, namely, those of ensuring that the boundary was respected between the sphere of the state and that of civil society—a boundary so memorably transgressed under the Third Reich. Free collective bargaining (*Tarifautonomie*) was maintained throughout this period. Above all, the FRG lacked many of the institutions that enabled a state like France to pursue its policies. The federal structure, which was, after all, designed to prevent this kind of concentration of power, gives considerable fiscal resources and planning instruments to the *Länder* and even the municipalities.

The central planning phase did not last long. Like its inception under Schiller, it owed its decline to a combination of circumstances and personalities. General disillusionment with grandiose schemes for the improvement of mankind was hastened by the oil-shock-induced recession of 1974–5 and in any case did not accord with Schmidt's problem-solving proclivities. It was in this context that the Bundesbank came into its own and became more and more of a public actor. For instance, it began to publish its monetary targets as a way of influencing wage negotiations; *Tarifautonomie* remained intact, but subject to greater pressures. Above all, as automatic growth became a thing of the past and unemployment an issue for the first time in twenty years, the Bundesbank's anti-inflationary interest rates policy became controversial. Those who felt that, under the new circumstances, unemployment was a greater evil than inflation blamed the Bank for prolonging the recession in 1973–4 and, after the second oil shock, in 1980–2, and for throttling the recovery in 1976. Schmidt, however, tended to side with the Bank, at any rate on the first two occasions. He did agree to an injection of public investment in 1976, but that was motivated partly by electoral considerations.

The domestic electoral cycle was, however, not the only political factor that Schmidt had to take into account. The emergence of the FRG as the major economy of Europe, accounting for 9 per cent of total world output, meant that whatever it did affected all its trading partners. It was, therefore, under continuous pressure to act as the 'locomotive' of Western prosperity by pursuing expansionary policies. Schmidt was sensitive to these demands. He was aware that many outside Germany regarded the FRG's rise to power, in the words of one of his own memoranda, as 'unwanted and dangerous'. He was aware, too, that the interdependence of modern economies obliged all players to co-operation and reciprocity. Equally, however, he was not prepared to risk the FRG's hard-won stability for the short-term benefit of less disciplined economies. This meant in particular more strained relations with the USA and a search for a replacement for the kind of stability that the Bretton Woods system had provided up to 1971—a replacement that might be either global or European.

One sign of transatlantic strains, and of the risk that economic policy divergences might spill over into other policy areas, came in West German reactions to the first oil shock. The USA was inclined to adopt a confrontational response towards OPEC. Continental European states, the FRG included, which were more dependent on Middle Eastern oil and had more to gain from trade with the oil-producing states, inclined towards conciliation and Schmidt took the lead in proposing a World Energy Conference. This was not, as we have seen, the first difference between the FRG and the USA on strategic trade matters: the pipeline dispute of the late 1960s had been a foretaste. But as West German dominance in the world economy increased and that of the USA declined, differences were likely to become more frequent and regular. A major long-term cause of these differences was the weakness of the dollar, exacerbated by the continuing high level of US oil imports and the failure of the USA to adopt a rigorous energy-saving policy. It was this failure that inclined Schmidt to ignore pleas to be a 'locomotive'.

The first outcome of these currency difficulties was a world economic summit in 1975, the forerunner of the later annual G7 meetings at which the USA, Japan, France, Great Britain, the FRG, Italy, and Canada meet. The immediate agenda was to resist French pleas for a return to fixed parities by persuading the USA to support its currency more strongly. When this undertaking appeared to be achieving little success, Schmidt and the French President Valéry Giscard d'Estaing decided on an alternative Europe-based strategy. They persuaded their fellow EC members to adopt a European Monetary System (EMS) with the aim of creating a stable European currency zone less dependent on the vagaries of the dollar. The confirmation of the new equilibrium between Europe and the USA, and of the FRG's pivotal role in it, came at the 1978 G7 summit in Bonn, at which Schmidt was able to play host and at which the FRG agreed to stimulate its economy in return for US energy-saving measures.

There was an irony in these German–American difficulties, for Schmidt was by instinct an Atlanticist, dedicated to the maintenance of the German–American partnership. In part the reasons for the rift were contingent. They were the domestic difficulties that American politics faced in the aftermath of the Vietnam War and of the enforced resignation of President Nixon in the wake of the Watergate affair, as well as the poor personal relationship between Schmidt and President Jimmy Carter. But there was no denying a longer-term drifting apart between American interests, on the one hand, and Western Europe, and the FRG in particular, on the other. In an increasingly multipolar world, the overlapping of priorities between the USA and its allies and between the Soviet Union and its allies could no longer be taken for granted. This trend emerged both in matters of defence strategy and in East–West diplomacy.

With the FRG's Eastern relationships regularized by the *Ostpolitik* treaties and the Helsinki Final Act, Schmidt and Genscher decided that the best they could do was to protect the new status quo. This meant above all that the eased position of Berlin continued to be preserved. It meant secondly that *Deutschlandpolitik*, which had been a major preoccupation of the superpowers, was now downgraded to being a primarily West German concern—another sign of the increasing policy autonomy that the FRG had derived from *Ostpolitik*. What did not occur in the course of the 1970s was any liberalization of the regimes of the Eastern bloc, which the Western powers had expected as a result of *détente* and Helsinki. Indeed, as we saw in Chapter 5, repression increased again in the GDR in the second half of the decade. Schmidt and Genscher were prepared to be patient: if the choice lay between stabilization and liberalization, they were prepared to settle for stabilization. Schmidt became a regular visitor to the capitals of the satellites and in 1981 there was even a Schmidt–Honecker summit, the first between the heads of government of the two German states since the Brandt–Stoph encounters of 1970. The timing of this summit illustrated, however accidentally, the extent to which 'normalization' was being interpreted on Soviet bloc terms. The meeting coincided with the declaration of martial law in Poland and the banning of the Solidarnósc trade union. But this major violation of human rights did not interrupt the summit: stability retained its priority.

The divergent evaluation of the human-rights question was another of the reasons for rifts between the FRG and the USA, especially during the Carter presidency. Another reason was the divergent evaluation of Soviet military policy. Anxious as Schmidt and Genscher were to avoid any disturbance of relations with their Eastern neighbours, they were nevertheless convinced that a condition of this relationship was the maintenance of the military equilibrium. When this was threatened, they insisted on countermeasures. As far as conventional ground forces were concerned, the FRG could act fairly independently and by 1975 the *Bundeswehr* had been built up to half a million men. Strategic weapons, however, still meant the US umbrella. The Soviet Union had begun not only to increase its ground forces in Europe but to replace its medium-range nuclear missiles with the more modern SS-20. The Soviet side claimed this updating was consistent with the Strategic Arms Limitations Treaty (SALT-I), signed by the two superpowers in 1971; President Carter reassured Schmidt that, even if this was not the case, it would be covered by SALT-II, at that time under negotiation. Schmidt was satisfied with neither argument and saw salvation in a new battlefield weapon, developed in the USA and approved by Congress in 1977—the 'neutron' bomb which, because it relied heavily on intense but short-range radiation for its destructive effect, appeared suitable as a tactical deterrent in European conditions. In accepting this reinforcement—indeed by formally requesting it—Schmidt risked heavy domestic opposition; what he reaped, when Carter cancelled the project in 1978, was humiliation. As a substitute, NATO embarked on its 'twin-track' decision of 1979, which threatened to instal cruise and Pershing-II missiles in Europe, specifically in the FRG, if the SS-20s were not withdrawn by 1983. This, too, represented a domestic political headache to Schmidt, as we shall see below, but strategically it achieved its aim in the long run: both systems were withdrawn under the terms of the 1987 Intermediate Nuclear Forces (INF) Treaty.

For the FRG government, the twin-track decision was a necessary evil. Schmidt's aim was arms reduction, not an arms race. Yet the fact that *Ostpolitik* in its late-1970s version survived this decision shows how compartmentalized relations had become in the multipolar world. The Soviet government and the GDR tried to mobilize West German opinion against the neutron bomb and the twin-track decision. Yet neither these episodes nor the declaration of martial law in Poland had prevented or interrupted the Schmidt–Honecker summit. The same applied to the Soviet intervention in Afghanistan in 1979. President Carter saw this as a major violation of the spirit of *détente*, suspended the ratification of the SALT-II agreement, imposed an embargo on grain exports to the Soviet Union, and urged all NATO members to boycott the Olympics scheduled in Moscow for 1980. Continental European governments—that of Giscard d'Estaing as much as Helmut Schmidt's—judged this an over-reaction, just as they had watched the victory of Cuban-supported rebels in Angola three years earlier with indifference. If events in Gdansk were not capable of shaking the West German commitment to East–West stability, those in Luanda and Kabul certainly could not.

Ostpolitik survived the twin-track decision, but domestically it was a nail in Schmidt's coffin. His growing international stature was not matched by electoral security. The Social–Liberal coalition scraped home with a majority of only ten in the election of 1976, fought as the FRG was just emerging from the recession. The government's platform of 'Germany as a model' (*Modell Deutschland*) was not quite convincing. But neither was the CDU's counter-slogan of 'freedom or Socialism' (*Freiheit oder Sozialismus*): the risk of a lurch to collectivist totalitarianism under Schmidt was rather low. The 1976 election, and the very narrow defeat of the CDU, which polled 48.6 per cent, was significant in another way. It was the first national election fought by the then Prime Minister of Rhineland–Palatinate, Helmut Kohl, a self-proclaimed man of the political centre and one of Germany's most formidable vote-getters. The more comfortable majority gained by the government in 1980 was a clearer indication of what the majority of West Germans did or did not want. On this occasion the CDU's Chancellor candidate was the confrontational Franz-Josef Strauß, now Prime Minister of Bavaria. The CDU's vote dropped by 4.3 per cent to 44.5 per cent; the main beneficiary of this defection was the FDP, which went up by 2.7 per cent to 10.6 per cent. It was evident that it was Schmidt and Genscher, not Strauß, who spoke for the silent majority that favoured the status quo over adventures or experiments. *Modell Deutschland*, as designed by Schmidt, was now more acceptable. But the failure of the SPD to benefit from the anti-Strauß vote was also a warning. Schmidt was widely respected and trusted, but his party was not. Much of the domestic political turbulence of the 1970s was concentrated on the Left. Whereas the CDU learnt the lessons of its 1969 and 1972 defeats and built itself a membership structure and national organization that it had neglected when it was in power, the Left was unable to overcome the divisions sown in the late 1960s.

The APO of those years dispersed in three directions. There were those whom Brandt integrated into the SPD, where they formed an increasingly formidable faction of ecological, pacifist, and anti-capitalist dissent. There were those who remained outside conventional party politics and constituted the various citizens' initiatives that eventually merged in the Greens. Lastly there was the terrorist fringe, whose activities dominated public controversy for much of the

1970s. The main terrorist group, the Red Army Faction (RAF), was led by Andreas Baader and Ulrike Meinhof and was informally named after them. Though they had begun their campaign of violence in the late 1960s and the Decree on Extremists of 1972 had been aimed at cutting off their support base, the main wave of terror came after 1972. The RAF's main victims were the Berlin CDU politician Peter Lorenz, whose kidnapping secured the release of six imprisoned terrorists, and the Chief Public Prosecutor Siegfried Buback and the President of the Dresdner Bank, Jürgen Ponto, both murdered. Although Baader and Meinhof were both captured and imprisoned, the 'anti-imperialist armed struggle for freedom' continued, climaxing in two events in September and October 1977. The first was the kidnapping of the President of the West German Employers' Federation (BDI), Hanns-Martin Schleyer, the second the hijacking of a Lufthansa jumbo jet which was forced to land at Mogadishu in Somalia. The aim of both actions was to secure the release of the RAF leaders. In this they failed. German commandos stormed the airliner and released the hostages. On hearing the news the three leading RAF prisoners, Andreas Baader, Gudrun Ensslin, and Jan-Carl Raspe, committed suicide in their high-security cells. But the police failed to rescue Schleyer; his corpse was found across the French frontier in Mulhouse.

With the failure of the 1977 actions, terrorism was put on the defensive and the sympathy that the activists had earned for their aims, if not their means, began to ebb. Acts of violence continued until 1992, when the remnants of the RAF declared a cease-fire, having been deprived of the logistical support of the GDR, but the new leadership was weaker and more confused and recruitment became more difficult. In one respect, however, they were successful: they provoked the authorities into further repressive measures and thus were able to lend some credence to the belief that the state had not abandoned the German tradition of repressiveness. Telephone-bugging increased, at times beyond what the law permitted, and after the Schleyer abduction limits were placed on contacts between terrorist suspects and the outside world, including their lawyers. The political violence of the 1970s came from the extreme Left, but that was not its only possible source. A reminder that the extreme Right was not dead came in 1980, when a bomb that exploded at the Munich

October Festival was traced to a neo-Nazi group. As a sign of things to come, hostels housing immigrants were attacked in the same year and a Jewish publisher murdered.

Though it was the terrorists who directly challenged the authority of the state with violence, it was a much broader subculture of protest that influenced the political agenda of the country more directly. The objectives of the protest varied. Some were permanent, in particular the environment, with opposition to nuclear power as the main component. Some, even though environmentally inspired, came and went, like, for instance, the protest against a new runway at Frankfurt airport. Some were directed against insensitive and anti-social urban redevelopment and took the form of mass squats. One other major respect in which the successors of the APO added to the syllabus of public issues was through the introduction of gender politics. Feminism was part of the challenge to the conservative public values that had prevailed until the 1960s; it was reinforced by the frustrations of trying for a thorough reform of the abortion laws.

Much of what held this subculture of protest together was a loose network of life-style communities, with its own shops, newspapers, cafés, and kindergartens. But if public policy were to be affected, more than this would be needed, more indeed than *ad hoc* petitions and demonstrations. Slowly protest politics became structured, first through Citizens' Initiatives to press particular local demands, then by the adoption of Alternative Lists, under one label or another, to fight elections. In 1980 the Greens emerged as a party with an organization at the federal level, but even before then they had begun to achieve electoral success. In the European elections of 1979 they had secured 3.2 per cent, though they did less well in the 1980 Bundestag election, when the SPD managed to squeeze the anti-Strauß vote. Beginning in Bremen in 1979, they had begun to clear the 5 per cent hurdle for entry into state parliaments.

The heyday of Green electoral victories came in the 1980s and will be considered below. Before that the post-APO staged one major public propaganda effort against the Schmidt government's policies which helped to bring Schmidt down—a series of 'peace rallies' against the twin-track decision and the installation of cruise and Pershing missiles. These were the biggest public demonstrations on military policy since the 'anti-nuclear-death' movement of the 1950s and indicated how central Green positions had become to German politics. Organizationally the protest subculture might be marginal to West German society—deliberately so—but its ideas were penetrating deep into the mainstream. Of the estimated 650,000 who turned up for the final demonstration in Bonn, a good many were neither Communists (who had had a hand in drawing up the manifesto) nor Greens; they came from the SPD or no party at all. In this respect the demonstration highlighted the structural crisis of the SPD, one that Brandt had tried to transcend, but that Schmidt was forced to face.

At the very time that the SPD chancellor and his cabinet were turning towards pragmatic and incremental problem-solving, the 1968ers, marching through the institutions, were turning the party in the opposite direction. That applied particularly to economic policy and defence policy. The Schmidt government's successful fight against inflation after the oil shock was bought at a price. Though growth recovered in the late 1970s, unemployment remained stubbornly high and did not fall below the one-million level until 1978. The virtuous circle of low inflation, steady growth, full employment, and a favourable balance of payments that had been the FRG's hallmark ceased to apply. In 1980 the balance of payments fell into deficit.

These difficulties led to a triangular battle between the trade-union wing of the SPD, the party's New Left wing, and the FDP coalition partner. The trade unions, though in other respects Schmidt's natural allies against both the SPD Left and the FDP, insisted on an active labour-market policy and the maintenance of all the welfare gains from the Brandt government. In the 1970s unions became more militant than they had been. They insisted on wage rises to make good the costs of the oil price rise; their resentment at the FDP-imposed compromise on co-determination led to their withdrawal from the Concerted Action; and 1978 saw strike waves in a number of industries. In all these matters the trade-union rank-and-file had the support of the predominantly middle-class anti-capitalist Left of the SPD. Under the impact of these pressures the conflicting claims between social expenditure and new capital investment were increasingly difficult to reconcile and the tax cuts of 1975 were reflected in a higher government borrowing requirement. As a result, in the ten years from

1969 to 1979 the state's share of GNP rose from 39 per cent to 48 per cent. More than any other issue, the question of public finance increased the strains between the coalition partners—strains that became even more marked after 1977, when the more aggressively pro-market Count Otto Lambsdorff became the FDP's Economy Minister; strains that were to become irreparable in 1982.

The unresolved disputes on economic management showed that in many respects the West German divide between Left and Right now ran not between the parties, but down the middle of the SPD. Though the line separating radicalism from terror became clearer after 1977, that between the SPD Left and the emergent Greens remained fluid and their support bases became increasingly interchangeable. If this was true in the matter of public expenditure, it was doubly true of the issues closest to the heart of the Left—the environment, above all nuclear power, and defence. The 53.5 per cent that the coalition parties won in 1980 may have been an index of the silent majority's support for *Modell Deutschland*; it did nothing to clarify the differences on policy within the coalition. The SPD was as divided as ever on defence and nuclear power, and Schmidt himself, for all his devotion to sound money, was distinctly less keen than the FDP on cuts in public expenditure. The FDP Foreign Minister Genscher began to fear that Schmidt could not deliver the votes of the SPD for the twin-track policy to which they were jointly committed. Lambsdorff lost whatever confidence he may once have had that the SPD would agree to slim down the state. He therefore threw down the gauntlet on 9 September 1982 with a memorandum that detailed the conditions on which the FDP would be prepared to remain in the coalition. To reverse the decline in investment activity and the growth of the public-sector share in both revenue and expenditure, the memorandum demanded radical reversals of policy: a priority for investment over consumption in public expenditure and the tax structure; reductions in subsidies; reductions in social-security expenditure, including unemployment benefit; a greater private-sector share in social insurance; and incipient deregulation of the business sector.

Lambsdorff's demands were designed to be unacceptable. The SPD duly obliged and the FDP ministers resigned from the government. Four weeks later a 'constructive vote of no confidence' took place in the Bundestag on the terms of Article 67 of the Basic Law—only the second time in the history of the FRG that it had been invoked. Helmut Kohl, the leader of the CDU, was elected Chancellor in the place of Schmidt by a majority of twenty-one—forty fewer than the joint strength of the CDU–CSU and FDP. As in 1969, the FDP was far from united on the change of partners, and a number of its leading members, including its General Secretary, Günter Verheugen, switched to the SPD rather than accede to the move to the Right. The way in which the change of government came about also revealed much about the way West German constitutional assumptions had evolved since 1949.

Thirty-three years had passed between the adoption of the Basic Law and the first successful use of Article 67. Previous changes of government—the formation of the Great Coalition in 1966 and that of the Social-Liberal Coalition in 1969—had also come about through switches of allegiance, not through an adverse electoral vote. Indeed, not only up to 1982 but in the whole history of the FRG no national government has been rejected by the electorate. In one important respect, however, the 1982 vote set a precedent. On the one hand, it was completely in accordance with the provisions of the Basic Law. But the constitution-makers of 1948–9 had assumed that the election of a parliament and the formation of a government were temporally and conceptually separate processes. The election they saw as a contest among the parties, government formation as a matter of subsequent negotiation. Chancellor democracy had undermined that assumption by emphasizing the connection between partisanship and governmental choice. The fusion of the two processes had been completed in 1972, when parties began to declare in advance their coalition preferences. Voters had become accustomed to electing not only a parliament, but a government. In 1980 the FDP had pledged continued support for Schmidt for the four-year length of a parliament, but had gone back on this pledge at mid-term. Was this a breach of constitutional convention? Did it diminish the legitimacy of Kohl's assumption of the Chancellorship? Kohl himself was uneasy about his position. Having formed a government in which Genscher remained as Foreign Minister and Lambsdorff as Economy Minister, he announced that this was a provisional administration only and that he would seek an early dissolution of the Bundestag. That was no simple undertaking, since the Basic Law had been drafted so as to prevent the frequent premature elections that had been one of the banes of the Weimar Republic. Only once the Constitutional Court had cleared the way on the grounds that the new Chancellor needed democratic legitimation could the Bundestag be dissolved. The election of 6 March 1983 did provide this legitimation. The CDU won a near-record 48.8 per cent and the FDP, which at one time looked like dropping below 5 per cent, won its second-lowest share of 6.9 per cent. The SPD, now led by Hans-Jochen Vogel, dropped 4.7 per cent to 38.2 per cent. The surprise of the election was provided by the Greens, who won 6.6 per cent and became the first new party to enter the Bundestag since 1953.

Kohl's election victory, which turned out to be the prelude to a Chancellorship that is likely to outlast Adenauer's, was less a reward for the Right than a punishment for the Left. Schmidt had lost the confidence of his coalition partner because he was losing the support of his party. The extent of the alienation between leader and members was shown by the Bonn 'peace rallies' in October 1983 which attracted an estimated 400,000 people and were addressed by the SPD's national chairman, Willy Brandt. On 18 November a special conference of the SPD voted by 583 votes to 14 against missile deployment. Four days later the Bundestag approved deployment by a majority of sixty; the conversion of the parliamentary FDP to the new coalition was as complete as the SPD's disavowal of the old coalition.

The conference vote confirmed the transformation of the SPD from the party of the Bad Godesberg programme to a party dominated by its 1968ers. A major factor in the party's anti-missile sentiment was its traditional anti-militarism. This had deep roots fed by the political role played by the Prussian–German army in the Empire and the Weimar Republic, but looked like being modified in the 1960s in the light of the more modest role of the new, depoliticized *Bundeswehr*. With Helmut Schmidt as Defence Minister from 1969 to 1972, the SPD–army relationship became almost cordial, but this cordiality faded as pacifism and anti-Americanism revived and the Greens and their sympathizers inside the SPD began to determine the agenda of the Left. The Greens' election success—repeated in 1987 and 1994, though not in the exceptional year of 1990—completed the realignment on the Left.

Especially in the *Landtage* and in local councils the Greens became increasingly strongly implanted and in 1985 they formed the first formal coalition government with the SPD in Hesse. The aim of the Greens was not merely to bring new issues to the fore, but to change the style of politics. Their commitment to representative parliamentary institutions was limited—indeed, among its 'fundamentalist' wing, led by Jutta Dittfurth and Rainer Trampert, it was non-existent. They preferred, instead, rank-and-file democracy (*Basisdemokratie*) and insisted on the biennial rotation of elected parliamentarians, which had to be abandoned once it turned out to be both impractical and unconstitutional.

All these developments amounted to a reversal of the ideological roles of the late 1960s. In the progressivist euphoria of those years, the Left was united by unlimited faith in the ability of politics to bring about human happiness. Rudi Dutschke even talked of realizing the dream of the Garden of Eden. Disappointment at the Brandt government's reform record, the impact of the Club of Rome's 1972 report on threats to the environment, *Limits to Growth*, the oil shocks, and the resumed nuclear arms race transformed optimism into fear and despair. Hope turned into paranoia and utopianism into apocalyptic vision, as when the Greens talked of the 'all-party coalition against the environment and peace'. Psychologically the reversal of mood was less great than the change of objectives might have indicated. Both the optimism of the 1960s and the pessimism of the later 1970s were absolute. As the disillusioned poet of the APO, Hans Magnus Enzensberger, pointed out, 'The idea of the apocalypse has accompanied utopian thinking from its outset. It follows it like a shadow . . . The notion of the end of the world is nothing other than a negative utopia.' Ironically, the New Left's despair facilitated a recapture of morale on the Right. The Right could now claim that it was capitalism that was truly progressive, that the rolling-back of the state would emancipate modern Germans, that the call for 'democratization' threatened a new totalitarianism by politicizing all aspects of civil society. It was the CDU that exuded confidence in 1983 with its slogan, 'Vote for recovery' (*den Aufschwung wählen*). By stressing that his new coalition represented the middle way ('die Koalition der Mitte'), Kohl established his claim to the inheritance of *Modell Deutschland*.

Buffeted by the oil shock, challenged by the New Left's rejection of the post-war consensus, undermined by terrorism, and divided by the measures to combat it, the FRG of the Schmidt period might well have seemed on the verge of destabilization. It certainly became more difficult to govern, though the talk then current of 'governmental overload' and 'ungovernability' seems in retrospect greatly exaggerated. What is true is that from the early 1970s onwards West German governments not only faced more complex policy challenges, but met greater institutional obstacles. The Social-Liberal coalition had safe majorities in the Bundestag, but not in the Bundesrat, which represented the *Länder*, in whose governments, for most of this period, the CDU–CSU predominated. A number of the government's proposals, including the extension of industrial co-determination and university reform, survived only as amended by the Bundesrat. The Constitutional Court was also invoked more often in the more polarized atmosphere of the 1970s and, though the Court gave crucial support to the government over the Basic Treaty with the GDR, it frustrated such measures as abortion law reform. Lastly, as we have seen, the Bundesbank became a more independent force in a period of inflationary pressures and currency turbulence and, though Schmidt and the Bank saw eye to eye more often than not, it was potentially a further constraint on the government's freedom of action. The increasing weight of the checks and balances has become a familiar feature of German politics and the Kohl government has been subject to them particularly since unification. But at the time they were a new factor and appeared to add to the burdens of maintaining the FRG's stability.

None of these difficulties seems to have diminished the legitimacy of democracy West German style. The longer the FRG lasted, the less its existence was questioned, so that it resembled Bertrand de Jouvenel's description of the French Third Republic in which agitated politicians ruled over a tranquil population. Pride in the FRG's achievements, which initially concentrated on economic reconstruction, now extended to its political life. While nationalism remained taboo, and the division of Germany appeared irreversible, the liberal constitutional order increasingly shaped a new political identity. The veteran political theorist Dolf Sternberger argued that out of 'a clear consciousness of the beneficence of this Basic Law . . . a new, second patriotism has imperceptibly evolved', one that he dubbed 'constitutional patriotism'. His Heidelberg colleague Rainer Lepsius coined the similar concept of a 'citizens' nation' in which 'legitimation [is] derived from civil rights', far removed from the traditional German ethnic criterion of nationality.

As a description of the prevalent political consciousness at the beginning of the 1980s, these theses were probably close to the mark. They did not, however, remain uncontested, for they touched one of the continuing themes of German public debate over nearly two centuries: how to define German national identity. Constitutional patriotism and the Citizens' nation were attractive to the Liberal Left not only for the high valuation they placed on democracy, but for the way they downgraded ethnicity, cultural exclusiveness, and historical continuity. That made these concepts less than welcome to sections of the Right. They saw in the new doctrine an encouragement to accept the permanent division of Germany and to forget the national past. There was no uniform response to the theses of the Liberal Left. Some, like the Berlin historian Ernst Nolte, sought to reintegrate the Third Reich into German history by 'historicizing' it; others, like the late Andreas Hillgruber, to restore the patriotism of those who fought against the Russian army in the Second World War; others still, like Michael Stürmer, at one stage Helmut Kohl's speech-writer, argued that Germans needed a new historical consciousness, since a German nation-state as a political unit was evidently beyond recall. These controversies became known as the 'historians' dispute', which raged between 1986 and 1988, and it was in this context that the concept of constitutional patriotism was launched into popular debate through a polemic by Jürgen Habermas. The emergence of this dispute was to some extent anticipated by the election of Kohl. On the one hand, Kohl was an unambiguous constitutional democrat; he could hardly be otherwise as the self-styled political grandson of Adenauer. On the other hand, though he acknowledged that there was no returning to the Bismarckian nation-state of 1871 to 1933, he also insisted that the German Question was still 'juridically open'. How and when it would be solved he could have no idea; but when the opportunity did present itself he was psychologically ready to seize it. Until that moment he did not always show a sure instinct in dealing with the past, as when he invited President Reagan on the fortieth anniversary of VE Day to the military cemetery of Bitburg, where both Waffen-SS volunteers and *Wehrmacht* conscripts were buried. In this respect, Richard von Weizsäcker, Federal President since 1984, demonstrated a less shaky judgement. He stated unambiguously that 8 May 1945 was a day of liberation for all Germans and that its anniversary was a day of remembrance: 'the more honestly we celebrate it, the freer we shall be.' He invoked constitutional patriotism: 'never has there been a better protection of the citizen's rights on German soil.' But he did not forget solidarity with the Germans of the GDR.

In the 1983 election campaign Kohl called for a 'turn-around', a *Wende*. In domestic politics this amounted to a more determined attempt to pursue his predecessor's objectives, rather than the implementation of Lamsdorff's agenda. Initially public expenditure was cut and the budget deficit reduced. The automatic indexation of pensions that had been the centrepiece of Adenauer's social-welfare package was modified, though the precedent for this had already been set in 1977. When Kohl proclaimed his government to be a coalition of the middle, he meant it. Despite some pressure from business and the FDP, he did not embark on the kind of neo-liberal counter-revolution that happened in Britain under Mrs Thatcher and in the USA under President Reagan. Of the three main commandments of monetarism, at best one-and-a-half were observed. The first—tight control of the money supply—was inherent in the powers of the Bundesbank. There was nothing new about that. The second—low taxation and low public expenditure—was half-observed. Taxes were cut in 1987, stimulating consumer demand, but public expenditure was not cut by an equal amount, with the result that the budget remained in deficit until 1989. Like the SPD, the CDU had powerful client groups; like the SPD, it felt it could not afford to offend electorally strong voter groups. Generous subsidies to agriculture, coal and steel, and aerospace remained untouched. On the liberalization of the labour market, the other main demand of monetarists, very little happened, though the government did legislate to end unemployment benefit to workers laid off by extraneous labour disputes. Indeed the continued bargaining strength of trade unions was shown by the move towards a thirty-five-hour week in which the metal-working industry took the lead. The main consequence of these policies was that the economy remained buoyant, but for most of the 1980s unemployment remained at over 2.25 million, some 8–9 per cent of the labour force. However, the record was sufficiently good to ensure the re-election of Kohl in 1987. While the CDU dropped back to near its average at 44.3 per cent, the FDP recovered. Of the opposition parties, the Greens went up by another 2.3 per cent, while the SPD, still divided on major issues, stagnated. At the end of four years there was not much sign of a policy turn-around. In so far as there had been a *Wende*, it had happened in 1974, when Schmidt took over from Brandt. Given the lack of dynamic in domestic policy, it is not surprising that Kohl's hold on electoral support remained uncertain. The CDU was shaken in 1987–8 by the Barschel Affair, a dirty tricks campaign by the Prime Minister of Schleswig-Holstein, Uwe Barschel, during the *Landtag* election, which resulted in the SPD capture of the *Land* government and the suicide of Barschel. A further blow was the death in October 1988 of Franz-Josef Strauß, the leader of the CSU and Prime Minister of Bavaria. Though Strauß had caused Kohl much anguish and pain by his attempts to pull the CDU to the Right, he was generally credited with integrating right-wing voters into the CDU–CSU. His death may have contributed to the rise of a new far-Right party, the Republikaner, led by a television journalist and former Waffen-SS officer, Franz Schönhuber. With a platform that concentrated on xenophobia and law-and-order, the Republicans were able to make sizeable gains in local elections during 1989 and to secure election to the European Parliament in that year by winning 7.1 per cent nationally. The Republicans' gains were a sign of general political discontent and the auguries for Kohl's chances in the 1990 Bundestag election began to be less and less favourable. But by the time that election took place, the world had changed.

If economic management followed well-worn paths under the new government, Kohl embarked on a number of important initiatives in foreign policy. The complex of problems he faced was not new: how to combine loyalty to the Atlantic alliance, maintenance of *Ostpolitik*, and a strengthening of the Franco-German axis in Europe. The most urgent need was to repair relations with the USA and here the departure of the SPD and the continuation in office of Genscher both helped. Above all, the personal friction that had existed between Schmidt and President Carter no longer applied. With the installation of the missiles in 1983 US fears that its European allies might be soft on security were laid to rest, as were European—and particularly German—fears that the USA might disengage itself from Europe. There were, nevertheless, a number of obstacles to the full renewal of the old German–American friendship. The close personal and ideological partnership that existed between President Reagan and Mrs Thatcher downgraded Kohl's influence; it was only when George Bush succeeded Reagan in 1988 that the FRG regained its place as America's premier European partner.

A second concern of Kohl's was one that he shared with Schmidt, and that arose out of the FRG's special relationships with the East. He could have wished for a less confrontational US stance towards the Soviet Union and was particularly disturbed by Reagan's adoption of the Strategic Defence Initiative (SDI or 'star wars'). A foolproof defence against Soviet missiles, if it turned out to be technically feasible, would again diminish the importance of Europe in the Atlantic alliance. Given the need to repair the transatlantic bridges and given Britain's enthusiastic support for SDI, Kohl suppressed his doubts and went for the next best option—namely, securing the maximum European participation and research contracts for West German high-technology firms. Paradoxically, the softening of superpower relations in the later 1980s did not improve the FRG's bargaining position. When Mikhail Gorbachev succeeded to the First Secretaryship of the CPSU in 1985, the trend towards *détente* returned, culminating in the INF Treaty of 1987 that led to the reciprocal withdrawal of the medium-range missiles. That this was achieved through bilateral American–Soviet negotiation, in contrast with the twin-track decision that had involved all NATO partners, showed that the strategic fate of Europe could still depend on extra-European forces. For twenty years the *détente* cycle had passed through bi-polar and multi-polar phases; it was, for the time being, back in a bi-polar phase.

Given the uncertainties of the West German–American partnership, Kohl also relied on the alternative Western insurance policy, that was underwritten by France. West German and French interests did not coincide at every point. There were from time to time differences of emphasis on energy policy, industrial policy, and, above all, world-trade policy in which France was considerably more protectionist than the FRG. The programme of 'Keynesianism in one country' that characterized the first two years of Mitterrand's presidency (1981–3) certainly ran counter to the FRG's preferences. But on crucial issues the two states were now bound to each other in an alliance within the alliance. Mitterrand supported Kohl's stand on the twin-track decision, though without agreeing to station NATO missiles on French territory; joint military manœuvres were intensified; and the EUREKA European space programme was initiated, partly out of fear that SDI might lead to an unbeatable US monopoly in space research. Above all it was France and the FRG that maintained the momentum of European integration, in particular in working towards the Single European Act, which opened the way to the Single Market inside the EC in 1992. In this matter, however, strong British support was also forthcoming.

If the FRG's relations with France and the USA gave rise to occasional incompatibilities, the West German desire to maintain *Ostpolitik* gave rise to more serious problems. Though Kohl's opposition to Communism was no more in doubt than Schmidt's and Genscher's, the need to keep an open line to Moscow retained its priority. Kohl himself had not been in sympathy with the CDU's hard-line objections to *Ostpolitik*; the election victory of 1983 therefore provided an opportunity for leading his party out of its oppositional cul-de-sac. Any move for further *détente* with the Soviet Union was difficult as long as the unmoveable Leonid Brezhnev was at the helm. His successor, Yuri Andropov, though by instinct a reformer, stayed in office for too short a period (November 1982 to February 1984) for new initiatives; his successor, Konstantin Chernenko, lasted only thirteen months. During this interim period the countries of Western Europe were able to take advantage of tensions between Moscow and its satellites to move closer to the latter. Honecker, in particular, having threatened a 'new ice age' if NATO missiles were installed, reacted remarkably mildly once they were in place, a stance echoed by both Hungary and Romania. Kohl was therefore encouraged to continue his predecessors' policy of embracing the GDR in order to foster diplomatic independence and domestic liberalization. Indeed, he managed to kill two birds with one stone. He offered credits of unprecedented generosity to the GDR, amounting to almost DM 2 billion, and appointed the bitterest critic of *Ostpolitik*, Franz-Josef Strauß, the messenger to bear the money.

The success of this policy was limited. The GDR regime continued to engage in pinpricks—for instance, by using the East Berlin airport of Schönefeld in 1986 to flood West Berlin with asylum-seekers. But there was also practical co-operation—for instance, in improving road access and in cleaning up rivers. Honecker was keen to visit the FRG, one motive being to see the family home in the Saarland again, but this was vetoed by Moscow. He finally came in 1987, but by then the leadership in Moscow had changed. Above all, *Ostpolitik* was, as before, also West German domestic politics and this made friendly noises towards Poland more expensive than those towards the GDR. The expellees from the Eastern territories, especially Silesia, were a vocal lobby on whose votes the CDU depended. Brandt and Schmidt had ignored them, but Kohl caused some embarrassment and confusion when he addressed their annual rally in 1985 at which the platform banner—removed before he spoke—declared, 'Silesia remains ours'. Ambiguities about the CDU's attitude to the Oder–Neiße frontier were not finally removed until after unification.

As long as the inflexible Brezhnev and his immediate successors directed Soviet policy, Honecker could pursue his own cautious *Deutschlandpolitik*, aimed at securing a special relationship with Bonn. The opportunity for this came to an end with the death of Chernenko. With the election of Gorbachev as First Secretary of the CPSU in March 1985 the initiative passed to Moscow again; as the INF Treaty showed, superpower *détente* regained its priority. With that the GDR could have lived, however regretfully. Gorbachev, however, went further, albeit with slow and uncertain steps. He became convinced of the need to reform the Soviet Empire, by liberalizing the regime of both the Soviet Union itself and the more Stalinist of its satellites. That, as Honecker appreciated more quickly than Gorbachev, the GDR could not live with. Whether Gorbachev was aware of de Tocqueville's warning that the most dangerous moment for a tyranny comes when it tries to reform itself we do not know. Its truth was once more borne out.

Slowly the contagion of *glasnost* spread into the GDR. In 1987 there was a riot in East Berlin when police tried to stop young people listening to a pop concert taking place on the other side of the Wall. At the time, that could be dismissed as an isolated incident, but instances of dissent multiplied. The next came on 15 January 1989, the seventieth anniversary of the murder of the founders of the German Communist Party, Karl Liebknecht and Rosa Luxemburg. The official commemoration was disrupted by placards and leaflets quoting Luxemburg's dictum that freedom means freedom for those who think differently. Eighty demonstrators were arrested. After the municipal elections in May of that year there were further protests at the falsification of the results, designed to conceal the high level of abstentions. In June there was discontent at the support that the regime gave to the crushing of the Tiananmen Square protest in Peking. Applications for permission to emigrate multiplied. However, the real opportunity for the population to turn its back on the regime came with the summer holiday season. Thousands of GDR tourists sought asylum in the West German embassies in Budapest and Prague with the aim of being transferred to the FRG. Hungary, where a reformist Communist government had dismantled the fortifications along the Austrian border, offered the best opportunity. After secret negotiations with Chancellor Kohl, the Hungarian Foreign Minister, Gyula Horn (Prime Minister since June 1994), opened the Austrian border to the East German applicants. In the next few weeks some 50,000 persons left for the FRG by this route, followed by a rather smaller number from Czechoslovakia.

While this individual dissent was gathering pace, collective dissent was organizing itself inside the GDR. The most important of the dissident groups was the New Forum (*Neues Forum*), formally constituted at the beginning of September and led by a formidable group of writers and intellectuals including the biologist Jens Reich and the painter Bärbel Bohley. Others included Democratic Awakening (*Demokratischer Aufbruch*) with strong links with the Lutheran Church, and 'Democracy Now' (*Demokratie Jetzt*), as well as numerous smaller local initiatives. All were concerned with civil liberties, including freedom of speech and freedom to travel, with anti-militarism, and with concern for the environment. More threatening still to the regime's claim to monopolize political activities was the formation of parties outside the approved 'anti-Fascist bloc', beginning with a reconstituted Social Democratic Party, banned since the enforced fusion into the SED in 1946; the example of the first semi-free elections in Poland in June, in which the re-legalized Solidarnósc trade union had won almost all the seats open to them, was evidently another source of contagion. Even within the SED, dissent was for the first time openly organized, round the lawyer Gregor Gysi and the film school director Lothar Bisky, who were to become leaders of the SED's post-Communist successor party, the Party of Democratic Socialism (Partei des Demokratischen Sozialismus (PDS)).

In the face of these internal and external pressures the GDR regime grew increasingly desperate. On 31 August the Minister for State Security, Erich Mielke, was forced to ask whether the GDR faced another 17 June. His regional commanders reassured him that everything was under control. In fact the GDR faced something much worse than 17 June: the total disavowal of the state by its population. In the course of September increasingly well-attended meetings and protest services took place in churches in East Berlin, Leipzig, and other towns. In Leipzig they were followed by peaceful processions every Monday, culminating on 9 October in a demonstration by 70,000 persons. Mielke was prepared to use force to crush it, as he had done on previous days in other cities, but in the end this did not happen. A number of intermediaries have claimed credit for the avoidance of bloodshed, including the conductor of the Leipzig Gewandhaus Orchestra, Kurt Masur, but the decisive factor was the unavailability of the Soviet army. The world had changed between the Berlin rising of 1953 and the peaceful processions of 1989, and Gorbachev was not prepared to impose a 'Chinese solution' in the centre of Europe. Whether or not it decided to use force, that was the day on which the regime's bankruptcy became manifest, for more had changed than the mood of the population. When Gorbachev visited East Berlin on 5 October for the celebration of the fortieth anniversary of the GDR, he warned the SED leadership that, unless they reformed, they would forfeit Soviet support. The crowds that welcomed him with cries of 'Gorby, Gorby', reminiscent of the calls of 'Willy, Willy' in Erfurt in 1970, showed that then as now they looked for salvation from outside the GDR. As it turned out, it was neither Washington nor Bonn that dealt the death-blow to the regime, but Moscow. On 18 October the Politburo of the SED saw the light. It deposed Honecker as General Secretary and elected Egon Krenz in his place. On 9 November the Council of Ministers promulgated an ambiguous statement about the liberalization of foreign travel regulations. The population of East Berlin took the hint and made its way to the Wall. Guards, confused by contradictory instructions, let the crowds stream into West Berlin. Physically the Wall still stood, but it had lost its political purpose. The GDR was at the beginning of its end. The provisional, which had come to look durable, turned out to be provisional after all.

8 A New Germany

Germany. A former country in central Europe.
(*Random House Dictionary of the English Language* (1967))

WITH the opening of the Wall, the GDR, as the world had known it, came to an end. Like the other events of 1989, which brought about the end of Communist rule in the satellite states of the Soviet Union, this one took both participants and observers by surprise. But the uncertainty took on a special dimension in the GDR. In Poland and Czechoslovakia, Hungary and Romania, the question about the future was straightforward: who would take power after the Communists had vacated it? It was the regime that was in question, not the nation-state over which it ruled. Poland would still be Poland and Hungary would still be Hungary. Only Czechoslovakia broke into two, without violence, and Yugoslavia with much bloodshed. But in both these cases the fragmentation was internal, with no outside power involved. The GDR was different. In the other satellite states the Soviet Union had imposed a regime; in Germany it had created a state. The GDR's *raison d'être* was the Soviet-style economic system; once that went, would there be any point in the state's survival? That was the question debated over the next year. The participants in the debate were, for the last time, the three parties that had combined to shape the fate of post-war Germany on every critical occasion: German politicians—this time from the East as well as the West; the German population—this time, too, from the East as well as the West; and the four victor powers.

To appreciate what the options were, we need to ask, however briefly, why the GDR collapsed. There were a number of necessary conditions, but none of them was, until 1989, sufficient to bring about the fall of the regime. The state lacked popular legitimacy; the anti-Fascist and Socialist idealism that stood by at its birth was exhausted; the economy was stagnating; freedom of speech and thought was more severely controlled than in at least some other parts of the Soviet bloc. Yet because nobody starved, because a modicum of private and family life could go on undisturbed, above all because there was no realistic prospect of change, the population remained quiescent. West German politicians, even those, like Chancellor Kohl, who talked of the German Question being open, gave no hint that they wished to change the status quo created by *Ostpolitik*. The SPD, now in opposition, sought even closer links than before with the SED, and in 1987 the two parties produced a joint paper on ideology and common security. This paper showed both the strengths and the weaknesses of the SPD's outlook. It underlined the SPD's commitment to civil liberties as outlined in the Helsinki Final Act and thereby evoked a favourable response from oppositional groups in the GDR. But the emphasis was on the joint obligation to peaceful coexistence, which took the SPD one step closer to acknowledging the equal status of the GDR. In the last resort, stability in the relations between states came first. The SPD was now close to regarding the 'two-state theory' not as a necessary evil but as desirable, a conclusion that proved a fatal handicap to it once the Wall was opened.

What turned the potential for revolt in the GDR into the real thing was contagion from outside: the examples of liberalization in Hungary and Poland and Gorbachev's policy of *glasnost*. These examples encouraged the opposition both outside and inside the GDR to organize; once this happened the population gained the courage to demonstrate in massive numbers; and once the regime abandoned the attempts to suppress the demonstrations by force, its weakness was plain for all to see. By October 1989 it was possible to speak of a consensus in the GDR against single-party rule and against the denial of free speech, free elections, the rule of law, and the right to travel. It was far from certain whether there was a consensus in favour of a particular alternative. Gorbachev, it was clear, wanted to save Communism by reforming it, and that meant, in the context of the GDR, a take-over by a reformed SED, possibly in coalition with other forces. The GDR opposition, led by the New Forum, also wanted a reformed GDR; it did not dissent from the ideals of the GDR, only from the way the regime had betrayed them. But what did the silent majority want? Its wishes emerged by stages, spread over several months. As the demonstrations became larger and larger, the participants proclaimed 'We are the people'. The agenda changed on 20 November when the slogan changed—no one quite knows how—to 'We are one people'. But which slogan had the stronger support? There was, as yet, no knowing.

What is surprising in retrospect is the slowness of the West German reaction. It is as if Kohl, too, was a prisoner of the two-state theory and had no contingency plan for the collapse of the GDR regime. Even those who desired national unification, which was by no means all West Germans, assumed that the process would be gradual and long drawn out. This was the implication of Kohl's Ten-Point Programme of 28 November, which foresaw a confederation of the two German states with eventual unification after a period that was unspecified, but generally assumed to be not less than two years. Meanwhile events moved faster in the GDR than in the FRG. Hans Modrow, First Secretary of the SED in Dresden and reputed to be a reformer, became Prime Minister on 13 November. On 3 December the Krenz era came to an end. Following protests by rank-and-file members the forty-five-day First Secretary, and with him the entire Politburo and Central Committee of the SED, resigned. Krenz was too closely implicated in the local election fraud and the support for the Tiananmen Square massacre to survive into the new GDR. Would a purged and reconstituted party after all have a say in the future of the state? The SED gave itself a new name, adding Partei des Demokratischen Sozialismus as a suffix (SED–PDS), and dropping the SED part two months later. It elected a new leadership under Gregor Gysi, a former dissident, as First Secretary. But, though the leading positions were now in the hands of new men, the membership structure lower down remained largely intact, as did the near monopolization of public administration and the economy by party members.

The mission of Modrow and the new SED leadership was to save what could be saved: as much as possible of the Socialist system as a prop for a continuing GDR; failing that, as much as possible of an independent GDR even without the Socialist system. If both these failed, it aimed to postpone German unification as long as possible and to negotiate it on the most favourable terms possible. That the last of these three options was the only viable one became increasingly probable even before the end of the year. Although the SED had made major concessions to democratic demands by striking the 'leading role of the SED' out of the constitution and making preparations for free elections, it remained discredited in the eyes of the majority of the population. More ominously, the idea of a surviving GDR in any shape or form seemed to be losing support. When Chancellor Kohl visited Dresden on 19 December he was greeted by a crowd of 100,000 demanding unification.

The device by which Modrow sought to broaden the base of his government was the Round Table, which met for the first time on 7 December. It consisted in equal parts of government delegates (i.e. the SED and the old 'bloc' parties) and the principal civil-rights organizations, as well as the newly reconstituted Social Democratic Party. It was easier to say what the Round Table was not than what it was. It was clearly not a representative or legislative body, for it was elected by no one and accountable to no one. It was not an alternative government. It was a consultative body and a watch-dog; above all, though the opposition members were the antagonists of the SED–PDS, they were unwittingly also its allies, for most of them were still prepared to reform their state rather than abolish it. It was in their reformist enterprise that they were most effective as watch-dogs. When Modrow dragged his feet over the abolition of the Stasi and proposed replacing it with a similar body, the Round Table passed a vote of no confidence in him. A crowd broke into the Stasi headquarters and there were threats of a general strike. Modrow gave in, but it was evident that the state needed a new set of institutions.

What replaced the Round Table was a 'Government of National Responsibility', which now contained members of the oppositional groups as ministers, though without departmental portfolios. Yet the strengthened formal position of the groups merely highlighted their inherent weakness—namely, their lack of legitimacy. The Round Table had already decided to bring forward the elections to the Volkskammer from the original date, 6 May, to 18 March, which made the new government's authority even more transitional. More and more the political running was being made by actors outside the control of Modrow, the PDS, and the government: power was shifting to the crowds on the streets, the mushrooming political parties, the politicians of the FRG, and the victor powers. As far as the street was concerned, there were first of all those who voted with their feet at the rate of 60,000 per month, now that there were no longer any physical obstacles to moving West. This migration alone put severe pressure on the West German authorities and the government. Those that stayed called increasingly for German unification, ironically quoting the line from the official GDR anthem, 'Germany—united fatherland', that had been taboo since the 1970s. Above all, a new theme now appeared in the chants, the call for economic unification. If the Deutsche Mark did not come to the East, the demonstrators argued, they would move to it.

While the Government of National Responsibility officially held political authority, political parties proliferated. The two most significant of the 'bloc' parties, the CDU and the LDP, had already left the 'Democratic Bloc' before the end of 1989, and the CDU had made efforts to renew itself by replacing the collaborationist leadership with a new team, headed by Lothar de Maizière, a lawyer who had defended dissidents and was a prominent member of the Lutheran Church. The LDP delayed internal reform until February 1990, when it bowed to the threat posed by rival foundations and formed an electoral alliance with these in the League of Free Democrats (Bund Freier Demokraten (BFD)). But it was the reconstituted SPD that attracted most attention and seemed to have the greatest chance of popular support, especially when it chose Willy Brandt as its honorary president. It felt at home in the traditional strongholds of German Social Democracy and its record, unlike that of the bloc parties, was clean. Conscious of the head start that the SPD had established, the CDU had little confidence that it could compete effectively. It therefore formed a pact—the Alliance for Germany (Allianz für Deutschland)—with two new parties, the opposition group Democratic Awakening, which had formed itself into a party in December 1989, and the German Social Union (Deutsche Soziale Union (DSU)), more right wing than either of its partners, which enjoyed the active support of the Bavarian CSU and had adopted the CSU's slogan of 'freedom instead of Socialism'. The Alliance stood for 'Yes to German Unity and the social market economy' and saw in Chancellor Kohl 'its reliable partner'. These, it turned out, were to be its trump cards. The last major party formation was that involving some of the remaining opposition groupings. Precisely because they saw themselves as informal popular movements, much on the lines of the early Citizens' Initiatives in the FRG, they were reluctant to enter on electoral competition, with all the organizational structures and parliamentary compromises that that implied. In the end, led by the New Forum, three of them combined to form one list named Alliance '90.

Though these parties were the formal participants in the competition for public favour, two men outside the GDR had more influence on the outcome than anyone inside it. They were Helmut Kohl and Mikhail Gorbachev. When Modrow visited Moscow on 30 January to seek Soviet support for his new government, he came away empty-handed. Gorbachev hinted that he now had no objection to the principle of all-German self-determination. When Kohl and Genscher visited Moscow eleven days later, they got a similar message. Nobody knows quite when Gorbachev became resigned to the prospect, or even the desirability, of German national unity, but it was probably in January 1990, when it became evident how fragile the authority of the GDR government had become. But, whenever the decision came, it was crucial for the history of Europe. All Germans, and certainly all German politicians, knew that from 1945 to 1990 the shape of German statehood had depended on the wishes and the vetoes of the four victor powers. Once that veto was suspended, and only then, could Germans themselves freely decide. Once the veto of the Soviets, who by 1990 had the biggest stake in a divided Germany, was suspended, the outcome was increasingly clear.

The emergence of an East German party system that closely resembled that of West Germany and the ever more intimate links between the Eastern parties and their Western patrons meant that the election campaign was being increasingly conducted on Western terms and indeed by Westerners. In part the reasons for this were purely technical. The Eastern party leaders lacked not only the expertise, but also the means for effective campaigning. Not only the money but the posters, the photocopiers, the personal computers, even the stationery and the paperclips had to come from the West. Moreover, since the media of the GDR were still predominantly in the hands of those sympathetic to the PDS, GDR citizens depended even more than before on Western sources for information and guidance. But the main reason for the Western domination of the campaign was that the politics of the GDR was now a major issue in the politics of the FRG. As the demands of the East German population for unification and economic aid became more insistent, West German politicians were under growing pressure to produce responses. On the procedures and timing of political unification it was still possible to be vague. On economic relations greater urgency was needed, if only because of the uncontrolled freedom of movement that now existed between the two German states.

It was in this context that Helmut Kohl, as head of the Federal Government, was not only able, but required, to take initiatives. He established a cabinet committee on German unity on 7 February and offered immediate economic aid to the GDR. But a condition for this aid was an East German commitment to economic reform and currency union. When Modrow failed to guarantee this, the aid package of DM 16 billion was withheld. In the light of the whip hand that Kohl succeeded in establishing over all-German politics, the outcome of the Volkskammer election is less surprising than it was to most observers at the time. Contrary to opinion-poll forecasts and media expectations, the Alliance for Germany won 48.1 per cent, almost an absolute majority. The CDU alone won 40.6 per cent. The SPD, which had gone into the election in the hope of at last entering into its inheritance, had to be content with 21.9 per cent. The PDS got 16.4 per cent, Alliance '90 2.9 per cent, and the remaining civic movements a further 2 per cent.

This election result answered a number of questions about the politics of the GDR: not only most obviously in terms of immediate policy preferences, but in terms of how the population saw their future and perhaps had always seen their future. The election outcome was a vote of confidence not so much in the nominal victors, the CDU of the GDR, as in Chancellor Kohl. The CDU's rather dubious past role as the lap-dog of the SED was overshadowed by its new link with the man best qualified to play Father Christmas. The CDU had triumphed over its structural weaknesses in the East, where none of the factors that favoured it in the West applied. There were few

Catholics; indeed observant Christians or even nominal church members were in the minority. There were no self-employed farmers and virtually no self-employed small businessmen. Group politics, as it is known in Western pluralist societies, did not exist. East Germans voted overwhelmingly for national unity, the rule of law, and Western affluence. It was also the absence of group politics that was the SPD's undoing. The working-class subculture that had once flourished there and that had sent the founder of German Social Democracy, August Bebel, to the Reichstag as long ago as the 1870s, was no more. It had been undermined by the Nazis and destroyed by forty years of Communism, its very symbols discredited through being appropriated by the regime. Willy Brandt remained a hero to much of the population, but he was the ambassador of a party out of power. Indeed, the most remarkable feature of the election was the SPD's failure to win the working-class vote. Throughout the GDR half the working-class vote went to the CDU and its allies. In the most industrialized south, in Saxony and Thuringia, two-thirds of the working class voted for the parties of the Right.

The election also went a long way to answering another question: what did those East Germans want who did not want the GDR? The answer turned out to be what many had long suspected, that the 'reference society' for most GDR citizens was the FRG; that they equated their state with the regime and wanted to be rid of both; and that those writers and intellectuals who in November 1989 had evoked 'a Socialist alternative to the Federal Republic . . . and the anti-Fascist and humanistic ideals that were our point of departure' were whistling into the wind. The substantial PDS vote represented some of these voices, but mainly those who had been the beneficiaries of the regime. The minuscule vote for the civic movements showed that the 'third way' was not a serious option. The immediate consequence of the election for the GDR was the creation of a coalition embracing the Alliance for Germany, the Liberals, and the SPD under the CDU leader Lothar de Maizière. The consequence for Germany was that talks on the modalities of unification could now begin seriously on both the relevant levels: the inter-German and the international. Given the new political constellation, with CDU-led governments in both East and West, the inter-German level was the easier. This had a dual agenda, economic and constitutional, of which the first was the more urgent, the second the more profound, in its implications.

Talk of economic convergence, or at least of currency union, was already in the air by the time of the Volkskammer election; with the outcome a clear vote for accelerated unification, negotiations moved into a higher gear. Economic rationality might have dictated that the economy of the GDR be reformed on market principles before being integrated with that of the FRG. This is the course being pursued by the other reform economies of Central Europe, with greater or lesser success, in preparation for their entry into the EU. Yet there were a number of reasons why this option was unrealistic. The first was that it would require a degree of patience that East Germans did not possess; indeed the election campaign had discouraged patience by the parties' competitive bids to accelerate unification. There were, moreover, no physical barriers any longer to *de facto* unification. The frontier between the two states had ceased to exist; the Deutsche Mark circulated freely in the GDR; the threat that East Germans would move to the Deutsche Mark if it did not come to them was real enough. The second reason was that the timetable of economic union was connected with that of political union. Those who wanted political union as quickly as possible—and that included Chancellor Kohl—had no choice but to move fast on the economic front.

The outcome of these priorities was the German Economic and Monetary Union between the two German states, which came into force on 1 July. It created, at a stroke, a single German economic area, with the Deutsche Mark as the sole legal tender, on the basis of the social market economy, private property, rewards based on competition, and free movement of labour, capital, goods, and services. All wages, salaries, benefits, and debts were converted from GDR marks to D-Marks at the rate of 1 : 1; personal savings at the same rate up to DM 4,000 (but DM 2,000 for those under 14 and DM 6,000 for those over 60); all other assets at the rate of 1 : 2. Of these items, the conversion rate was the most controversial. It was opposed by those who feared that by overvaluing East German wages and prices it would make much of the East German economy uncompetitive, fears that were in part realized. It was also opposed by those who feared that the increase in the money supply and the release of pent-up consumer demand would stoke inflation. This was above all the fear of the President of the Bundesbank, Karl-Otto Pöhl, whose publicly expressed misgivings caused the biggest open row between the government and the Bank in the history of the FRG. Pöhl's forebodings on this score were not fully realized. The savings of the East German population were relatively small. The money supply as measured by M3 went up by DM 160 billion or about 13 per cent, whereas the East German population amounted to 20 per cent of the whole, and by no means all of the newly released purchasing power went into immediate consumption. He was, however, nearer the mark in anticipating that the costs of quick economic union would be high. The whole episode illustrated the limits of the Bundesbank's power. Treaty-making was a political matter, even when it had monetary implications. The Bank could advise and try to influence, but in the end had to accept the government's sovereignty, just as the government had to accept the Bank's independence in its wide, but limited, field.

Underlying the speed with which economic union came about there was a political agenda. The promise of swift economic union undoubtedly helped the CDU to victory on 18 March. But its achievement was also a pre-condition for swift political union. Here we witness a repetition of the process by which the FRG had been created in 1948–9. It was the currency reform and the economic union of the three Western zones that had been the crucial events in the division of Germany; thereafter the foundation of a West German state was both inevitable and almost an anti-climax. So now it was the economic and currency union that was the crucial event in ending the division of Germany; political union was bound to follow sooner rather than later.

Nevertheless there was no unanimity on either the speed or the form that political unification should take. The Basic Law permitted two possibilities. Article 23 provided for the simple accession of 'other parts of Germany' to the FRG. Article 146 provided for the adoption of a new constitution on the basis of the 'free decision of the German people'. Initially there was considerable support for the Article 146 road, to symbolize a new political start for a unified Germany and to avoid the suggestion that the GDR was simply being annexed. Two of the Justices of the Federal Constitutional Court lent their weight to this argument. In the end, however, the advocates of Article 23 won out. This method had the advantages of speed and simplicity on its side, but also those of legitimacy. The Basic Law was, in the words of the editor of the Liberal weekly *Die Zeit*, 'the best German constitution of all times': why not accept it for the whole of Germany, especially since the FRG was, for the majority of the GDR population, a 'reference society' not only economically but politically? Those in the GDR who did not like Article 23 in the main did not want a single German state. Though Germans on both sides of the Iron Curtain had dreamed of the end of division for forty years and had been genuinely delighted at the fall of the East German dictatorship, the prospect of instant national unity traumatized many of them. It was, as we noted in Chapter 1, yet another discontinuity in German national life, yet another shock to the structure of German statehood. Reactions to this challenge varied with rather blurred boundary lines between them. On the Right there were nationalist formulations which saw the restoration of a German nation-state as historical justice and the ending of an undeserved abnormality. On the Left there were those who viewed the prospect of a restored German nation-state with dismay, given the past record of such states. Between these two poles there was a broad spectrum of those best described as 'constitutional patriots', who welcomed national unity as the satisfaction of a basic human right and were happy to see the tried and tested institutions of the FRG extended to the East.

The actual negotiations between the two German states on political union took even less time than those on economic union. The GDR Volkskammer voted in favour of unification on the basis of Article 23 on 23 August, less than eight weeks after the currency union had come into force. On 23 September the two German parliaments accepted the Unification Treaty, to come into force on 3 October. That was the day on which the GDR ceased to exist, 329 days after the opening of the Wall. Five of the former members of the GDR government joined the Federal Cabinet as ministers without portfolio. On 18 October elections took place in the five *Länder* of the former GDR, reconstituted after their abolition by the Communist authorities in 1952. They largely confirmed the verdict of the Volkskammer election. One final outcome of the unification process that scarcely anyone would have dared to forecast when the Wall was opened was that the Bundestag election scheduled for 2 December became an all-German one—-the first to be held under free conditions since November 1932.

As these momentous events unfolded, Chancellor Kohl, who had been as hesitant as any of the participants in the autumn of 1989, showed an increasingly bold command of them. Yet the climax of German unification could not have happened without the agreement and, in the end, the active support of the victor powers. As at the time of the creation of the FRG and the *Ostpolitik* treaties, the map of Europe was determined within a framework designed by the super-powers and with the collaboration of those German politicians who seized the opportunities offered. With each stage of the evolution of the German Question the bargaining power of the West German players increased. Just as Brandt held a stronger hand than Adenauer, so Kohl held a stronger hand than Brandt. Each stage not only re-flected the degree of policy autonomy that West German policy actors enjoyed, but also increased it. In 1990 three men made German uni-fication possible: Mikhail Gorbachev, George Bush, and Helmut Kohl. Gorbachev and Bush, together with President Mitterrand and Mrs Thatcher, held a veto over this process, however theoretical that might in the end be. What was significant about the evolution of their attitudes was the way in which they found themselves reacting to events in Germany, rather than shaping them.

Germany's immediate Western neighbours were the least enthusiastic about the prospect of a single German state, given the obvious imbalance that that would create in the European state sys-tem. Mitterrand showed this in an ostentatious official visit to the GDR in December 1990. But by the time of the Dublin summit of the European Council in June 1990 he had concluded that the way to save the Franco-German axis was to influence German unification rather than oppose it. The British Prime Minister was not so easily per-suaded. She feared an 'overmighty bull in a china shop' and was in any case less enamoured of France's solution to the china shop's security problems—namely, closer European integration to limit Ger-man sovereignty. But on the appointed day both Britain and France signed, because there was no holding out against a formula agreed by Gorbachev, Bush, and Kohl.

What was it that those three did agree on? It became increasingly obvious even in the early months of 1990 that the question was ceasing to be whether Germany might be unified, but on what terms. Each of the participants therefore concentrated on maximizing his interests in what had manifestly become an unstoppable process. The first of the four victor powers to recognize that German unity was not only unstoppable but worthy of support was the USA. This was consistent with the shift of priorities under President Bush, who preferred a Bush–Kohl axis as the basis of US foreign policy to the Reagan–Thatcher axis that had dominated the 1980s. In this he was encouraged by his ambassador in Bonn, Vernon Walters, who seems to have foreseen the denouement of the German drama even before Chancellor Kohl. Mikhail Gorbachev, as we have seen, was resigned to the probability of German unification in early 1990. The remaining questions for the victor powers, and above all the victor superpowers, were: who should participate in the process of designing German unity? and on what conditions would German unity be acceptable?

The first question was answered by the 'Two–plus–Four' formula agreed in February 1990. The two German states were to participate with the four victor powers in determining the future of Germany. This decision alone showed how far the world had moved since Potsdam, when Germany was not only the subject but the object of the victor powers' decisions. The second question was more complicated, for it involved the security concerns of Germany's neighbours and of the superpowers. It was a question with several components. One of them was whether the FRG's existing international commitments, such as membership of the UN, the EC, NATO, and many others too numerous to list, would still apply to a united Germany. This was the international version of the domestic dispute over Article 23 *versus* Article 146: was united Germany to be a new state or an extension of the FRG? The FRG's Western allies, it was evident, preferred the Article 23 road; their pressure reinforced the Chancellor's own strong preference for this solution. But—and this was a further component of this question—if the whole of a united Germany was to belong to the EC and NATO, should that be subject to any conditions or restrictions? The resolution of this delicate matter rested on bilateral negotiations between the FRG and the Soviet Union, for it was the Soviets who had most to fear from a Westward extension of the Western economic and security systems—a 'One-plus-One' sub-plot in the 'Two-plus-Four' drama.

It was the resolution of the sub-plot that revealed that Gorbachev needed Kohl at this stage as much as Kohl needed him. Gorbachev was presiding over a Soviet Union that was rapidly losing political and military control over its periphery and over an economy that was visibly in collapse—a situation quite different from that of Stalin at Potsdam or Brezhnev at the time of *Ostpolitik*. The objective to which Soviet policy-makers had given priority ever since 1945, that of securing international recognition of the frontiers and regimes they had imposed at the end of the Second World War, was no longer an option. The terms on which the victors and the defeated concurred on the shaping of post-Cold War Europe were agreed at the Kohl–Gorbachev summit in the Caucasus on 14–16 July. Soviet troops were to withdraw from Germany within four years. The whole of post-unification Germany would be a member of NATO, but German troops stationed on ex-GDR territory would not, for the time being, be under NATO command. German conventional forces would be restricted to 370,000 personnel, less than the pre-1990 *Bundeswehr*. In return, the FRG, the Soviet Union's largest creditor, would help to stave off its debtor's bankruptcy. Kohl had already provided a loan of DM 5 billion in May. In September a further DM 12 billion was made available, as well as an additional DM 3 billion to cover the costs of the remaining stay of Soviet military forces in Germany and of their removal to the USSR. One other matter remained to be settled: the Oder–Neiße frontier with Poland, long recognized as a 'frontier of peace' by the GDR, but regarded as 'open' by the FRG until there was a peace treaty. That there was no altering that frontier after a *de facto* existence of forty-five years Kohl knew as well as anyone else, but for reasons of campaign politics he did not want to commit himself to this until the all-German elections were out of the way, a decision much criticized outside Germany. The matter was finally settled by the German–Polish treaty of 16 January 1991.

The Caucasus summit virtually set out the terms of the 'Two-plus-Four' Treaty, which was signed on 12 September 1990. It was not the Peace Treaty promised at Potsdam, but it was the nearest thing to it. It marked the Allies' formal agreement to end the division of Germany. More importantly, it marked the restoration of full German sovereignty. The Allies gave up their remaining occupation rights and ended the special status of Berlin, which became fully integrated into the new Germany as the sixteenth *Land*. The last of the occupation forces withdrew, as promised, in 1994.

Shortly after the fall of the Wall, Chancellor Kohl assured his allies that Germany would not 'go it alone'. Strictly speaking he kept that promise. Equally there is no denying that as time went on the initiative lay in his hands, with much of the detailed diplomacy dealt with by Foreign Minister Genscher and his foreign-policy adviser in the Federal Chancellery, Horst Teltschik. With US support declared at an early stage, it was the Soviet Union and France that needed persuading and the persuasion came predominantly from the German side. The combination of 'Two-plus-Four' and the Unification Treaty was the joint achievement of all involved, but it was a triumph for Kohl and Genscher. That triumph was reflected in domestic politics. The CDU, which had been trailing in the opinion polls since shortly after its victory in the Bundestag election of 1987 and which had been particularly badly hit by the scandal in Schleswig-Holstein, drew level with the SPD in the autumn of 1989 and the FDP once more overtook the Greens in the spring of 1990. Once the treaties were signed, the SPD embarked on the Bundestag election campaign facing certain defeat. Its standard-bearer, the Saarland Prime Minister, Oskar Lafontaine, was an able administrator and effective orator. At any other time he might have done well. But his warnings on the costs of unity were interpreted in both East and West as lack of enthusiasm for the cause of unification. In this first all-German election East and West voted separately, so as to maximize the chances of locally implanted parties. The Kohl–Genscher coalition won hands down in both regions, with 54.9 per cent in the old *Länder* (i.e. the former FRG) and 54.7 per cent in the new (i.e. the former GDR). The SPD suffered its worst defeat since 1957, with 35.7 per cent in the old *Länder* and 24.3 per cent in the new. The PDS, which had a following only in the East, secured election thanks to the electoral law, but lost one-third of its support since the Volkskammer election—11.1 per cent instead of 16.4 per cent. The fate of the smaller parties was significant. The West German Greens, who had declined to form a joint list with the East German Alliance '90, suffered from the general backlash against the Left and failed to get back into the Bundestag, whereas Alliance '90 cleared the 5-per-cent hurdle in the East. The Republicans, who had beaten the nationalist drum most loudly during their brief surge in 1989, found themselves completely sidelined by the reality of unification, winning only 2.1 per cent.

The re-election of the Kohl–Genscher government marked yet another link between the FRG of 1949–90 and the new German nation-state. But unification, it turned out, was the easy part; growing together would be much more difficult. The two societies that faced each other once their states were merged differed radically in many respects. That of the West was bourgeois, internationalized, and cosmopolitan. As the years passed the continuities with the older Germany had faded and the values of a liberal open society came to prevail. What many observers took to be a restoration in 1945–9—the more or less intact survival of the bureaucratic and judicial apparatus and an economy based on private property—showed itself to be much more adaptable. The old aristocracy, its privileges already undermined under the Third Reich, ceased altogether to be a force. The Marxist-inspired proletarian subculture, which both resulted from the segmentation of German society and helped to perpetuate it, was also weakened under the impact of affluence and mass culture. Above all, in the course of time the norms of the Basic Law, with their emphasis on the rule of law and political accountability, gained almost instinctive acceptance, turning the great majority of West Germans into 'constitutional patriots'. In the GDR the discontinuities were both greater and less. The changes in the socio-economic structure were much more profound. An independent property-owning, managerial, and professional class—a bourgeoisie, in other words—all but disappeared. What remained was the older German authoritarian state tradition in which a privileged stratum ruled a nation of subjects. Above all, the travel restrictions and censorship served to isolate the population from the new globalized culture. The East Germans whom West Germans encountered after 1990 were therefore in many respects more traditionally German than the Westerners.

Nor was it clear what new national identity, if any, the new German state would create. Unification was acceptable as a process because it managed to satisfy a whole range of political demands. It appealed to nationalists, who had never given up the German people's claim to form a nation-state again. It appealed to the much larger segment who saw in it the realization of a right to self-determination, the triumph of the Basic Law over arbitrary government. Much of the euphoria of 1989 was not a chauvinistic spasm, but understandable joy at the fall of a dictatorship and the disappearance of an iron curtain. There were also the sceptics who feared the impact of capitalist triumphalism, and those who, like Günter Grass, thought that the idea of a German nation-state was so discredited by its historical record that the experiment should never be repeated. But the fact that the post-1990 German nation-state rested, in contrast with all its predecessors, on a liberal-democratic consensus meant that in this respect at least the new Germany really was new.

The fashioning of a new identity would have taken a long time even without additional difficulties, but the fall of Communism bequeathed a whole series of problems—economic, constitutional, diplomatic, and military—that heightened discontents and disillusionment in both the old and the new *Länder*. One of the most persuasive arguments for a slow-speed unification lay in the adjustment trauma that the East German economy, and those dependent on it, would suffer if it were integrated overnight with that of the FRG—but, as we have seen, the political pressures in favour of a quick fix and an unrealistic currency conversion rate were irresistible. The adjustment problems were made worse by two sins of omission and one of commission that were made in the crucial transitional phase. The first, and the most excusable, was to underestimate the gap between the East and West German economies. In the absence of reliable data, but also because no experts had anticipated the prospect of an economic merger, the reality that East German productivity was a mere 30 per cent of West German came as an additional blow. The second, and the least excusable, lay in the electoral imperative to play down the sacrifices that unification would enforce. In the course of the election campaign Chancellor Kohl evoked the future 'flourishing landscapes' of the new *Länder* and assured his audiences, in East and West, that nobody need be worse off as a result of unification, either through higher taxes or through lower real incomes. When both of these occurred, many Germans, East and West, felt betrayed. The third, and the most easily avoided, related to the property question in the ex-GDR. There had, as we have seen, been several waves of expropriations in the East. The first, conducted by the Soviet occupation authorities until 1949, was irreversible: Gorbachev had (allegedly) insisted on this as a condition of his 'yes' to unification. The remainder, conducted by the GDR, as well as the Nazi expropriations between 1933 and 1945, could be made good in one of two ways: compensation or restitution. Compensation would have been expensive, but also quick. The FDP, however, insisted that the principle of sanctity of property be observed, with the result that Article 41 of the Unification Treaty gave priority to restitution over compensation. This led not only to long delays in the settlement of claims but to much bad blood, as former owners or their heirs turned up to view properties in which the occupants had long felt secure. The deadline for lodging claims was 31 December 1992; by then 2 million claims had been registered to 1.1 million properties covering half the land area of the former GDR. Pessimists think it may take thirty years to clear the backlog.

Burdened by the consequences of these decisions, the government faced a number of other dilemmas in determining how best to restore the East German economy. The most important of these were:

- stimulating the speed of investment *versus* encouraging local ownership;
- maximizing competitiveness *versus* maintaining real incomes;
- killing off lame ducks *versus* maintaining a reasonable level of employment;
- injecting non-inflationary aid *versus* shielding the taxpayer.

What was out of the question for both political and economic reasons was the kind of shock therapy adopted in Poland. The newly sovereign states of Eastern Europe could survive this therapy by taking advantage of their low wages, offering special inducements to investors, and maintaining exchange controls. East Germans, in contrast, had been led to expect a rapid equalization of living standards; moreover, Germany as an EC member was restricted in the market distortions it could engage in. To try to resolve its dilemmas the government undertook a number of initiatives.

The most important was the creation of the trustee body, the Treuhandanstalt, to administer the state property of the former GDR, with a remit to privatize its assets. The difficulties it encountered were an indication of the general problems that the East German economy faced. The initial estimate of its assets at between DM 800 billion and DM 1,000 billion had to be scaled down to DM 200 billion. Many privatization bids were held up by uncertainties over property titles. Given the lack of capital inside the new *Länder*, new investment had to come from the old *Länder* or elsewhere in the West, leading to the suspicion of a take-over by carpet-baggers. In many cases the Treuhand bent the rules, either by anticipating the resolution of a property question, or by writing off the debts of a firm (as, for instance, those of the prestigious Jena optical firm), or by sharing the costs of cleaning up land contamination. Above all, it soon realized that giving absolute priority to market principles would result in an unacceptable level of bankruptcies and redundancies. It therefore found itself delaying plant closures and keeping on work-forces for whose production there was little demand. It experienced in an acute form the dilemma all modern governments are faced with: how high a social price is it permissible to pay for economic efficiency? how high an economic price is it permissible to pay for social peace? Some of the Treuhand's delaying tactics paid off: sections of East German industry that looked unrescuable in 1991, such as major chemical and steel plants, did find buyers. But there is no such thing as a free rescue plan. When the Treuhandanstalt was wound up at the end of 1994 it bequeathed a debt of DM 275 billion.

The Treuhandanstalt was only one of the burdens the state had to bear through taking over the East German economy. Under the terms of the Economic Union Treaty a German Unity Fund was created, one-third of its resources coming from the Federal Government and the old *Länder*, the remainder raised in the market. This increase in the public debt was controversial from the beginning, being criticized by the SPD opposition, which would have preferred higher taxes, and by the Bundesbank, which would have preferred matching cuts in public expenditure. The main consequence of what the markets saw as fiscal laxity was a rise in interest rates, with the Bundesbank fixing the discount rate at 8.75 per cent in July 1992—a post-war high. Try as the government might, however, there was no avoiding some tax increases. These duly emerged in the form of a 7.5 per cent 'solidarity surcharge', as well as increases in VAT and fuel excise duty. They have caused great resentment, not merely because they were tax increases but because they contradicted Kohl's campaign promises. The 'tax-lie' charge came to haunt him.

The cost of unification did not merely put a greater burden on public finances; it also changed the way government worked. In theory, the Unification Treaty transferred the structure of government from the FRG to the whole of Germany; in practice, this structure had to adapt to the new needs and circumstances, just as it had constantly evolved between 1949 and 1990. The adaptation applied particularly to federalism. The accession of the five new *Länder* and Berlin raised the number of *Länder* from ten to sixteen. The newcomers were not only poorer *per capita* than the others; they were also in the main smaller. The whole of the GDR had a population less than that of the largest Western *Land*, North Rhine–Westphalia. But because the *Länder* are not represented in strict proportion in the Bundesrat, the new *Länder* (without Berlin) have nineteen votes there and North Rhine–Westphalia has six. That has enabled the Bundesrat to become more of the regional voice it was originally intended to be; votes within it are based as much on the clash of interest between rich and poor *Länder* as on party lines, in contrast with the more partisan trend before 1990. However, the size of the transfer payments has meant that the financial role of the *Länder* has, however temporarily, diminished, making Bonn the main channel of redistribution. This was underlined by the Solidarity Pact of 13 March 1993, designed to provide the Eastern *Länder* and municipalities with a further DM 13.7 billion. The additional sums were to be produced by the Federation through taxes and borrowing, because the Western *Länder* refused to increase their contributions. Indeed, strict interpretation of the principle of redistribution would have meant that the poorest Western *Länder*, Bremen and the Saar, hitherto beneficiaries of redistribution, would have become net contributors. The Solidarity Pact was intended to provide temporary relief, not to transfer power permanently to the Federation. Under the terms of the Unification Treaty the rules on redistribution of resources among the *Länder* were to apply fully to the new *Länder* from 1995 onwards; to make this arrangement acceptable, the Solidarity Pact decreed that the *Länder* share of VAT revenue was to rise from 37 per cent to 44 per cent by 1995, a shift that would be dependent on the federal government's success in cutting its own expenditure. Whether the balance between *Länder* and Bonn intended by the constitution can survive the imbalances brought about by unification will in the end depend on the success of these plans.

One cause of the economic difficulties of the new *Länder* that was touched on in the talks on the Solidarity Pact, but in which the government was careful not to intervene, was the rapid rise in labour costs. Free collective bargaining was, after all, one of the fundamentals of the social market economy. In the euphoria of unification, unions and employers had agreed that wages in the old and new *Länder* were to be fully harmonized by 1996, an undertaking that became increasingly difficult to implement as productivity failed to rise sufficiently. In March 1993 the engineering employers in Saxony unilaterally repudiated an agreement that would have granted a 26-per-cent wage increase—the first such action in the history of post-war Germany. Steel employers in all the new *Länder* followed suit, leading to strikes in May—the first in that part of Germany for sixty years. The eventual agreement provided for a postponement over two years of wage harmonization, but underlying the dispute was a power struggle between unions and employers that called into question the social peace that had been such a dominant characteristic of the FRG. The wage dispute illustrated one significant feature of the impact of unification on German politics. Apart from the obvious East–West problem, few of the questions that troubled German policy-makers were new. The rising public debt had already been a source of concern in the 1980s, as had the high labour costs of German industry. What unification had done was to aggravate these problems. The same applied to other issues that were a hold-over from before unification: immigration, abortion, and Germany's military role, though the fall of Communism had admittedly added new dimensions to these.

Up to 1989 there had been three types of immigrant into the FRG: workers recruited mainly from the Mediterranean countries, classified as migrants (*Gastarbeiter*) even if settled in the FRG with families; refugees from the GDR (*Übersiedler*), the flow of whom never dried up even after the building of the Wall; and ethnic German resettlers (*Aussiedler*), whose numbers swelled from the late 1980s onwards, especially from the Soviet Union and its successor states and from Romania. A fourth category, whose numbers escalated largely as a result of the collapse of Communism, were real or alleged asylum-seekers (*Asylanten*), attracted by the liberal provisions of Article 16 of the Basic Law. By 1992 opinion polls were recording that, in the old—but not the new—*Länder*, immigration was seen as the biggest single problem. What was more disturbing was the increase in acts of violence against asylum-seekers and other foreigners, culminating in a five-day riot in August 1992 in the East German city of Rostock. At the same time parties of the extreme Right, including the Republicans who had faded at the time of unification, revived and made striking gains in *Landtag* and municipal elections. Whether these were due solely to the immigration question will be discussed below. The authorities and public opinion reacted with delay to this crisis, but impressive demonstrations against xenophobic violence took place in major cities, especially Berlin and Munich. A number of extreme Right organizations were banned by the government. Some restraint on asylum-seeking, however symbolic, became politically inescapable, and an amendment to the Basic Law was adopted on 26 May 1993, supported by the government parties and most of the SPD. By putting the onus of proof on the individual applicant, it stemmed the flow somewhat and the issue gradually lost salience.

The abortion controversy had been bubbling for even longer, ever since reform of the extremely restrictive §218 of the Criminal Code became the main demand of the women's movement in the 1960s. What complicated the controversy, as we saw in Chapter 6, was the involvement of the Federal Constitutional Court. The question became acute again at the time of unification, because the GDR had a radically different law, permitting abortion on demand in the first three months of pregnancy. The Unification Treaty left the question open for later legislative solution, which the Bundestag and the Court have been wrestling with ever since. On 26 June 1992 the Bundestag approved a compromise bill which legalized abortion in the first three months, after compulsory counselling, for the whole of Germany, but this was once more rejected by the Court. The controversy on abortion is not only substantive, it is also symbolic. It illustrates the potential conflict between parliament and public opinion, which strongly supported the Bundestag bill, and the Basic Law, as interpreted by the Court. But this is not new. It also illustrates the extent to which gender politics is an integral part of the public agenda and a determinant of voting behaviour. But this is not new either. What was new was the differential effect of unification on men and women. Abortion rights were one aspect of this, but for most women this was of abstract importance only. The main effect was on jobs and income. In the GDR 78 per cent of women of working age were in employment (91 per cent if students and trainees were included), compared with 55 per cent in the FRG. It does not follow that all women in the GDR regarded the economic pressure to pursue full-time employment as liberating, though it did offer the opportunity for gaining qualifications. Moreover, women's incomes were on average one-quarter lower than men's. Following unification, non-working persons of both sexes, e.g. pensioners, became better off, as did most wage- and salary-earners. But the employment shake-out hit women much harder than men and working couples also suffered as the automatic entitlement to day nurseries ceased to operate. All major changes since 1990 have affected the East German population unevenly, but on no sector of the population has the effect been more uneven than on women.

The most obvious change in German politics resulting from unification, as far as the outside world is concerned, is in the country's international status. This is formally the product of the decisions of others, though, as we have seen, the 'Two-plus-Four' Treaty was predominantly a response to the pressure of events inside Germany. Domestically the changed international status has been as divisive as the social and economic turmoil. On the one hand, there have been those who argue that, since Germany is now a sovereign state, it must act with full responsibility for its status on the world stage, or at least the European stage. Opposed to them are those who argue that Germany must never again play a military role. The second point of view prevailed at the time of the Gulf War in 1991 in ensuring that the somewhat ambiguous provisions of Article 87a of the Basic Law on national defence were interpreted as restrictively as possible. As in other matters, such as abortion and taxation, the Federal Constitutional Court has become more interventionist and it has gone some way towards resolving the disputes between the CDU and majority opinion in the other parties on 'out-of-area' operations by German armed forces—that is, for other than defensive purposes within NATO. In April 1993 the Court ruled that German participation in non-combatant surveillance flights over Bosnia was consistent with the Basic Law. In July 1994 the Court went further in permitting German forces to participate in any operations sanctioned by the UN, subject to specific Bundestag approval.

The controversy over a German military role illustrates the continuing anxiety over the burden of history and the country's image abroad. When, on the occasion of the ratification of the Unification Treaty, President von Weizsäcker said that 'for the first time we Germans are not an object of conflict on the European agenda', he was expressing an aspiration rather than a fact. The emergence of a bigger Germany in the centre of Europe has provoked misgivings, whether justified or not. Fears of a remilitarized or expansionist Fourth Reich faded quickly. Article 23 of the Basic Law has been replaced: there are now no further 'parts of Germany' that would qualify for joining the Federal Republic. When the Foreign Minister, Klaus Kinkel, declared after the 1994 Court verdict on military participation that German policy would continue to be based on a 'culture of restraint', he reflected the wishes of most Germans, though not necessarily the preferences of all Western foreign ministries or the Secretary-General of the UN. The economic role of the new Germany has been more controversial, though fears that Germany would reconstruct the East European economic hegemony it had enjoyed in the 1930s or before 1914 also turned out to be exaggerated. Only in the Czech Republic and Slovenia is Germany the principal foreign investor. More disturbing was the ripple effect of the Bundesbank's high-interest policy in 1992 and 1993, which, by obliging other European central banks to follow suit, undoubtedly held back recovery from the recession.

As Germany wrestled with the consequences of unification, doubts arose both inside and outside the country about its ability to cope with them and about its future as a dependable partner. Preoccupation with domestic problems could well lead to a downgrading of external obligations: the high-interest policy of the Bundesbank was often cited as one example of this. Another fear was that, with nation-state status recovered, Germany would lose interest in the continued integration of Europe and would rediscover longings for national sovereignty and for going it alone. The most pervasive fear, however, during the difficult initial period of unification, was that the government would lose control over events; that the dual cement that had enabled the FRG to cohere—fear of Communism and integration in the West—would crumble; that Bonn would, all previous indications to the contrary notwithstanding, turn out to be Weimar again.

The operation of the economic cycle added to these fears. The post-unification boom, from which not only the West German economy but that of its trading partners benefited, was short-lived. The surge in consumer demand in the Eastern *Länder* subsided and Germany became caught up in the world-wide recession. All-German GDP rose by only 1.1 per cent in 1992 and fell by 1.1 per cent in 1993. Unemployment peaked at 3.5 million in March 1993, affecting 7.4 per cent in the West and 15.5 per cent in the East. The real unemployment situation in the East was much worse, for the official figures did not take account of short-time working, retraining, or early retirement. When one added the immigration crisis and the wave of xenophobic violence to the psychological and economic adjustment problems of the new Germany, one could be forgiven for wondering whether the foundations of post-war German democracy were still firm.

Party and electoral trends lent some support to these doubts and worries. In the early stages of unification party organization and party affiliation seemed to point to stability. The main parties of East and West—the CDU, the SPD, and the FDP—had amalgamated even before the Bundestag election of 1990. The Western Greens and Eastern Alliance '90 belatedly followed suit in 1993. Even though politicians from the East are under-represented in the leadership positions of these parties, Eastern influence can make itself felt in other ways. All three parties know that they cannot win without Eastern votes, something that showed most clearly in the Eastern input into the final version of the Solidarity Pact. What faltered during the trough of confidence in 1992 and 1993 was the ability of these parties to keep the confidence of voters. Fragmentation of the party landscape seemed a real threat.

The first minor party to recover after 1990 was the Greens, who reverted to their old level of support in *Landtag* elections. Moreover, as their more radical personalities left for the wilderness, the Greens emerged more and more as pillars rather than subverters of the system and by early 1994 were represented in three *Land* coalitions. More ominous for the stability of the system was the revival of the Republicans, who reached double figures in the election to the Baden-Württemberg *Landtag* in April 1992. Even more extreme parties, like the neo-Nazi German People's Union (Deutsche Volksunion (DVU)), also did well in *Landtag* and local elections. Since their rise coincided with both the immigration crisis and the recession, it is difficult to know which was the weightier cause of their success; but whichever was the explanation, it lent support to those who feared that German democracy was a fair-weather construction only. The third symptom of party fragmentation came from the East, where local elections in Brandenburg in December 1993 showed that the PDS, far from continuing to decline, had stabilized itself as a regional protest force. There was therefore a prospect of a five-party and possibly six-party Bundestag after the 1994 elections, which would leave no choice but a Great Coalition at the national level—a cartel of the traditional parties with no constructive opposition to offer an alternative government. This electoral volatility, especially at the expense of the classical parties, as well as the lower turn-out, led to much talk of German disillusionment with politics as such—*Politikverdrossenheit*. Indeed the Society for the German Language proclaimed *Politikverdrossenheit* to be the word of the year for 1993.

The outcome of the 1994 election did not confirm these fears. Chancellor Kohl, whose party held majorities in only two *Land* governments by 1994 and had at one stage sunk to the low twenties in opinion polls in the Eastern *Länder*, once more showed his skill at presenting himself as the national unifier. He was by now the longest-serving head of government in Europe and the sole survivor of the stirring events of 1990. Foreign Minister Genscher departed in 1992 and was succeeded by the less charismatic Klaus Kinkel, who also took over as chairman of the FDP. President von Weizsäcker's term of office came to an end in 1994. He was replaced by the President of the Federal Constitutional Court, Roman Herzog. Once Kinkel and the FDP had supported the election of Herzog and declared for a continuation of the coalition with Kohl, the only alternative was a combination of the SPD and the Greens. This lacked appeal. The Greens, though acceptable as *Land* coalition partners, were still suspect on foreign and defence policy, having retained their pacifist and neutralist stances. The SPD's new standard-bearer, the Prime Minister of Rhineland–Palatinate, Rudolf Scharping, was a lacklustre campaigner. But most important of all, the recession was over and the 'tax lie' forgiven, even if not forgotten. By the spring of 1994 Kohl was again popular and in the European elections of 12 June the CDU led the SPD by 6.6 per cent. In the Bundestag election of 16 October the CDU–FDP coalition won an absolute majority of ten seats over all other parties. Both government parties lost in relation to their triumph in 1990; the SPD and Greens recovered some of the ground lost in the disaster of 1990; the PDS, though failing to clear 5 per cent nationally, won 20 per cent in the Eastern *Länder* and returned to the Bundestag by virtue of winning four constituencies in Berlin. The far-Right vote collapsed: the Republicans got 1.9 per cent, less even than in 1990.

As Chancellor Kohl embarks on his fourth full term of office, none of the problems of post-Communist Germany has been solved, but they have begun to appear solvable. Experience between 1990 and 1994 reminded us that the post-war West German political order was designed not only to provide firm government, but also to prevent the abuse of power, and that the checks and balances of federalism and judicial review might on occasion obstruct the first imperative. In the year of unification German institutions showed themselves to be wonderfully flexible; thereafter they returned to their habitual slow-moving ways. On transfers to the East, on immigration and unemployment, there was improvisation, but little long-term strategy. On abortion, on European integration, once the Maastricht Treaty was in place, and on the revision of the Basic Law, as enjoined by the Unification Treaty, there has been virtually no movement. What has helped is that Germans have become more patient and have lowered their expectations. In the old FRG, that change began in the 1970s after the oil shocks. In the GDR, patience had always been a habit, to be momentarily swept aside in the brief euphoria of liberation. The East German economy bottomed out in 1993. In 1994 and 1995 it registered growth rates of 8.5 per cent, but it has not reached self-sustained take-off and remains dependent on transfer payments. The equalization of living standards prescribed by the Basic Law is unlikely to be reached before 2010. The party system in the East is less stable than that in the West and associational life there has not recovered: party and trade-union membership remains low compared with the old *Länder*. The Bundestag and *Landtag* elections of 1994 have left only three parties in place in the new *Länder*: the CDU, the SPD, and the PDS. The last of these, though accepted as a legitimate component of political life by the majority of East Germans, retains the neo-Stalinist faction of the Communist Platform; as long as that is there, the PDS will live in isolation, excluded from any level of government except the municipal.

The problems of unification in the second half of the 1990s are as much psychological as organizational. Whatever government is in power needs to reassure East Germans that they count as equal citizens and West Germans that their burdens are both necessary and equitable.

Conclusion

BEFORE becoming Chancellor in 1969, Willy Brandt complained that the Federal Republic, which had become an economic giant, remained a political dwarf. Even before unification this distinction had lost much of its validity. The Federal Republic owed its influence in the world to its economic strength and the stability of its currency. In the post-Cold War world military power is even less relevant as a measure of political influence, and a strong economy is even more the *raison d'état* of the new Germany. The demilitarization of the pursuit of German national interest is one post-1945 development that has come to stay. The other is the convergence of national identity and democracy. For much of the nineteenth century and the first part of the twentieth those who wanted to build a German nation-state or to enhance its power were only too ready to subordinate the construction of political liberty to this aim. Those who gave priority to political liberty were only too readily dismissed as 'scoundrels without a fatherland' ('vaterlandslose Gesellen', in the words of Kaiser Wilhelm II). That the dichotomy between nationhood and democracy has finally been overcome is shown by the way Germany was unified in 1990. The instrument of national unity was the Basic Law of the Federal Republic, 'the best German constitution of all times'. The accession of the GDR on the terms of Article 23 was a victory for constitutional patriotism. But those who dissented from this device and wanted a new constitution under the provisions of Article 146 did so on the grounds that that was the more democratic path. Bismarck, the first unifier of Germany, declared in 1862 that the great decisions of the day would be made not by speeches and majorities, but by blood and iron. In 1990 it could not have been more different.

If Germany was unified peacefully and by consent, it was also unified in haste. This is the other formative influence on the Berlin Republic, which has taken the place of the Bonn Republic. Given the pressure to unify quickly, little thought could be given to adapting the structures of the FRG to the needs of the enlarged and more heterogeneous state. Since many of these structures were already over-burdened before 1989, it is not surprising that governing the Berlin Republic has proved difficult. The institutions that adapted most smoothly in the first five years of unity are the political parties. As the outcome of the 1994 election showed, there has been no fragmentation of the party system, though there has been some regionalization. The two main parties, the CDU and the SPD, are spread more evenly over East and West than in 1990; the FDP and the Greens have become predominantly Western parties and the PDS remains an overwhelm-ingly Eastern party. At the national level this distribution of voting strength causes few problems; at the sub-national level the chances of confusion are greater. At the beginning of 1995 the sixteen *Länder* had seven different types of single-party or coalition government, which could make majority building in the Bundesrat more difficult.

Indeed, it is in those many areas in which the federal govern-ment is not completely sovereign that the addition of the new *Länder* has caused the greatest problems. The most important of these are the federal structure and associational life. The checks and balances of West German federalism worked tolerably well until 1989, given the relative homogeneity of the old FRG and the conventions that had grown up regarding fiscal burden-sharing. Even so, strains were be-ginning to show. The increasing gap between the rich and the poor *Länder* made the burden-sharing more difficult; the growing share of the GDP taken by the federal government altered the balance between federation and *Länder*; the proliferation of 'common concerns' be-tween federation and *Länder* has shifted the balance further in favour of centralized government. Unification, by necessitating a much higher level of transfer payments, has tipped the balance still further towards the central government. The increased share of VAT that the *Länder* will receive when the Eastern *Länder* become full members of the inter-*Land* transfer mechanism may reverse this trend, but only if the increase is sufficient for Eastern needs.

The FRG's system of subsidiarity meant that many major public-service tasks were left to the *Länder*, including school and higher education and broadcasting. Notwithstanding some party patronage, universities and radio and television corporations maintained and developed a fair degree of autonomy. The absence of autonomous structures in these spheres in the GDR means that they had to be created after unification—which means, paradoxically, that there is a heavy Western tutelary role which, in turn, diminishes autonomy. Time may heal this defect, but as long as it lasts it reinforces the Eastern sense of having been colonized.

What applies to these autonomous public institutions applies even more to associational life and professional organizations, which, as in all advanced countries, have considerable formal and informal policy functions in Germany—in particular in the legal system and the health service. Here there was a dual pressure for speedy assimilation of East and West—from the state, in the interests of legal uniformity, and from the professional organizations, in the interests of preserving existing structures. The consequence is again that, for the short term at least, not only Western norms but Western personnel predominate.

The balance of power within the federal system, the autonomy of public-service and educational bodies, the policy-making role of professional bodies—all these had been problems in the old FRG. The addition of five new *Länder*, with greatly different experiences, needs, and resources, has put additional strains on the inherited structures. Above all, it has put a new strain on the office of Chancellor. The fact that one man, Helmut Kohl, held the office both before and after unification has helped to disguise the way in which it, too, has had to bend to new demands. Even before 1990 the old model of 'chancellor democracy', as it had come to be understood in the early years of the FRG, had become inadequate. Public opinion had become more diverse and less malleable; organized interests had become more entrenched and confident in their power; the Bundesrat had gradually extended its competence over nearly half the total federal legislation. That meant that the Chancellor had to be more of a negotiator and conciliator, less of a policy initiator. In addition, the gradual emergence of the FRG as a major international actor means that the range of the Chancellor's responsibilities has expanded, without being matched by an equal expansion of powers: currency policy involves the Bundesbank, defence policy may involve the Federal Constitutional Court. The office is changing, even while the officeholder provides the illusion of permanence.

There are no miracles in this world: it was not a foregone conclusion that German unification, whatever its blemishes, would work as well as it has. It will be a long time before the shape of the new Germany stabilizes itself. But Bonn was not built in a day either.

Appendix I.
Tables of Election Results

TABLE 1. *General election results, FRG 1949–1987, Germany 1990–1994* (% of votes cast)

Year	Turn-out	CDU–CSU	SPD	FDP	KPD*	DRP[†]	Greens
1949	78.5	31.0	29.2	11.9	5.7	1.8	
1953	85.8	45.2	28.8	9.5	2.2	1.1	
1957	87.8	50.2	31.8	7.7	——	1.0	
1961	87.7	45.3	36.2	12.8		0.8	
						NPD	
1965	86.8	47.6	39.3	9.5		2.0	
1969	86.7	46.1	42.7	5.8		4.3	
1972	91.2	44.9	45.8	8.4		0.6	
1976	90.7	48.6	42.6	7.9		0.3	
1980	88.6	44.5	42.9	10.6		0.2	1.5
1983	89.1	48.8	38.2	6.9		0.2	5.6
1987	84.4	44.3	37.0	9.1		0.6	8.3
					PDS	Republicans	
1990[‡]	77.8	43.8	33.5	11.0	2.4	2.1	5.1
1994[‡]	79.0	41.4	36.4	6.9	4.4	1.9	7.2

* Extreme Left parties.
[†] Extreme Right parties.
[‡] All-German elections.

Source: Statistisches Bundesamt.

TABLE 2. *Election results in former GDR, 1990–1994* (% of votes cast)

Election	Turn-out	CDU	SPD	FDP	PDS	Alliance '90
Volkskammer 1990	93.2	48.0*	21.9	5.3	16.4	2.9
Bundestag 1990	74.7	41.8	24.3	12.9	11.1	6.0
Bundestag 1994	72.6	38.5	31.5	4.3	19.8	4.3

* Including allies.

Source: Statistisches Bundesamt.

Appendix II. Figure of Economic Performance

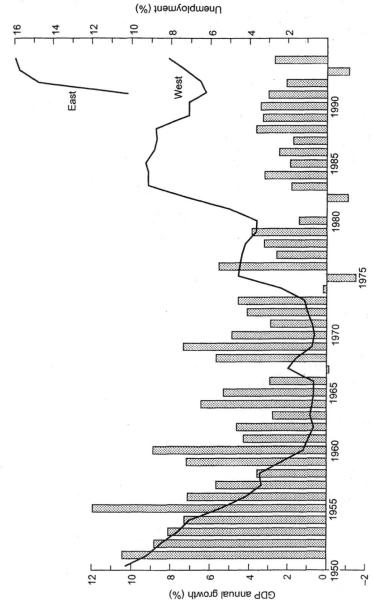

Suggestions for Further Reading

General

BARK, DENNIS L., and GRESS, DAVID R., *A History of West Germany* (Oxford, 1989; 2nd edn., 1993).

BERGHAHN, VOLKER, *Modern Germany: Society, Economy and Politics in the Twentieth Century* (Cambridge, 1982; 2nd edn., 1987).

FULBROOK, MARY, *The Divided Nation: A History of Germany 1918–1900* (Oxford, 1991).

PATERSON, WILLIAM E., and SOUTHERN, DAVID, *Governing Germany* (Oxford, 1991).

SMITH, GORDON, et al. (eds.), *Developments in German Politics* (Basingstoke, 1992).

TURNER, HAROLD A., *Germany from Partition to Reunification* (New Haven, 1992).

The Division of Germany

DEIGHTON, ANNE, *The Impossible Peace: Britain, the Division of Germany, and the Origins of the Cold War* (Oxford, 1990).

LITCHFIELD, EDWARD H. (ed.), *Governing Post-War Germany* (Ithaca, NY, 1953).

MARSHALL, BARBARA, *The Origins of Post-War German Politics* (London, 1988).

MERKL, PETER H., *The Origins of the West German Republic* (New York, 1963).

Politicians and Parties

BRAUNTHAL, GERARD, *The German Social Democrats since 1969: A Party in Power and Opposition* (Boulder, Colo., 1994).

BURNS, ROB, and VAN DER WILL, WILFRIED, *Protest and Democracy in Western Germany* (Basingstoke, 1988).

HEIDENHEIMER, ARNOLD J., *Adenauer and the CDU* (The Hague, 1960).

KOLINSKY, EVA, *Parties, Opposition and Society in West Germany* (London, 1984).

MARKOVITS, ANDREW S., and GORSKI, PHILIP S., *The German Left: Red, Green and Beyond* (Oxford, 1993).

PADGETT, STEPHEN (ed.), *Parties and Party Systems in the New Germany* (Aldershot, 1993).

PRIDHAM, GEOFFREY, *Christian Democracy in Western Germany* (London, 1977).

STÖSS, RICHARD, *Politics against Democracy: The Extreme Right in West Germany* (Oxford, 1991).

Economy and Society

DAHRENDORF, RALF, *Society and Democracy in Germany* (London, 1968).

KATZENSTEIN, PETER, *Policy and Politics in West Germany* (Philadelphia, 1987).

KOLINSKY, EVA, *Women in Contemporary Germany: Life, Work and Politics* (Oxford, 1989; 2nd edn., 1993).

MARKOVITS, ANDREI S., *The Politics of West German Trade Unions* (Cambridge, 1986).

MARSH, DAVID, *The Bundesbank: The Bank that Rules Europe* (London, 1992).

NICHOLLS, ANTHONY J., *Freedom with Responsibility: The Social Market Economy in Germany 1918–1963* (Oxford, 1994).

OWEN SMITH, ERIC, *The German Economy* (London, 1994).

Foreign Policy

BARING, ARNULF (ed.), *Germany's New Position in Europe* (Oxford, 1994).

HANRIEDER, WOLFRAM (ed.), *West German Foreign Policy, 1949–1979* (Boulder, Colo., 1980).

—— *Germany, America, Europe: Forty Years of German Foreign Policy* (New Haven, 1989).

KRIPPENDORF, EKKEHARD, and RITTBERGER, VOLKER, *The Foreign Policy of West Germany: Formation and Contents* (London, 1980).

MORGAN, ROGER, *The United States and West Germany 1945–1973* (London, 1974).

STENT, ANGELA, *From Embargo to Ostpolitik* (Cambridge, 1981).

WURM, CLEMENS (ed.), *Western Europe and Germany: The Beginnings of European Integration 1945–1960* (Oxford, 1995).

Unification and After

DALTON, RUSSELL J. (ed.), *The New Germany Votes: Unification and the Creation of a New German Party System* (Providence, RI, 1993).

GARTON ASH, TIMOTHY, *In Europe's Name: Germany and the Divided Continent* (London, 1993).

GLAESSNER, GERT-JOACHIM, and WALLACE, IAN (eds.), *The German Revolution of 1989: Causes and Consequences* (Oxford, 1992).

GROSSER, DIETER (ed.), *German Unification: The Unexpected Challenge* (Oxford, 1992).

HUELSHOFF, MICHAEL G., *et al.* (eds.), *From Bundesrepublik to Deutschland* (Ann Arbor, 1993).

MARSH, DAVID, *Germany and Europe: The Crisis of Unity* (London, 1994).

POND, ELIZABETH, *Beyond the Wall: Germany's Road to Unification* (Washington, DC, 1993).

Index